Governors State University
Library Hours:
Monday thru Thursday 8:00 to 10:30
Friday 8:00 to 5:00
Saturday 8:30 to 5:00
Sunday 1:00 to 5:00 (Fall
and Winter Trimester Only)

Best Ideas for Teaching with Technology

Best Ideas for Teaching with Technology

A Practical Guide for Teachers, by Teachers

Justin Reich and **Thomas Daccord**

WITH A FOREWORD BY ALAN NOVEMBER

M.E.Sharpe
Armonk, New York
London, England

Library of Congress Cataloging-in-Publication Data

Reich, Justin, 1977-
  Best ideas for teaching with technology : a practical guide for teachers, by teachers
/ Justin Reich, Thomas Daccord.
      p. cm.
  Includes bibliographical references and index.
  ISBN 978-0-7656-2131-3 (cloth : alk. paper)
  1. Computer-assisted instruction. 2. Educational technology. 3. Internet
in education. I. Daccord, Thomas. II. Title.
  LB1028.3.R437 2008

  371.33'4—dc22   2007052922

Printed in the United States of America

The paper used in this publication meets the minimum requirements of
American National Standard for Information Sciences
Permanence of Paper for Printed Library Materials,
ANSI Z 39.48-1984.

♾

EB (c)   10   9   8   7   6   5   4   3   2   1

Publisher: Myron E. Sharpe
Editorial Director: Patricia Kolb
Editorial Assistants: Nicole Cirino, Katie Corasaniti
Project Manager: Ana Erlić
Text Design: Carmen Chetti
Desktop Publishing Specialist: Zeph Ernest
Cover Design: Jesse Sanchez

Contents

Foreword

In *Best Ideas for Teaching with Technology: A Practical Guide for Teachers, by Teachers,* Justin Reich and Tom Daccord use their considerable teaching experience and technological expertise to show educators—in a clear and accessible manner—how to use technology to empower students to do meaningful work and develop essential skills. Throughout their book, Justin and Tom introduce and explain powerful educational tools and strategies that teachers can apply immediately to their own teaching. Regardless of content area or level of expertise, *Best Ideas for Teaching with Technology* is an extremely valuable resource for teachers hoping to realize the tremendous opportunities that technology offers for powerful learning in the twenty-first century classroom.

With the emergence of Web 2.0, or the "Read/Write Internet," teachers have an unsurpassed opportunity to provide students with the tools necessary to solve problems in creative ways and to collaborate globally. Justin and Tom understand that Web 2.0 technologies provide new and exciting opportunities for enhanced collaboration with the outside world. They point out that publishing to authentic audiences motivates students to work in powerful ways. *Best Ideas for Teaching with Technology* introduces several Web 2.0 tools and platforms that help put students at the center of the learning process and nurture an environment where students take ownership over their learning. This book is an important step toward empowering students to learn.

Justin Reich and Tom Daccord are master practitioners of the teaching craft and understand how technology can reshape the relationship between teacher and student. Though they use technology, they are fundamentally interested in becoming better teachers. They are "in-the-trenches" leaders in a revolutionary shift of control from the school to the learner. With his creative incorporation of email, blogs, and other tools, Justin creates collaborative, student-centered projects and activities that emphasize student ownership of the learning process. Tom's inventive and team-oriented uses of wikis, podcasts, and other technologies spur student engagement and creativity. His emphasis on "donating" to others the knowledge his students construct serves as an important model of community-service learning. I have had the pleasure of watching Tom present projects from his classroom and have seen first-hand the excitement and creativity he brings to technology integration. This excitement and creativity, coupled with the confidence he demonstrates in his students, represent important ingredients of the successful twenty-first century classroom teacher.

Best Ideas for Teaching with Technology gives teachers the tools and strategies to be leaders who help students and colleagues move to a collaborative and student-centered learning environment. Justin and Tom demonstrate a clear awareness of the skills to be cultivated in the classroom—critical thinking, problem solving, communication, and collaboration—and a dedication to the global economy skill set. Their book shows teachers how to use tools such as email, blogs, and Skype to progress from a relatively insular classroom environment to a community-based networked environment. Justin and Tom make it clear that teachers need not be technology gurus, but they must think creatively about how the best practices of great teaching can benefit from the collaborative power of modern technology.

Information literacy is an essential ingredient of the twenty-first century citizen. Today's youth live in a world that gives them access to almost unlimited amounts of information online. If students do not understand the basic conventions and grammar of the Internet they can be manipulated by people who do. *Best Ideas for Teaching with Technology: A Practical Guide for Teachers by Teachers* provides needed tools and strategies to learn information literacy. Our students must know how to access and validate information, and Justin and Tom help train teachers and students in this fundamental skill.

In *Best Ideas for Teaching with Technology,* Justin and Tom share examples and lesson plans from their classrooms and from master teachers in other disciplines. They provide you with numerous suggestions for incorporating activities in your classroom, whether you are a novice or an advanced technology user. At their Web site, Justin and Tom provide online video tutorials and podcasts with practical "how-to" demonstrations of various technologies. With this book and the Web site, you are well equipped to help your students become productive and successful twenty-first century citizens.

I am sure Justin and Tom would love to hear from you as you apply your own thinking around these powerful tools. Get in touch at edtechteacher@gmail.com.

Alan November
alan@novemberlearning.com

Introduction

About This Book
How to Use This Book
Zen and the Art of Teaching with Technology
The Two Big Questions: Why and How?
A Quick Word on Tutorials

ABOUT THIS BOOK

This is a book for teachers and future teachers who want to quickly, simply, and easily incorporate technology in their classroom. This book was written by teachers who, like you, have families, big piles of papers to grade, and a garage that has needed a major cleaning since September. We want to give you some ideas about technology that might take a weekend afternoon to figure out and set up and then can be used without much time investment afterward. We also want to give you some tools and lesson plans that you can use for your 8 A.M. class even if you pick up this book at 7:30. We want technology to add to the learning going on in your classroom—for you and your students—and we don't want technology to suck up your time.

Have fun with this, and let us know what you think at: edtechteacher@gmail.com.

HOW TO USE THIS BOOK

We've broken this book up into chapters based on the things that teachers and students do:

- Lectures
- Discussion and Communication
- Note Taking and Organization
- Guided Inquiry
- Open Research
- Homework
- Writing
- Presentations
- Grading and Assessment
- Class Management

Most books on technology take a different approach—they are organized around specific tools or programs. In our experience, though, that's not how teachers incorporate technology into their classrooms. No teacher wakes up in the morning saying "Hmm," I really need to learn something about screencasting." But all good teachers decide from time to time that we want to deliver better lectures, encourage more conversation, or assign more varied student presentation projects (screencasting is a great tool for student presentations; look for it in Chapter 8). We hope that our chapters will guide you toward new technologies that relate to the aspects of your teaching that you hope to improve.

One consequence of this approach is that we sometimes repeat ourselves a bit. We've done this intentionally so you don't have to read the book from start to finish; you can skip around, see what catches your eye, and experiment with ideas in any order you choose.

Features of Each Chapter

In each chapter we'll give you a series of ideas for incorporating technology into your classroom. We'll discuss the opportunities presented by emerging technologies, and we'll give you tips on new ways to employ older programs and services that you may already use. We'll share plenty of examples and lesson plans from our classrooms and from trusted colleagues, and we'll give you suggestions for making those activities work in your room.

For each tool, program, or activity, we will explain how to get started and how to integrate it in your classroom, and provide hints and tips to help things run smoothly. For more complicated tools, we'll provide illustrated, step-by-step tutorials to help you find your way.

For many activities in this book we'll provide you with **Tech Specs,** where we evaluate the activity on four scales:

> **Tech Specs**
> **Set-up Time:** *How much time will it take you to set this up?*
> **Keep-Up Time:** *After the initial investment, how much time will it take you to keep this up?*
> **Class Time:** *How much time in class will this activity take?*
> **Tech Savvy:** *How much technological fluency will you and your students need to be able to do this?*

These scales can help you decide whether the activity we describe is right for you, based on your comfort with technology and your skill level.

Connecting with Our Web Sites

The best way for us to teach you about using new technologies would be for us to sit down next to you and show you some things. In fact, it would be pretty fun for you to join us at our summer workshops, or for us to come out to your school and work with you there (check out http://www.edtechteacher.org/workshops.html for more info).

But in the meantime, you should visit our Web sites for video tutorials, annotated links, and more. At EdTechTeacher (http://www.edtechteacher.org) we have a wide variety of video tutorials and podcasts showing us doing a bunch of stuff starting a blog, recording a podcast, setting up a chat room, putting an image in a PowerPoint presentation, and all sorts of other things. At Teaching History with Technology (http://www.thwt.org) and Teaching English with Technology (http://www.tewt.org) you'll find tips and guides specific to those subjects. Finally, at The Best of History Web Sites (http://www.besthistorysites.net) you'll find an extensive collection of history-related Web sites that we have evaluated and annotated. We have written this book with the intention that if you find a topic that intrigues you, then you should be able to head right to our Web sites to learn more.

WEBSITE: As you read along, look for these boxes when you want to learn more about a topic. This is where we'll let you know about additional resources you will find on our Web sites.

ZEN AND THE ART OF TEACHING WITH TECHNOLOGY

Starting new endeavors is always a little nerve-racking, and for many of us introducing technology into the classroom is scary because things we don't understand can go wrong. Here are some tips to keep you sane as you start using technology in your classroom.

1. The more you use technology, the fewer problems you will have. Stick with it.
2. Practice beforehand from both the instructor and the student point of view. Some problems can be eliminated with a little practice.
3. Assume that something could go wrong. Have a pencil and paper backup plan.

PENCIL: In these boxes, with the nifty pencil symbol, you will find pencil and paper backup plans for activities that rely on computers or the Internet. As you start using more technology in the classroom, have these backup plans ready to go.

4. When things go wrong, remember this is a teaching moment. Every day you ask your students to get out on the edge, take risks, and try new things. Sometimes they make mistakes. They have much to learn from how you handle the bumps of learning.
5. When things go wrong, ask students to help. These days just about every class has at least one technological genius. See if they can solve the problem. Remember when you used to set up the VCR for your teachers? (If you are old enough that students were helping you set up the VCR in your classrooms, then we are really impressed that you are using this book!)

6. Find a mentor. Chances are that others in your school are using technology in their classrooms. See if you can get them to sit in on some of your classes.

THE TWO BIG QUESTIONS: WHY AND HOW?

This book has plenty of tutorials, explanations, and examples, and not so much Ed school jargon and theory. We do, however, have answers to two essential questions for this venture: *Why teach with technology?* and *How can we best teach with technology?*

Why Teach with Technology?

Our first tenet is that no one should use technology just for the sake of using it. Technology should not take away from all the terrific things you do in the classroom. There are lots of places where pencils, paper, and old-fashioned face-to-face conversation are all that a great class needs. We are on the look out for specific ways that technology can surpass or enhance the best practices in our classrooms. With that in mind, here are three good reasons and one OK reason for using technology in the classroom:

1. **Whoever is doing most of the talking, or most of the typing, is doing most of the learning (and the more people listening, the better).**
   - Computers can help us take responsibility for learning off our shoulders and put it onto our students. Technology can get students teaching themselves and communicating with the world outside the classroom.
2. **The more different ways we put things in our brain, the more likely we are to learn and remember.**
   - Computers let students interact with information in so many different ways— watching, listening, touching, moving, writing, creating. This diversity especially serves some students with particular learning needs, but ultimately we think diverse teaching techniques help every student.
3. **We cannot always leave the classroom to go out into the world, but we can bring the world into our classroom.**
   - Computers allow us to access documents, images, ideas, sounds, and people from all over the world. Getting students out of the classroom during the school year is a logistical feat, but bringing the world into the classroom through the Internet is now an ordinary task for many teachers.
4. **Sometimes technology makes things easier; sometimes . . .**
   - We have to be careful with this one. Playing with technology can have you fall down bottomless holes of time. We've fallen down those holes so that you don't have to. This book is about using tools that have significant benefits with minimum or moderate investments of our time.

How Can We Best Teach with Technology?

If Daniel H. Pink, author of *A Whole New Mind,* is correct, modern society is shifting from an Information Age to a "Conceptual Age" where successful participants in our fast-changing, globalized economy will increasingly be required to use right-brain characteristics such as inventiveness, synthesis, and empathy.[1] Currently, our schools are largely geared toward left-brain characteristics such as detail retention, order and pattern, and logic. That's what standardized tests assess. In this era of "teaching to the test," our schools are not doing enough to develop in our students the ability to design and create original products, work and collaborate with varied individuals, and grasp the underlying significance of what they are learning.[2] In our experience, technology-based projects are excellent vehicles for teaching these essential skills.

The design of our educational technology projects has been influenced by Professor Ben Shneiderman's "Collect-Relate-Create-Donate" e-learning framework. Professor Shneiderman, author of *Leonardo's Laptop: Human Needs and the New Computing Technologies,* argues that effective technology integration is "user centered," promotes human interaction and creativity, and empowers individuals to serve others. In the "Collect" phase of his framework, students begin an e-learning project by researching and collecting facts and information. Next, in the "Relate" phase, students work in teams and develop communication and management systems, identify and clarify problems, and work toward successful solutions. In the "Create" phase students work individually and collectively to create content for the project. In essence, "they create to learn and learn to create." Finally, in the "Donate" phase, students disseminate their product and offer it as a service to others.[3]

We think that the best uses of technology come about when we do less of the teaching and students do more of the learning. To put it another way, we feel that technology projects and activities that empower students by putting them at the center of the learning process are especially worthwhile. Technology projects that foster creativity and lead to published student work are especially motivating to students. To cite a few ideas, students might create a multimedia magazine on the 1920s, record a radio show about hobos in the Great Depression, shoot and edit a digital poetry movie, blog about an independent research project, build a virtual tour of ancient Athens, or collect and edit oral histories on the Vietnam War. In each of these cases students create the final product and the teacher serves as a facilitator or guide. In this e-learning model, students work individually and collectively to gather information, manage communication, identify and work through problems, and create a product that can be shared with others. As you read the chapters ahead, you'll find that many of the tools and techniques we discuss can culminate in these kinds of student-centered projects.

A QUICK WORD ON TUTORIALS

Through this book, we walk you through many different software programs and online services. During these tutorials, we'll use italics to denote what you need to click or type. For instance, if we say "Hit *Control-F* to enter the Find window," then we'd like you to simultaneously press the *Control* key and the *F* key on your keyboard. If we say "click *OK,*" then we'd like you to click the button on the interface that says *OK.* We use arrows to denote when we'd like you to go through the menus available in a program. For instance, if we write, "go to *File →Save,*" then you should to the File menus and choose Save.

We also need to alert you in advance that changes will undoubtedly take place in the time it takes to print this book. In the process of writing, we have had to make changes to several sections of the book as new versions of software and Web sites are unveiled. The technologies we discuss change so fast that by the time you are reading this, undoubtedly some of the products we discuss will have gone through upgrades and updates that render some of our advice incorrect. In these cases, we encourage you to visit our Web site, http://www.edtechteacher.org, where we hope to maintain a section of changes and errata. We have also chosen to present all of our Microsoft tutorials using the 2003 products rather than the new 2007 products. If your school has upgraded to Word or PowerPoint 2007, you will need to use the ribbon rather than the menus we reference in the tutorial. In general, many of the functions are the same.

That's enough introduction. Flip through the table of contents, look for an aspect of your teaching where you'd like to have more ideas and resources, and let's get started.

NOTES

1. Daniel H. Pink, *A Whole New Mind: Moving from the Information Age to the Conceptual Age* (New York: Riverhead Press, 2005.)
2. Ben Schneiderman, *Leonardo's Laptop: Human Needs and the New Computing Technologies* (Cambridge, MA: MIT Press, 2003.)
3. Doug Johnson. "Are 21st Century Skills Right Brain Skills?" *Education World* (2006), http://www.education-world.com/a_tech/columnists/johnson/johnson006.shtml (accessed 8 August 2007).

Best Ideas for Teaching with Technology

Chapter 1

Lectures: Enhancing Teaching and Learning with Multimedia

INTRODUCTION

Professor Don Sadoway, instructor of a popular freshman Chemistry course at the Massachusetts Institute of Technology, tells his teaching assistants that the two most significant developments in education over the last generation have been computers and Sesame Street. Computers radically changed how we access and present information, but it was Sesame Street that redefined young people's conception of learning. The generation of kids raised on Ernie and Elmo has come to believe that learning is meant to be loud, musical, colorful, and energetic. For better or for worse, teachers who want to reach out to the Big Bird generation need to use media to grab and sustain attention.

Older educational technologies have made it possible to use multimedia in the classroom for decades. Radios delivered audio, televisions displayed video, slide projectors showed images, and overhead projectors allowed reusable class notes. If you have ever used any of these tools, then you are already teaching with technology.

Computers offer three main advantages over these older tools. The first is that these media are now bundled, so only a single computer, rather than a cartful of equipment, is required to present everything. The second bonus is that computers connected to the Internet can find almost unlimited media for the classroom, much of it free. The final exciting benefit of computers is that they make it possible for you to create and modify your own multimedia presentations based on your passions, tailored to state standards, or focused on connections to your local community.

In many classrooms, the only computer in the room belongs to the teacher, and this book starts with an exploration of how a single computer attached to a projector can help teachers create more engaging lectures and presentations that reach out to students with a variety of learning styles. Great teachers use different media because the more ways you try to sneak information into the student brain, the more likely it is to actually get in and stay there.

MULTIMEDIA PRESENTATIONS WITH IMAGES, VIDEO, AND AUDIO

It's one thing to read Robert Frost's "Birches," but it's quite another to hear Frost read it (http://town.hall.org/radio/HarperAudio/012294_harp_ITH.html). It's one thing to read Martin Luther King's "I Have a Dream" speech, but it's quite another to watch him deliver it (http://www.mlkonline.net/video.html). Educational technology allows teachers to bring the best sources from our disciplines easily into the classroom. When our voices start becoming the mumbles of Charlie Brown's teacher, we can draw on other voices and images to energize our teaching and engage students with different learning styles.

Prepared Presentations with PowerPoint, Impress, and Keynote

Presentation software has become a standard accompaniment to lectures in education, business, government, and science. Microsoft PowerPoint is the most popular choice for presentation software, and we'll use it as our example in this chapter. PowerPoint allows you to create slides that incorporate text, images, audio, and video to accompany lectures or discussions. PowerPoint presentations are easy to design, and pre-made presentations are easy to find on the Web.

Ten Ways to Enhance Lectures with PowerPoint

1. Include visual evidence in your lectures with images of art, artifacts, and architecture.
2. In discussing authors, include audio and video clips of them reading their work, which can be put directly into PowerPoint.
3. Include charts, graphs, and figures to supply statistical support to an argument.
4. Show a sequence of maps that demonstrate change over time.
5. Compile short examples of student writing to critique or edit.
6. Sum up the essential points or questions of a lecture in an outline slide.
7. Use charts, diagrams, and matrices to help students see relationships among ideas or information.
8. Use portraits or photographs so students can see pictures of the people you discuss.
9. Include cartoons or funny illustrations to inject humor into your presentation.
10. Use slides with titles and subheadings to help listeners follow the argument in longer lectures.

Warning!!
PowerPoint can be used to deliver some extremely bad teaching. The classic parody of terrible PowerPoint was created by Google programmer Peter Norvig, who rewrote the Gettysburg Address as a PowerPoint presentation. The complete results can be found at http://www.norvig.com/Gettysburg/index.htm, but even one slide says it all.

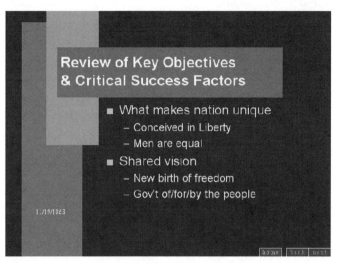

This PowerPoint presentation demonstrates that technology is not always an improvement.   *Source:* Courtesy of Peter Norvig.

As you can see, technology has the capacity to make lectures and presentations much, much worse. Computers are like any other tool: used well they can create works of beauty, but used thoughtlessly they can ruin things as well.

Finding and Borrowing PowerPoint Presentations

Because PowerPoint has become so popular among teachers and professors, many PowerPoint presentations can be found for free on the Web. If you are just starting to teach with PowerPoint, borrowing one of these presentations can be a first step to bringing more multimedia into your teaching. Be sure to role model good citation by giving the original author credit when using someone else's material.

Finding PowerPoint Presentations with Google's Advanced Search

We will have much more to say about searching with Google in Chapter 5, "Open Research," but Google has the perfect feature for finding PowerPoint presentations on the Web. When you go to the Google homepage, http://www.google.com/, just to the right of the search bar you will see a small link for *Advanced Search.* Click on that link and you will see a variety of powerful search options. One of those search options is *File Format,* where you can choose to ask Mr. Google to look only for PowerPoint presentations. Select this option, put your search terms in at the top, and for many topics you will have links to dozens of ready-made PowerPoint presentations to choose from.

If you click on a link to a PowerPoint, your Web browser will ask you if you would like to open the PowerPoint or download it to your hard drive. If you click on *View as HTML,* you will be able to view the PowerPoint slides on a single Web page, though some of the

Google's Advanced Search provides the option of searching for only the PowerPoint file format. *Source: Courtesy of Google.*

animations, sounds, and other features will be disabled. This is a useful method for previewing PowerPoint slides and is much faster than downloading many presentations.

Viewing PowerPoint Presentations in Class

Viewing PowerPoint presentations in class is quite straightforward. Open the PowerPoint presentation, and then hit *F5* (only on PCs) or click *Slide Show →View Show.* You can advance the slides with a mouse click, with the *space bar,* or with the *right arrow key.* Use the *left arrow key* to go backward, or quit at any time by hitting *Escape.*

As you start using PowerPoint, you should practice projecting presentations before you show them in class to ensure that your text is large enough, that the images are high enough resolution to be clear, and that everything works the way you expect it to. Sit in the back of the room and make sure that everything can be seen, even from the cheap seats.

The PowerPoint Slide Show Viewer

To be able to edit PowerPoint slideshows, you need the very expensive PowerPoint software. Anyone, however, can view a slideshow using the free PowerPoint Viewer. You can download the viewer at, http://office.microsoft.com/en-us/downloads/CD010798701033.aspx, or just Google search for "PowerPoint Viewer." With these viewers, your students should be able to watch and print your PowerPoint presentations, even if they don't own PowerPoint. You can also open PowerPoint presentations and edit them in OpenOffice.org's Impress.

PowerPoint's Competition

There are several great alternatives to PowerPoint. For Apple users, Keynote in the iWork suite is a great alternative. And for everyone, Impress from http://www.openof fice.org/ is a free alternative to both. If getting PowerPoint or other Microsoft products for everyone is a financial burden for you or your students, switch to Impress and the OpenOffice suite. Support for movies and sounds inside the presentation is weaker in Impress, but if you are using just images and text, it's pretty much just as good as the expensive stuff. If all the material for your presentations can be found on the Web, you might also consider using just tabbed browsing to create a BrowserPoint presentation, discussed toward the end of this chapter.

FEATURED PRODUCTS

Keynote
Web site: http://www.apple.com/iwork/keynote/
Developer: Apple
Cost: Keynote comes as part of iWork, which retails for around $80.

Apple's version of PowerPoint, which many reviewers find better than PowerPoint.

Open Office Impress
Web site: http://www.openoffice.org/product/impress.html
Developer: OpenOffice.org
Cost: Totally free

Open Office is an open-source project where software developers have created free versions of the standard suite of Microsoft Office or Apple products. It's probably not quite as good as the retail stuff, but when you look at the price tag, it becomes a whole lot more attractive.

Microsoft PowerPoint
Web site: http://office.microsoft.com/en-us/powerpoint/default.aspx
Developer: Microsoft
Cost: PowerPoint 2007 retails for $229; the full Microsoft Office suite costs $399.

The world's standard presentation software.

Tech Specs: Microsoft PowerPoint

Set-Up Time: Finding and downloading PowerPoint presentations from the Web takes only minutes. Creating and modifying your own can be time-consuming, especially if you get finicky about details and appearance.

Keep-Up Time: PowerPoint files are easy to change and update from year to year.

In-Class Time: Plan on a few minutes to open PowerPoint and load your presentation. Presentations can be as simple as a single image or as sophisticated as a full multimedia class.

Tech Savvy: Low to medium—text and images are easy; fancy presentations with animations and transitions can get complicated.

Making and Editing PowerPoint Presentations

Whether you are editing a presentation that you got from a colleague or found on the Web or whether you are starting your own presentation from scratch, these suggestions and tutorials should get you started with great presentations in short order.

Guidelines for Effective Presentations

The following are a few tips for crafting effective presentations. Review these before we get into the nuts and bolts of how to do it:

1. **Use PowerPoint to present what is not possible with a chalkboard.** Presentation software is great for displaying art, architecture, graphs, and maps. Many great presentations need nothing more than images and titles to reinforce the lecture or discussion in class.

2. **Use text as prompts.** In general, keep the text on your slides to a minimum. We have been in both middle school and graduate classes where students dutifully copied every word on the screen into their notebooks verbatim. Those students can't possibly listen to the conversation, probe their own thoughts, and practice being stenographers at the same time. Rather than putting all your lecture notes on the screen, put just a few words that will help students follow the day's conversation, perhaps supplemented with some new vocabulary or other important dates. If a lecture has a particular thesis or main point, it can be helpful to emphasize that on one slide as well. Putting questions on a slide is a great way to foster conversation. But on the whole, concisely present only the most important text. (Lecture outlines can be shared in other ways. See Chapter 2, "Discussion and Communication," for posting lecture notes on a blog, or Chapter 10, "Class Management," for posting notes on a class Web page).

3. **Use simple designs.** For most presentations, consider using the default white screen–black text template. Spend your time working on teaching a great class rather than fussing too much with the design of your slides. If you do choose a template, pick from the simplest, least distracting ones. For presentations with lots of images, use a light background and dark text. If you plan on presenting mostly text, consider a green background with white text. That works for highway signs, right?

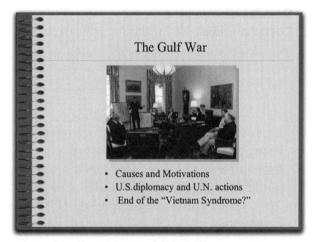

The slide above is clear, concise, and uncluttered. The background design is simple and nondistracting, while the slide's content (text + image) is equitably balanced by open areas or "white space." Moreover, the light design background contrasts well with the dark Oval Office photo.

Source: Microsoft product screen shot reprinted with permission from Microsoft Corporation.

4. **Avoid fancy animations and graphics.** Before you have that image zoom in with a curlicue pattern from the bottom of the screen, think to yourself: is this really going to help anyone learn? The occasional funny sound or gimmick might wake up some dozing minds, but these quickly devolve from novelty to distraction.

The Basics of PowerPoint in Ten Steps

Step 1: Start a new presentation. To get started with a new PowerPoint presentation, open the program and click *File →New.* This will bring up the New Presentation Menu in the sidebar. Choose either *Blank Presentation* or *From Design Template.*

> **Tip:** If possible, work with only one version of PowerPoint and don't try to alternate between a PC and a Mac. If you work on the same project on computers that have different versions of PowerPoint, or if you move your PowerPoint back and forth between a Mac and a PC, you may see some discrepancies in how PowerPoint displays content.

Step 2: Choose a design. The simplest template is the blank one. If you do choose to click on *From Design Template,* a menu of possible templates will appear in the sidebar. As you choose one, remember that images often show up better on lighter templates and that the more design junk (borders, lines, frames, etc.) in the template, the more likely the junk will get in the way of your text and images.

Step 3: Create a title slide. Once you make your slide design choice, a title slide will appear. Click on the *Title* and *Subtitle* boxes to insert text. This would be a good time to save your presentation. Do this by clicking *File →Save.*

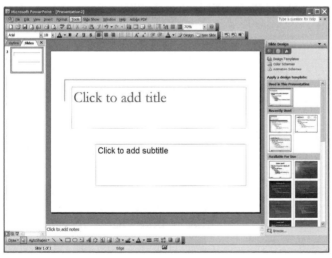

PowerPoint comes preloaded with a variety of slide designs, but it's best to stick with the simplest ones.

Source: Microsoft product screen shot reprinted with permission from Microsoft Corporation.

Step 4: Insert text. Most slides will have preset boxes where you can insert your text. If you choose to add text somewhere else, just click *Insert → Text Box* and you can draw a box with your cursor and put the text anywhere. After you create the text box, you can drag it around or click on a corner to expand or shrink the box. You can change the font, font size, and other features of the text inside the box like you would with a word processor using the toolbars at the top of the PowerPoint interface or by going to *Format →Font.*

Step 5: Create a second slide and choose a slide layout. To go to the next slide, click on the *New Slide* button or click on *Insert →New Slide,* and the sidebar menu will display a long list of possible choices. The two most useful ones are probably

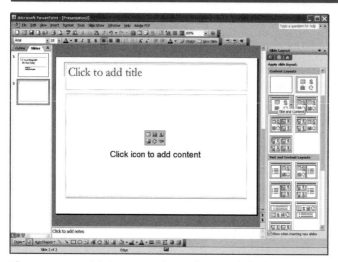

There are many slide layouts to choose from, and all of them can be customized.   *Source:* Microsoft product screen shot reprinted with permission from Microsoft Corporation.

the Title and Content slide, which is set up for a title and one image or graphic and the Title, Text and Content slide, which has a title at the top, text on the left, and space for an image on the right.

While these layouts automatically place text and images in certain places and configurations, you can easily move things around to your liking.

Tip: As you design your presentation, keep the "66 rule" in mind for each slide: maximum six lines of text and six words per line. Adhering to this guideline will help keep your PowerPoint slides uncluttered. Some argue for a "666 rule" (the Devil's Rule?): six lines of text, six words per line, and only six slides per PowerPoint! The message is to keep your PowerPoint presentations short and primarily visual.

Step 6: Insert an image. There are several ways to put an image into your slide. You can click the little mountain icon in the bottom left of the box above *Click icon to add content.* Then you can go the top menu and click *Insert→Picture→From File* and choose an image from your files. You can also find an image from your files or from the Web and simply copy the image in another application and then paste it into PowerPoint. Finally, if your screen has room to hold two open applications, then you can just click on an image from a program like a Web browser, hold the button down, and drag the cursor onto PowerPoint, when you release, the image will drop into the slot.

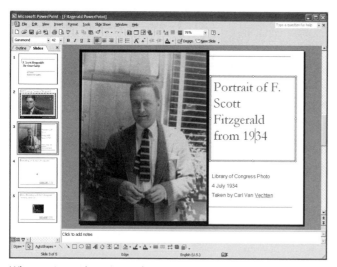

When an image has a vertical orientation, enlarge it to take up a full half of the frame.

Source: Microsoft product screen shot reprinted with permission from Microsoft Corporation.

Often when you copy an image onto the slide, it will take up only part of the slide. In order to help people see the image, it is best to make an image take up as much of the slide as possible. If the image has a horizontal orientation, stretch it the length of the slide. If it has a vertical orientation, like a portrait, then move the title to the right side of the slide, and let the image take up the whole left side.

> **Troubleshooting:** If you drag an image onto your slide, or copy and paste, and the silly "Click icon" box is still there, you can safely ignore it. It won't show up when you present. To get rid of the silly box, just click on the outside gray-hashed border of the box and hit the *Delete* key. Silly box.

You can try to copy and paste just about anything from the Internet onto your slides, not just pictures but also tables, graphs, or maps as well. Usually these are saved onto Web sites as image files, and so they copy easily. We'll discuss how to search for images using the Google Image search a little bit below.

> **Tip:** Microsoft PowerPoint also allows you to create simple graphs, charts, and other graphics for your slides. Click on the buttons above *Click icon to add content* and see what you find.

A DIVERSION INTO FILE FORMATS

Before we get into importing audio and video into PowerPoint, we need to discuss file extensions. Different types of files are saved in different formats. Each **file type** has a file extension, a code that gets attached to the end of a file name after a period. For Microsoft Word documents, the extension is .doc; MP3 audio files have the file extension .mp3.

There are many different file types and file extensions for image, audio, and video files. They represent different file sizes, levels of quality, and compatibility with different programs.

For presentations, the most common image file extensions are .jpg and .gif. For audio, they are .wav and .mp3. For video, .mpg and .avi are the most common standards. If you stick to these common extensions, you will have less trouble getting things to work in PowerPoint. It is possible to get files with other extensions to work in PowerPoint, but you may need to install other programs on your computer, and you may want to ask your IT staff for help. To learn more than you ever wanted to know about file extensions, visit http://filext.com.

Step 7: Insert an audio clip. If you want to incorporate MP3 clips into your PowerPoint presentation, click *Insert → Movies and Sounds → Sound from File* and choose a clip from the files on your hard drive. Once you do, PowerPoint will ask you if you want the clip to play automatically as the slide comes up or when clicked. Choosing the

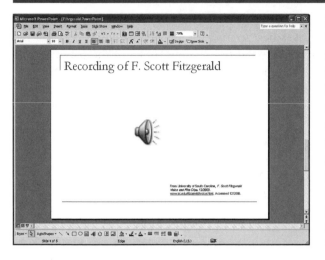

latter provides you with more flexibility about when you want to start the clip. You will see a funny little half-megaphone icon that is the link that you click to start the sound file. You can click the link to start the recording both in the design view and while playing the presentation. You can also record sounds in another program, such as Sound Recorder, Audacity, or GarageBand (see Chapter 8, "Student Presentations," for more on these programs), and then insert that recording into your presentation.

Now, here's the tricky part: if the sound file that you "insert" is greater than 100 kilobytes, PowerPoint won't actually insert it—it will just link to it. That means that if you move the PowerPoint presentation from one computer to another, you will need to move the sound file as well. For simplicity's sake, it's best to keep the PowerPoint presentation and all associated media in the same folder.

Step 8: Insert a video clip. If you would like to include video in your PowerPoint presentation, then you have two options: you can link to a video that you find on the Web or you can embed a file in your presentation.

In most cases, the easiest and least problematic option is to hyperlink to the Web page where the video clip is found. Just keep in mind that linking to a video on a Web page means that the video is not actually part of the slide show. To link to the video, click *Insert →Hyperlink.* Add the URL of the Web page you are linking to in the box that accepts a file name or Web page name. Another option is to search your list of "Browsed Pages" in the Insert Hyperlink dialogue box. When you click on the hyperlink during the presentation, your Web browser (such as Internet Explorer or Mozilla Firefox) will open to the page with the video, and you can play the movie from your browser. When you are done with the video, switch back to PowerPoint.

The alternative to linking to a video online is to insert the video directly into a slide. If you already have a video file on your computer, then inserting it into a slide is simple and similar to inserting an audio file. Click *Insert →Movies and Sounds →Movies from File.* Search for your file and select it, and it will appear as a storyboard. PowerPoint gives you the option of automatically playing the video when your slide appears or activating the video file manually by clicking on it during the presentation.

If you don't already have a video file ready to insert into a PowerPoint slide, you may be able to find what you are looking for on the Internet. We have lots of ideas on searching for multimedia later in this chapter.

Some file formats don't work in PowerPoint, and some older files of an accepted file format don't work, so sometimes trying to embed a movie file into PowerPoint can get very frustrating very quickly. Again, the simplest option may be to just hyperlink to a video on the Web.

CONVERTING FLASH FILES FOR POWERPOINT

Unfortunately, PowerPoint doesn't accept every type of video file format, including the Flash format. Flash is an increasingly popular file format for Internet video because its files are relatively small, are good quality, and can load quickly. For instance, Google's YouTube.com videos are in the Flash format. Fortunately, there are some clever people out there who have figured out how to help you to convert the Flash video into a format that PowerPoint does support. For instance, Vixy is a free online video converter that can be found at http://vixy.net, though it is still in the beta testing phase, so the service can be spotty. When you go to Vixy's Web site, you'll be prompted to insert the URL for an online video, and then Vixy can convert the video into a PowerPoint-compatible format such as .avi. Download the converted video, and insert it into your presentation like any other movie clip.

Flash video can be embedded successfully into many types of web pages, including blogs and wikis. (Learn more about embedded multimedia in Chapter 8, "Student Presentations".) David Strasburger, a physics teacher at the Noble and Greenough School in Dedham, Massachusetts, embeds Flash into his course wiki to create engaging presentations. See the Flash slideshow he created to show students how to solve one-dimensional elastic collisions with almost no math at: http://nobilis. nobles.edu/tcl/doku.php?id=courses:science:physics:ap_physics:1dcollisions

One final reminder: movie files are not actually embedded directly into the PowerPoint file; PowerPoint links to the file on your computer. That means that if you send the presentation to a different computer, you need to transfer the movie file as well, and you may be prompted to find the movie file when you try to play the presentation on the new computer.

Step 9: Set up custom animations. Custom animations can be used to control the entry and exit of objects, such as text and graphics, into your PowerPoint slides. (Note: slide animations can be distracting and can draw attention away from the slide's content.) An effective way to use custom animations is to control the entry of text in your slides. You can present one line, one word, or even one letter at a time. For instance, if you have a slide with five lines of text you may wish to introduce the lines one by one, pausing to discuss each point with your class. If you present all slide text, at once, students may be scrambling to jot it down and may lose focus on you and your immediate point.

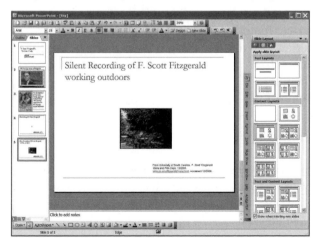

Videos will appear in your slide as still images of the first frame. Click on the image in the editing view or in the presentation view to play the movie.   *Source:* Microsoft product screen shot reprinted with permission from Microsoft Corporation.

To create a custom animation, click *Slide Show → Animation* from the top menus. Select an element of the slide, such as text or an image, and then choose an Entry Effect. Keep your animations relatively simple. You can view the effect by clicking on the *Preview* button. When you are satisfied with the effect, click the *OK* button. There are many options for animations—different effects, different timing options—limit how many you use to avoid wasting precious planning time.

Step 10: Print your slides as handouts. One of the most useful, hidden functions of PowerPoint is the ability to print handouts for your PowerPoint presentations with space and lines for taking handwritten notes. Click *File → Print*, and then in the bottom left of the window choose *Handouts* under *Print What*. The secret is that you must choose to print handouts with three slides per page. Choose any other number of slides, and you won't get the little space for notes. We don't know why this useful feature is so hard to find, but now you have the secret.

PENCIL: If you print out handouts for your classes to use during your presentations, then if your computer or projector fails, you can still deliver your presentation with students looking on at your slides, albeit itsy-bitsy versions of them.

COPYRIGHT AND FAIR USE: HOW MUCH CAN YOU BORROW?

The Internet has developed much faster than intellectual property law, and it can be hard to apply older copyright fair use guidelines to the new world of the Internet. To be sure you are respecting the legal rights of others, we recommend that you hire an army of lawyers to scrutinize your every move, or better yet, get to work on an intellectual property law degree at night.

Until you can finish up that degree, though, here are a few simple guidelines (which should not under any circumstances be construed as legal advice; that's what the army of lawyers is for):

1. Credit all the sources that you use in handouts and presentations. Role model good citation, especially if your students will be writing later. Get them used to seeing all those strange footnote notations.
2. Using things from the Internet for your in-class presentations is generally OK if you don't use too much from any individual work—and as long as you don't sell your presentations.
3. Copying things from the Internet to be put on a secure, password protected Web site is generally OK, again if you use only a little bit from any one work. But don't republish anything from the Internet onto a public Web site without permission.
4. For multimedia that are integrated into a student product, students are limited to using 10 percent of a work, with a 30-second maximum for music and a 3-minute maximum for video. There are other more specific rules that apply to different media types; again consult your librarian or army of lawyers for more help.

WEBSITE: For more information on copyright and fair use, go to http://www.edtechteacher.org/chapter1.html for some links to interpretations of the law.

PowerPoint as an Activity: Engaging Students with Presentations

Many students equate PowerPoint presentations with long, dull monologues during which they serve as passive (and bored) recipients of information. But it doesn't have to be that way. Images and textual prompts in presentations can serve as launching points for discussion and analysis.

A simple way to involve the students in active learning with PowerPoint is to have them analyze images you include in the slides. PowerPoint is an excellent vehicle for analyzing historical art and architecture, political cartoons, maps, and more. Remember, PowerPoint should be used primarily to present visual information, not text. Moreover, PowerPoint should not turn your typically student-centered and collaborative classroom into a teacher-dominated one.

In the slide below students are asked a simple, but challenging, question: What is the cartoonist's message? The students examine this Gilded Age cartoon closely for clues (clothing as indicators of socioeconomic class, the empty carcass on the "prosperity" plate, etc.) and use critical thinking skills to determine the point of the cartoon. Students could brainstorm ideas, work in small groups, and try to write their own caption. Or the teacher could provide possible captions for the cartoon and have the students debate which is the actual title:

a. "To the Victor Belong the Spoils"
b. "After the Feast: The Working Man Gets What's Left"
c. "Social Darwinism at Its Finest"
d. "Rags to Riches: Social Mobility and the American Dream"

Slides like this one challenge the students to think critically. The actual caption, by the way, is *b*, "After the Feast: The Working Man Gets What's Left."

If students can access your PowerPoint presentation on a computer, then you might consider inserting hyperlinks in your slides to turn your PowerPoint presentation into an activity. To insert Web links into a PowerPoint presentation; simply type the entire Web address including the "http://" into the text box, and PowerPoint will automatically transform the URL into a link (you can also go to the *Insert* menu and choose *Hyperlink*). Students can click on these links as they move through the PowerPoint slides and will be directed to other pertinent Web sites.

Another simple way of encouraging learning is to pose questions to the students either in the middle or at the end of a PowerPoint presentation. These questions can be in the form of a quiz, or can simply be a means to check for their understanding (and the quality of your teaching!). Questions should be designed to prompt students to reflect on

---

SMART Board

A SMART board is an (expensive) interactive whiteboard with a touch-sensitive surface that turns your computer into a powerful tool for presentations and activities. You can write and draw on the board, edit/highlight select material, save notes to a computer, and more. Tilesy Harrington, a math teacher at the Noble & Greenough School in Dedham, Massachusetts, is one of many teachers that makes effective use of a SMART board (and complimentary tools) to construct engaging in-class presentations and activities. She combines a calculator emulator with the SMART board so students can see her pushing keys on the calculator and can visualize results. She looks and talks directly to her students as she performs the steps instead of looking down into her palm (using "old" overhead projector panels). Ms. Harrington's students can also go to the SMART Board "all the time" during class so that they can help a particular student find elements like the right window for a graph, or the right menu for the operation they are trying to perform.

---

the content in the presentation. One effective strategy is to pair students up and then ask them to summarize the main themes presented in the PowerPoint presentation. Collective brainstorming, whether in a small group or among all the students, is an effective active learning technique that can easily be incorporated into a PowerPoint presentation.

Another technique to promote active learning with PowerPoint presentation is to insert a blank slide at strategic points, or to simply turn off the projector at times. This has the effect of directing all student attention toward you and provides you with an opportunity to encourage reflection and check for understanding. You may also use this opportunity to have students compare notes and to check if they are absorbing the information you are attempting to convey. It can provide an excellent opportunity to identify gaps in knowledge or misconstruction of the information.

A blank slide should always appear at the end of your PowerPoint presentations, and not just to indicate the end of your slides. Here is an opportunity to ask students: if they could ask a single question about the PowerPoint presentation, what would that question be? This provides an opportunity for reflective learning as students ponder the significance or importance of the topic.

SEARCHING FOR IMAGES, AUDIO, AND VIDEO: HOW TO FIND ALL THAT GOOD STUFF IN THE FIRST PLACE

Every day, thousands upon thousands of movies, audio clips, and images are added to the vast storehouses of the Web. If you can imagine a picture or a sound, however strange or esoteric, chances are you can find it on the Internet.

Tech Specs: Google Image Search

Set-Up Time: Depends on what you are looking for, but well-known images can often be found very quickly.

Keep-Up Time: None.

In-Class Time: We'll discuss Google searching for students more thoroughly in Chapter 5, "Open Research".

Tech Savvy: Low—Google's simple interface is what led it to victory in the search engine wars.

Google
Web site: http://www.google.com
Developer: Google
Cost: Free, with advertising

The current king of search engines. If it's publicly available on the Web, you'll find it with Google.

Searching for Images with Google Image Search

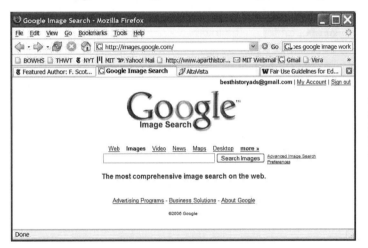

Google's image search engine can sort through the millions of pictures uploaded to the Web. *Source:* Courtesy of Google.

Google Image Search, found at http://images.google.com, is probably the handiest way to search for images on the Internet. Google tracks down images by looking at the name of the file, information embedded in the file, the text next to the image, the caption of the image, and all sorts of other things so that when you put in a search string, Google has a pretty good chance of returning the results that you are looking for. You can find pictures of just about anything you can imagine using Google Image Search, from photographs of recent events to images of art and architecture from long ago. Here are a few tips:

1. The more details you can put in the search box, the better. To find pieces of art to put in slide shows, put the name of the artist and the title of the work in the search box. It can also be helpful to know the museum where the work of art is housed.
2. For best results, use the Advanced Search. If you look just to the right of the Search Images box, you'll find the *Advanced Image Search* link. Click that first. We'll discuss Google's Advanced Search functions more fully in Chapter 5, "Open Research."
3. Your search results will be a series of small images called thumbnails. These are very small files and usually have very poor resolution when enlarged. Don't copy these files. Instead, click on the image and look at the top of the page for a link that says *See full-size image.* Click on that link, and you'll be taken to a page where you will be able to copy that larger image. If you find that the link to the full-size image is still a small image, the resolution might be too low for a presentation. To copy an image from the Web, right click (or *Control-click* for Apple) on the image and choose *Save Image As.*

PUBLIC DOMAIN IMAGES

Many of the images that you might use in a PowerPoint presentation will have copyright restrictions. If you are planning to show copyright images within the confines of your classroom, then your usage more than likely falls within the scope of educational "fair use." More educators are making their PowerPoint presentations available online, and this practice raises some important copyright issues. If you make your PowerPoint publicly accessible on the Internet without the express written permission of the authors of the copyrighted images, then you have most likely infringed on copyright protection. One way to make your PowerPoint presentations accessible to your students, but not the general public, is to place them on your school's local area network where only authorized students can access them. (You might ask the IT specialist at your school to set up a folder on the local area network where you could deposit your PowerPoint presentations.) Since the PowerPoint slides will not have to be accessed via the Internet, the students will not experience the delay that often accompanies loading Internet pages. Fortunately, there are numerous Web sites that offer visitors copyright-free public domain images. These images may be included not only in in-class PowerPoint presentations but also in presentations disseminated on the Internet and in other public forums.

WEBSITE: We have compiled an extensive list of Internet sources for public domain images, with an eye toward the humanities. The list can be found at http://www.edtechteacher.org/chapter1.html.

A great source of public domain images is Creative Commons at http://creativecommons.org/. Creative Commons helps you find free public domain media that you can legally use and share. Through the Creative Commons website you can search multiple content-rich directories, such as Yahoo and Flickr. Flickr is especially valuable for finding images. Flickr, located at http://flickr.com/, is a free web-based photo-sharing service where members upload pictures and make them available for others to see. Flickr contains millions of pictures, and many members make their pictures available for download and display on other Web sites. A Flickr image has a sidebar category called "Additional Information" where you will find out what rights the photographer has reserved. If you see a link to *Some Rights Reserved*, you can click on the link to see how you are allowed to use the image (usually educational uses are fine if the image is properly attributed). You can explore Flickr categories or "tags" (categorizing terms) for photos or just use the Flicker search engine.

Searching for Audio and Video with AltaVista

Tech Specs: AltaVista Search
Set-Up Time: Typically, finding audio and video will take longer than finding images or Web pages.
Keep-Up Time: None.
Tech Savvy: Medium—it can be a little tricky to figure out which file extensions will work with which programs. See more below.

FEATURED PRODUCT

AltaVista
Web site: http://www.altavista.com
Developer: AltaVista, now owned by Yahoo! Inc.
Cost: Free, with advertising

For regular searches, it's tough to beat Google, but AltaVista is a good option when looking for audio and video.

Back in the search engine wars of the 1990s, you might have put your money on the AltaVista search engine, which was a contender for a while, though it was ultimately Google's clean interface, relevant hits, and massive index that won the hearts of America's computer nerds. But AltaVista is still a good choice for searching for audio and video files.

Searching for Audio with AltaVista

For anyone who is a frequent user of Google, this search engine will look suspiciously familiar. But finding audio is a snap. Select the file extensions you want to look for (Microsoft PowerPoint won't recognize Real or AIFF files, but many music players will) and then type in your search terms. You will then get a listing of Web sites that are hosting your sound file. You may need to do a little searching on the page to find your file.

Tip: Remember that you can search the contents of any Web page by pressing *Control-F* (*Apple-F* on a Mac) and then typing in the words that you want to search for within the page.

DOWNLOADING AND STREAMING MEDIA FILES

There are two basic types of media files on the Internet—those that you can download in their entirety and those that can only be streamed. Streaming means that you cannot put the file on your computer; you can only listen to it or watch it through the Internet. You can play these files in class through a media player or Web browser, but you cannot put them in a presentation.

To stream any type of file, typically you just need to click the link. Sometimes the file will open right in your browser and start playing, and other times it will open your media player, such as Real Player, QuickTime, or the Windows Media Player.

To download a file, instead of clicking on the link, you will need to right click (*Control-click* for Apple machines) and choose *Save Link As*. If what you download is a tiny file—maybe just a few kilobytes—that cannot be opened, the file can probably only be streamed. You will be able to view it through your Web browser, but not through PowerPoint.

Tech Terms

Streaming is a method of sharing multimedia content. When something is streamed from the Internet, a computer won't download the whole file, just the part of the file you are watching or hearing.

Searching for Video with AltaVista

AltaVista's video search scours the Web for video clips. *Source*: Courtesy of Yahoo!.

Video searching is equally simple. Chose the file extensions that you want to search for—again, PowerPoint will only be happy with MPEG, AVI, and Windows Media, but you can find players for all of the extensions—and then type in your search terms. This time your search results will be screenshots from different video clips, and once again you will need to go to the linked Web sites to find the videos.

Searching for Audio and Video with Google

If you cannot find what you want with AltaVista, try using Google by searching for both a term, like "E. O. Wilson," and a file extension like .mp3 for audio or .mpeg for video. Or you can just use "audio" or "video" as search terms.

If you are willing to constrain your search to just videos posted on Google Video and YouTube, you can also go to http://video.google.com. Google purchased YouTube in 2007, so now searches in Google Video find videos from both sources. If you can dodge all of the PG-13 videos on the most popular list, type your search terms in the window, and you will find that many people have posted historical material of significant merit. For instance, you could use Google Video and YouTube to show Walter Cronkite's influential 1968 news editorial on Vietnam, Martin Luther King Jr.'s "I Have a Dream" speech, a Toni Morrison interview, as well as television footage of the Tet Offensive.

Ten Ideas for Teaching with Multimedia

Here are ten ideas for ways to use all these new media in your classes. In Chapter 8, "Student Presentations," we provide more ideas for ways for your students to use the new media.

1. **Incorporate visual evidence.** Make a presentation of art, architecture, and cultural objects for each time period you study. Ask students to explain how specific details in the projected images connect to the larger themes you are studying.

2. **Compare poetry readings.** Ask two students in your class to read a poem. Encourage the second student to try to read it differently from the first. Then find a clip of the author reading the poem, and ask students to make observations about how the mood or meaning of the poem changes with different readers.

3. **Start class with a news clip.** In a new twist on the age-old plan to start class with a current event, instead of bringing in a clipping from the newspaper, show a video clip of important or relevant events. Most American network and cable news programs offer free clips from their programs, and several international sources do as well, notably the BBC.

4. **Tell the story in maps.** Put several maps in a PowerPoint presentation or in several tabs in a single Web browser. As you lecture, you can switch from map to map. It's like those old map stands in your classroom, you just have thousands to choose from and you don't have to jump to flip them over.

5. **Show a few short clips from a movie**. With a DVD player that has a bookmarking option, it is very easy to show clips from a film starting from anywhere in the film.

6. **Use visual evidence to place students in an author's world.** As you are reading Henry David Thoreau's *Walden,* create a presentation with pictures of nineteenth-century Concord, Thoreau's neighbors, the architecture of nineteenth-century Massachusetts, the re-creation of his cabin from Walden Pond State Park, the steam engines of his day, and other images of his life and times.

7. **Use music to set the mood**. Especially in those first few minutes of class where kids brains are still stuck in Biology class, play a little music to transport students into the world of your class.

8. **Prep for a field trip by touring the Web site.** Before you go out into the world, familiarize yourself by touring the site through its Web site. You can even use a map program like Google Maps or Mapquest to see satellite images of where you are going.

9. **Use clips from documentaries to spark discussion.** The PBS series *Frontline* and *Nova* and the Chicago Public Radio series *This American Life* both make many of their shows available for free streaming online.

10. **Record yourself when you can't be there.** Fire up a digital video camera, give your presentation, send the file to a colleague, and ask him or her to play it during class. You never need to miss a class again!

Example: Presenting The Grapes of Wrath *with Multimedia*

Here is an outline for an interdisciplinary introductory presentation on *The Grapes of Wrath* by John Steinbeck.

- Begin with a historical introduction to the Great Depression using public domain images available via the Library of Congress American Memory exhibition: http://memory.loc.gov/ammem/fsowhome.html. Select a few images to include in a PowerPoint slide show and add a question or two to each slide that will encourage students to analyze and discuss the emotional toll of the Great Depression.

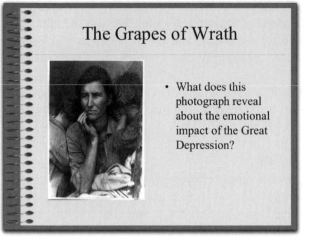

The Grapes of Wrath

• What does this photograph reveal about the emotional impact of the Great Depression?

Including photographs can force students to imagine the physical and emotional tol of the Great Depression.

Source: Microsoft product screen shot reprinted with permission from Microsoft Corporation.

• Direct students to read personal histories of Americans living during the Great Depression, such as those found at the New Deal Network: http://newdeal.feri.org/index.htm and PBS's *Surviving the Dust Bowl* at http://www.pbs.org/wgbh/amex/dustbowl/. If your students are teenagers, consider having them read the stories of teenage hobos who were "riding the rails" in the 1930s: http://www.pbs.org/wgbh/amex/rails/.

• Listen to audio interviews of Americans who lived during the Great Depression. Visit the Library of Congress's "Voices from the Dust Bowl" collection at http://memory.loc.gov/ammem/afctshtml/tshome.html for mp3 files.

• Listen to a "Fireside Chat" by President Roosevelt and discuss what impact these chats had on the American public. You can find select Fireside Chat audio recordings at the American Rhetoric Web site: http://americanrhetoric.com/.

• Use Google Earth to follow the Joad family as it travels to California. A *Grapes of Wrath* "Google Lit Trip" is available from: http://web.mac.com/jburg/iWeb/GoogleLit/9 12/9–12.html (See Google Earth in Chapter 4, "Guided Inquiry").

• Watch the trailer for the 1940 movie *The Grapes of Wrath* starring Henry Fonda available at http://www.imdb.com/title/tt0032551/trailers. Obtain the DVD and watch select scenes from the movie.

As you can see, even for topics from the first half of the twentieth century, we can find an incredible wealth of audio and video to help immerse students in another era.

For more lesson plan ideas, go to http://www.edtechteacher.org/lessons.html

USING VIDEO IN THE CLASSROOM

While short clips work reasonably well inside presentations, larger video clips take a very long time to load when embedded in presentation software. Fortunately the Web is increasingly full of streaming video clips that can be played right off of the Internet. Most major news outlets have plenty of clips on their Web sites. PBS's documentary series *Frontline* has made its entire library of recent episodes available online for free.

Another big player in streaming video is Discovery Education's United Streaming. Already available in more than half of all U.S. schools, United Streaming has over 5,000 full-length videos broken up into 50,000 clips, all available on demand for educators.

These videos can even be downloaded and inserted into PowerPoint presentations. Go to http://www.unitedstreaming.com/ or speak to your school's librarian or IT staff to learn more.

Typically streaming clips is easy enough. Just click on the link, wait for a player to pop up, and wait for the clip to download.

Tip: Don't wait until you want to play a clip to start loading it; sometimes it can take a while. Instead, get your clips all loaded up before class, and then put them on pause. When you are ready to use the clips, just press play. You'll save yourself from those awkward, waiting-to-load moments.

Bookmarking

If your computers have Mac OS X, then you have one of the best tools for playing DVDs in class: DVD Player. This software has a feature, Bookmarks, that will change the way you show videos in class. Take a video home, find the scenes you want to show in class, and then bookmark those starting points with names for the scenes. To use the bookmark feature, play the DVD in DVD Player, and at the start of the scene you would like to book-mark, move your mouse to the top of the screen and click on *Controls →New Bookmark.* Then give that scene a name that easily identifies it. You can create as many bookmarks as you wish, and then, when you are ready to play the DVD for your class, simply start play-ing the DVD, move your mouse to the top of the screen, and click *Go →Bookmarks* and choose that scene that you would like to play. If you have four 60-second scenes from all different parts of the movie, you can easily show all four in class without a lot of jumping between chapters, fast-forwarding, going too far, rewinding, and so on.

BROWSERPOINT: SIMPLE WEB SITE PRESENTATIONS WITH TABBED BROWSING

If all the information that you want to present in a lecture is easily available on Web sites, then don't bother to make up a whole PowerPoint presentation. Instead, use tabbed browsing to prepare your presentation, and call it a BrowserPoint presentation.

There are some things that Web sites can do much better than PowerPoint. For instance, some online multimedia timelines show the same map at several points in history and do a great job of showing the development of areas and regions. Certain art history sites also have great collections of art by a single artist that would just be a waste of time to copy into PowerPoint (check out http://www.besthistorysites.net/arthistory.html for some great links). Some sites are also set up for viewing several multimedia news and documentary clips, and both TV and print media are creating more Web sites with this type of presentation. All of these things are more easily viewed from a Web browser than from PowerPoint.

The new technology that allows for these types of BrowserPoint presentations is the **tabbed browser**. This means that in a single window, you can have "tabs" with differ-ent preloaded Web sites. This makes it quite easy to jump backward and forward among several different sites. Weaving together a few different Web sites into a single presenta-tion has never been easier, as long as you have access to the Internet in your classroom. Some browsers also make it easy to share groups of pages, which means you can share your BrowserPoint presentations.

Creating BrowserPoint Presentations

These four tabs at the top are different web pages open in the same browser. It makes it easy to quickly flip between the pages.

Tabbed Web browsing allows you to pre-load several Web sites to show during a single class presentation.
Source: Microsoft product screen shot reprinted with permission from Microsoft Corporation.

Mozilla's Firefox (http://www.mozilla.com/) is a free Web browser that is good for setting up tabbed browser presentations, although the new Internet Explorer from Microsoft has a few additional features that make it a better choice for BrowserPoint presentations. If you have not yet downloaded Internet Explorer 7 (IE7), you can do so at this address: http://www.microsoft.com/windows/downloads/ie/getitnow.mspx.

Here are some basic steps to creating a BrowserPoint presentation using tabbed browsers in Internet Explorer 7.

Step 1: Create a new folder in Favorites. Find the first page you would like to use in your presentation. Click on the *Add Favorite* button, which is a star with a plus on the left-hand side. You will be prompted to put the new *favorite* in a folder. Use *New Folder* to create a new folder for your presentation.

Step 2: Add pages to your new folder. Search for the Web sites you want to use, and save them to your new BrowserPoint folder. In IE7, click on *Add Favorites* and then choose to put the Web site in your presentation folder.

Step 3: Name your links. To simplify your presentation, you will probably want to rename your links. Rename them starting with "Slide 1," "Slide 2," and so forth, and things will be easy to organize.

Step 4: Open the presentation. Once you have all of your sites chosen and placed in your folder, preparing the presentation is easy. Just open a new Web browser, and open your Favorites folder by clicking on the yellow star in the upper left-hand corner.

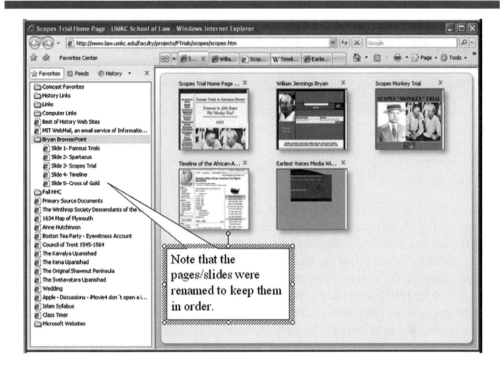

(You may also want to click on the green arrow in the upper right-hand corner of the Favorites sidebar, which will pin your Favorites folder to the screen.) Then right-click on the BrowserPoint folder, select *Open in Tab Group,* and, *voilà,* all of your pages/slides will open.

Step 5: On with the show! To deliver your presentation, just click on each tab to advance your presentation. If you ever get lost or need to jump back a few slides, IE7 has a handy *Quick Tabs* button, just to the left of all the open tabs. Click this button (or press *Control-Q*) and you will get a handy visual index of your tabs, very reminiscent of the Slide Sorter in PowerPoint.

> **Tip:** If some of your pages are too small to read, there is a handy *Zoom* function under the *Page* menu in the top right of the toolbar. You can also just enlarge the text by adjusting the *Text Size* option in the *Page* menu.

Advanced BrowserPoint

If you want to add some text to accompany your BrowserPoint, just create some new posts on your blog (remember to use a large font size for easy viewing), and then add those pages to your BrowserPoint folder. (See Chapter 2, "Discussion and Communication," for more on blogs.) You could also create Web pages using Google Pages, with text for your BrowserPoint presentations. (See Chapter 8, "Student Presentations," for more on Google Pages.)

If you want to add some audio commentary to your BrowserPoint, like instructions on what students should look for in the sites, create a podcast with a tool like Odeo, and then add that page to the folder in Favorites. (For more on Podcasting, see Chapter 8, "Student Presentations.")

PENCIL: One disadvantage of BrowserPoint is if the Internet goes down, you are out of luck. Whenever you are planning to use the Web in class, be sure to plan some backup activities in case your Internet connection fails.

Examples in BrowserPoint

Modern Events

Many events since the 1950s have been captured by TV and radio, and much of this footage can be found on the Web. Recently Tom used tabbed browsing and Internet media to present a lesson on the Watergate scandal. He used a special report called "The Watergate Story" available at the *Washington Post* Web site: http://www.washingtonpost.com/wp-srv/onpolitics/watergate/splash.html.

To introduce his students to the Watergate scandal, he first played a video at the Web site that provides an overview of the story. As his class reviewed the key events and individuals involved in Watergate, he played a section of the infamous Nixon Oval Office tapes that was available at the Web site. Students listened and discussed its contents. He also had students watch an Internet video discussion of Watergate featuring Bob Woodward, a key *Washington Post* reporter during Watergate. The class also listened to various CBS news reports from 1973 and 1974 available at the same *Washington Post* Web site.

Instead of clicking around the site during class to find each section he wanted to present, Tom simply set up browser tabs to various sections of the Web site. In this way, he was able to move immediately to the various multimedia he wanted to present. Before class he made sure he loaded all the audio and video because multimedia files often load more quickly after the first play.

During these kinds of multimedia presentations, be sure to pause at strategic junctures to ask questions and to test for understanding. Also, periodically put the cover on the projector's bulb to focus students' attention exclusively on the question at hand. These techniques will help make your presentations more engaging and interactive; remember, whoever is doing most of the talking is doing most of the learning.

Maps and Change over Time

Tabbed browsing is also especially effective when you want to present a series of events that demonstrate change, such as the physical growth of a region. With tabbed browsing you could present geopolitical changes in Europe through the medieval and early modern periods through a series of maps. There are public domain maps available for free from the Medieval Internet History Sourcebook: http://www.fordham.edu/halsall/sbookmap.html. Set up a series of tabs in your Web browser with pages in chronological order. For example, your first tab could point to a map of Europe in 476, the next to a map of Europe in 800, the third to a map of Europe in 1099, and another to a map of Europe in 1360. In this manner you could present the geopolitical changes quickly and ask students to explain the changes that took place.

PROJECTORS: SHARING YOUR SCREEN WITH THE CLASSROOM

Tech Specs: Projectors

Set-Up Time: If you are new to using projectors, you should spend 20–30 minutes figuring out all of the features before you start using it for class. Ideally, you should find someone to walk you through it.

Keep-Up Time: None, once you figure it out.

In-Class Time: Budget a minute or two to plug in to a projector, and another two minutes or so for the bulb in the projector to warm up. It's a great time to check in with students or ask if they have questions about the previous night's work.

Tech Savvy: Low to medium—some models are bare bones and just need to be turned on; models with more bells and whistles may be more complicated.

To start using computers in your class, you will need a projector to make your computer screen available to the whole class. In a sense, the projector is like a second monitor attached to the computer, but one that the whole class can easily see. With a projector, you can easily show portraits, news clips, landscapes, charts, tables, and graphs to enhance the visual elements of your teaching.

Getting Started with Projectors

Since there are dozens of projector models out there, it would be hard to say exactly what yours will look like or exactly how it will work. So instead, here is a list of questions that you should ask the IT staff at your school so that you can know everything you need to know to get started.

1. **Power** *Where is the power switch?*
2. **Power** *Where are the cords to plug in the projector?*
3. **Connection** *Where are the cords to connect the projector to my computer? Where do the cords connect to my computer? Do I need any special adaptor for my Apple computer?*
4. **Connection** *What buttons do I press on the projector so that it will recognize my computer?* Most projectors can take input from several different sources, like DVD players or computers. Be sure that you know what to do to tell the projector to find your computer.
5. **Connection** *Do I have to do anything on my computer to get the image to display through the projector?* Most Apple computers will automatically display through a projector when they are connected. Some PC computers will as well, although sometimes you need to go into the *Display* settings and tell the computer to display through the projector. Some brands of laptops have a special button (sometimes *Function-F8*) that will rotate between the monitor, the projector, and both displays.
6. **Audio Connection** *Does the projector have speakers? If so, where are the cords to connect my computer to the projector?* Many projectors now have built-in speakers. Usually you will need a cord with one end that plugs into the speaker/headphone jack on your computer, and another end that has red and white connectors to the projector.

7. **Getting Started** *How long does the projector take to warm up?* Many models take a few minutes to actually display an image.

8. **Getting Started** *How do I focus the image? How can I make it larger or smaller? How can I adjust the brightness? How can I adjust the volume?*

9. **Troubleshooting** *How do I restart the projector?* As with much of technology, when things are not working, the first thing to try is a re-boot. Oftentimes turning the projector and computer off, waiting a few minutes, and then restarting will solve the problem.

10. **Troubleshooting** *How do I replace a burned out bulb? Where are the extra bulbs?*

Arm yourself with these questions when you first learn how to use your projector, and you should eliminate most of the common problems encountered when starting to use computers in the classroom.

> **PENCIL:** Even with all of this planning, something is likely to not work at some point. When you have something planned to project in class, always have a backup plan ready, whether it be lecture notes, discussion questions, or every student's favorite, the pop quiz. A pop quiz may provide you enough time to call an IT person or fellow teacher to come help you out, and kids love the chance to prove how well they are doing their homework!

WEBSITE: Still having trouble? Look for links to other troubleshooting sites at http://www.edtechteacher.org/chapter1.html.

The Natives Are Restless: Dealing with Native Resolutions

Sometimes when you connect to a projector, it will change the size of all of the icons and windows on your screen. All screens and projectors have a "native resolution," which basically means that they are viewed best at a certain level of detail and resolution. Most projectors have a native resolution that is lower than most computer screens, so you may find that when you connect to the projector, the computer automatically adjusts itself to the settings of the projector and resets itself when it disconnects.

If your computer is not automatically making these changes, you may want to have someone show you how to change the resolution of your computer screen to match the resolution of your projector. For PCs, this means fiddling with the *Display* settings in the Control Panel, or the System Preferences for Macs. If you are always going to be using a particular computer with a particular projector, you may just want to set the computer to the same resolution as the projector.

Tech Terms

Pixel: The term "pixel" comes from the phrase "**pic**ture **el**ement," and a single pixel is a single point of color in an image.

Resolution: When referring to monitors and projectors, resolution refers to the number of pixels that fit in a given area. When resolution numbers are larger, that means an image is made of more pixels, which creates a finer image, but also demands more from the computer processors.

When your computer gets reset to the projector's native resolution, some applications, like Web browsers, will look somewhat different at the new resolution. You'll find that "less" of the browser fits on your screen, as if you had zoomed in. Most presentations, such as those in PowerPoint or Keynote, should look the same.

Should You Buy Your Own Projector?

Because of the disgraceful state of educational funding in this country, the wealthiest in world history, many teachers know all too well that sometimes being able to teach well means taking money from your own pocket.

When wrestling with the question "Should I plunk down nearly a thousand dollars [half that price on eBay] for a projector?" consider the main advantage of having your own: you can take it home and watch movies with it. Whether you spend the extra hundred dollars for a screen or just tack up a white sheet, they look awesome and cost much less than a big TV. Other advantages include always having it available for your class and getting to know its quirks and moods. Remember, your TV probably isn't tax-deductible, but that LCD projector that you bring to class sure is!

GETTING DATA INTO YOUR CLASSROOM

Unless you have the good fortune to be able to do 100 percent of your planning in the same room you teach in, you will need to develop a system for moving files from your home to your office and classrooms. In this section we'll look at several means of transferring your computer data among different rooms.

Lugging the Lappy

Sales of notebook computers are quickly outpacing sales of desktop computers, so chances are if you own a computer, then you own a laptop. If you do, then toting your laptop between home and the classroom is probably the easiest way to move your data. You can plan classes at home, in your office, or in a tree house, and then you can bring your laptop into your classroom to teach. If you don't have a laptop, here are a few other ways of moving presentations, audio, and video around with you.

Thumb Drives

Tech Specs: Thumb Drives
Set-Up Time: None.
Keep-Up Time: None.
In-Class Time: Almost none—even large files should upload and download from the drive very quickly.
Tech Savvy: Low.

Tech Terms

Byte: A single unit of data. A typical text email message might be 2 kilobytes (2,000 bytes), a typical mp3 song might be 3 megabytes, (3 million bytes) and a small hard drive might store 60 gigabytes (60 billion bytes).

USB or Universal Serial Bus: A standard type of connection between computers and peripheral devices. It's a rectangular plug and slot about 1 centimeter wide.

Sometimes called USB drives, flash drives, or memory sticks, these devices are little hard drives that are about the size of your thumb, and can hold a gigabyte of data for less than $20. For most presentations, even with some audio and video, that is more than you would ever need.

Thumb drives can store several gigabytes of information on a tiny stick, which is perfect for transporting data.

These devices plug into your computer, act like an extra hard drive, and usually are compatible with both Apple and PC computers. You plug the device into one of the USB slots in your computer (if you don't know which one, just keep poking things until it fits), and then you should see a new icon appear—either right on the desktop for Apple machines or in the *My Computer* folder for Windows. Drag files into the folder for your thumb drive, and they will be saved on your little device.

Remember: Always safely disconnect the drive before you unplug it. You can lose data or mess up your drive if you yank it out while it's running. To safely remove the drive on Apple machines, just throw the drive icon in the trash before you unplug it. On Windows machines, look in the bottom right hand corner of your toolbar for the *Safely Remove Hardware* icon.

Click this icon, click the device you want to remove, and then click *Stop*. Sometimes you have to confirm which device you would like to remove and click *OK*. Once that's all done, it's safe to remove your thumb drive and put it in your pocket.

When shopping for a thumb drive, some of the most useful features are those that help you keep track of the little devil. Consider buying a thumb drive attached to a key chain and look for drives where the cap cannot be lost either. For most teachers, 1 gigabyte should be plenty of storage for everyday needs.

Portable Music Players as Hard Drives

Tech Specs: Portable Music Players

Set-Up Time: 20–30 minutes to read up on the Web and change your settings.

Keep-Up Time: None.

In-Class Time: Almost none—even large files should upload and download from the player quickly.

Tech Savvy: Low to medium depending upon which brand you have purchased. iPods are pretty easy to set up.

That iPod that you are jamming out to is really not much more than a hard drive with a small operating system on it. With some simple changes, you can tell your iPod or other portable music player to store data alongside your music. For instructions on using an iPod as a storage device, go to http://docs.info.apple.com/article .html?artnum=61131. For other players, look in the product documentation or on the product Web site.

Online Storage and Saving

If you have an Internet connection at home and in the classroom, you don't even need a device to move your files back and forth. There are many ways to save things on the Internet, and the easiest is probably just by attaching files to an email. If you have a Gmail or Yahoo mail account, you can send files up to 10 megabytes, which is enough for most presentations. (For more uses for email, see Chapter 2, "Discussion and Communication.")

If you want to have access to bigger files at home and at work, you might want to try using an online storage service. These services basically let you have some hard drive space on the Internet. Xdrive is a currently a free service from AOL that lets you store up to 5 gigabytes of data online and access it from anywhere. You can even make files accessible to others, which would be useful if you wanted to show presentations in class, and then make them available to your students. MediaMax, formerly Streamload, is another online service that offers 25 gigabytes of free data storage. It is available at http://www .mediamax.com/.

Tech Specs: Xdrive

Set-Up Time: 10 minutes to register for an account; uploading lots of files can be very time-consuming.

Keep-Up Time: Uploading and downloading files can be slow, especially if you don't have a broadband connection

In-Class Time: Too long—plan on having everything downloaded before class starts.

Tech Savvy: Low—the system looks very much like the folders in Windows or Mac OS.

FEATURED PRODUCT

Xdrive Online Storage
Web site: http://www.xdrive.com/
Developer: AOL.com
Cost: 5 gigabytes free

Xdrive offers up to 5 gigabytes of free, secure online storage. Your files can be easily shared with others as well.

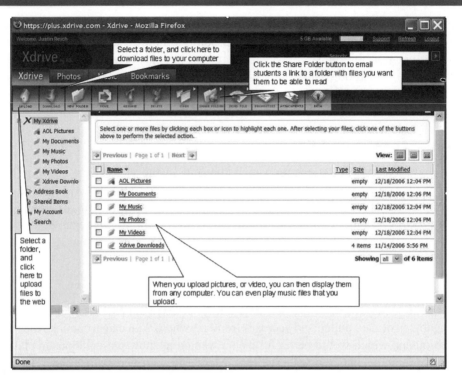

Xdrive provides an online option for backing up files, grade books, and syllabi.
Source: © 2007 Xdrive LLC. All Rights Reserved. Used with permission.

To start using Xdrive, go to http://www.xdrive.com/, and use either your AOL or AIM screen name or register for one. Set-up is easy and the interface is pretty simple. One other advantage of using this system is you can back up your important files, like your grade book or syllabi. Even if your computer crashes, your files will still be safe on the Internet (and if the Internet crashes, then you will probably have bigger problems than your gradebook . . .)

FINAL THOUGHTS

Great teachers sometimes use technology, but technology alone doesn't make great teachers. A certain private boarding school has recently completed an extremely expensive new building of special classrooms with all kinds of fancy computers, projectors, smart boards, and windows that darken at the touch of a finger. As one faculty member said of it, "We spent all this money, but you can go to a class and still see kids sitting in the back of the classroom, half asleep, with a little drool coming out of the corners of their mouths."

If we simply replace our own droning on in front of the blackboard with new droning on in front of a PowerPoint slide, then we haven't made any educational progress. As we experiment with the exciting possibilities of new media, we must remember that the fundamentals of great teaching—mastery of our subjects, compelling questions for students, and passion for learning—have not changed much since Confucius was keeping students on their toes in China. Combine these fundamentals with the immersion and engagement made possible by digital media, and teachers have at their hands a potent recipe for excellent teaching and learning.

Chapter 2

Discussion and Communication

Introduction
Creative Uses of Email
Educational Uses of Blogging
Chatting
Bringing the World into Your Room: Skype and iChat
Final Thoughts

INTRODUCTION

Effective discussion is at the heart of every successful History and English classroom. The sharing of information and ideas encourages students to engage actively with course materials and to articulate opinions based on sound critical thinking. Fortunately, computers and the Internet open the doors to a variety of exciting new ways to discuss and communicate with your students. And unlike in the physical classroom, you won't be limited by space and time. In this chapter, we'll discuss new ways to generate discussion with your students both in and outside of class and to communicate more effectively with the world outside your classroom walls.

CREATIVE USES OF EMAIL

Electronic mail is a popular and easy-to-use communication medium that teachers can adopt for a number of classroom purposes. If your school does not provide you with a shared platform for emails between teachers and students, see Chapter 10, "Class Management," for some ideas. One of email's advantages is that communication is virtually instantaneous and messages can be stored and archived. Teachers can email students homework assignments, class notes, multimedia files, and various other course materials, and students can store these materials electronically and indefinitely. And that's just a start. Creative uses of email can help spur discussion and active learning. This section is devoted to outlining just such uses.

Using Email to Jump-Start a Class: Daily Warm-Up

Short journal-style writing assignments are great ways to get class started. They quiet the room, give students time to reset their brains to your class, and allow class discussions to emerge from ideas developed in writing.

Tech Specs: Email Daily Warm-Up
Set-Up Time: None (maybe 15 minutes to set-up an extra "turn-in" e account).
Keep-Up Time: 10 minutes (to think up warm-up questions and send email).
In-Class Time: 10–15 minutes.
Tech Savvy: Low.

Tech Terms
1–1 or One-to-one computing refers to situations where every student has access to a computer—such as a computer lab, a classroom with a laptop cart, or a school where every student is required to have or be provided with a laptop.

If you work in a 1–1 computing environment, email is a great way for students to write these kinds of journal assignments. Rather than scratching their thoughts in a notebook, they'll send them directly to you. Even if you only occasionally read through them and grade them randomly, your students will have a much greater incentive to write thoughtfully than they might if they were just writing in their notebooks. Perhaps more importantly, when students are emailing something to another reader, they are more motivated to do better work.

To simplify receiving a classroom full of emails, it's very helpful to set up a separate "turn-in" email. This can be as simple as setting up a Gmail, Yahoo, or Hotmail account like TurnInReich@gmail.com or setting up a special turn-in account on your school server. That way students can email questions and issues to your main email account and assignments to your turn-in account.

Using email for a daily warm-up is simple. Send students a question about the previous night's assignment, or a thought question about the topic of the day, or even a "pre-question" about a new topic, and have them respond to your email.

Sample Exercise: The Daily Warm-Up

In the following example, Justin set up a mailing list for one of his World History sections. Most email systems make it very easy to store groups of email addresses as a single list, which is very handy when emailing classes.

Students are instructed to forward the email to Justin's TurninReich account. If students forward the email, then the original text is preserved so they don't need to retype the question. Typically, students would be given 5–10 minutes for this exercise. If students finish quickly, encourage them to improve their paragraphs by rewriting the topic sentence or including more evidence.

Once time is up, ask students to send their answers via email, and start class with a conversation about the Daily Warm-Up. If you have students who are reluctant to speak up in the midst of a heated discussion, this can be an excellent time to call on them to share their thoughts, since they have had a chance to rehearse their ideas in writing.

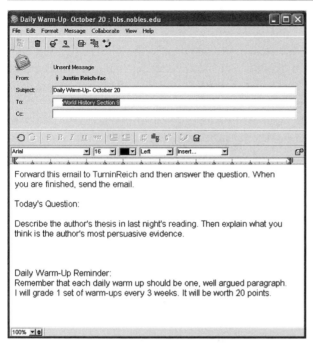

A typical Daily Warm-Up email for one of Justin's World History classes.

Every month or so, go through your turn-in email account and correct a random assignment. You can email students back with comments on their responses and grades. With everything on email, this can be an entirely paperless assignment! Grading these warm-ups occasionally will keep students on their toes.

PENCIL: If any student has a problem receiving or sending an email, they can always write their response on paper.

Reaching Outside the Classroom: Emails to Authors and Other Professionals

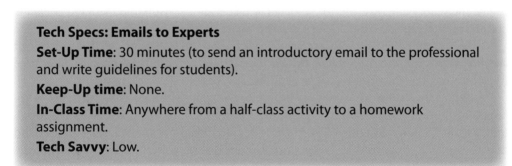

Tech Specs: Emails to Experts
Set-Up Time: 30 minutes (to send an introductory email to the professional and write guidelines for students).
Keep-Up time: None.
In-Class Time: Anywhere from a half-class activity to a homework assignment.
Tech Savvy: Low.

Many assignments respond to a particular article or book. Why not direct those writings toward the author? Many online newspapers now include the author's email address in the header of the article. For books written by professors at universities, author's emails can often be found by searching for them on the college or university Web site, and sometimes they can be found by putting the author's name in a search engine. Authors often have their own Web sites and many of them read and respond to email. If you are reading works from a popular author, chances are there is an association dedicated to studying that author's works that may entertain questions and host forums.

Before having a class email a professional, send that person an email warning him or her of the impending deluge. You might have more luck getting a response if you mention that you would be grateful if the author would be willing to send a response to the entire class. As we have experimented with this approach, we have had a variety of responses ranging from silence to a response to one student to a response to the whole class. Whether or not you do hear back, students, in general, put more effort into their writing if they are writing to someone specific and know that their work will be judged not just by their teacher but also by a member of the public.

Students need to be warned in advance of this assignment that respectful criticism is encouraged, but any inappropriate or disrespectful language will earn them a failing grade.

Writing Letters to the Editor and Submitting Editorials

Tech Specs: Emails to the Editor
Set-Up Time: Generally 10–15 minutes is sufficient to find an email address to your local opinion editor. Again, it can be useful to send the recipient a warning if he or she will be receiving eighty letters on a topic.
Keep-Up Time: None.
In-Class Time: One homework assignment or one class-length activity.
Tech Savvy: Low.

Publishing your opinions in a local newspaper is one of the great means of contributing to a democratic community. With the advent of email, submitting your thoughts is easier than ever. Many Language Arts classes have units devoted to persuasive writing, and it can be incredibly empowering for students to take a shot at using the media to persuade not just their classmates, but also their entire community.

Visit the Opinion Section of your local paper online and look for links that say *Submit a Letter to the Editor* or *Submit an Op-Ed.* These links will often lead you to guidelines for submitting these writings and email addresses for the relevant editors.

Letters to the editor are typically printed in response to published articles or on issues of regional importance. Papers often accept letters up to 250 words, though they will often edit them down. The best letters to the editor are snappy, concise, and direct. Drafting them so that every word counts is an excellent exercise for budding writers.

Op-Ed pieces are longer, typically around 700 words. They are columns that address issues in the news, but they do not respond to particular articles like letters to the editor do. Op-Ed literally stands for "opposite the editorial page," since most opinion columns are published opposite the editorial page. While most of these columns are written by professional writers, pundits, and community leaders, students and teachers have as much chance of getting their thoughts published as anyone else.

An excellent resource on submitting letters to the editor and Op-Eds is the Web page on the topic published by the Communications Consortium Media Center at http://www.ccmc.org/oped.htm. The page includes helpful tips for writing opinion pieces and email addresses for opinion editors at the 100 largest circulating papers in the United States. You may not have much luck getting your work published in your local paper, but sometimes its fun to go for the gold!

Using Email to Connect Your Students to the World: ePals

Tech Specs: ePals School Networking
Set-Up Time: Two hours—one to set up an account and learn about the ePals Program, and another to plan once you have connected with another school.
Keep-Up Time: Regular emails with your ePal classroom.
In-Class Time: Variable, depending on your investment with the other school.
Tech Savvy: Low.

Email also provides an excellent opportunity to communicate with schools around the country and around the world. Some of the best email pen-pal exchanges might come from connections you have with friends who are teaching across the country or overseas. If you need help finding pen pals in other parts of the world, one great resource is http://www.ePals.com/. On an average day, twenty-five new schools join the ePals community, and you can search pen pals by country. ePals connects schools across the world and can provide language translation services and content filtering. The connecting service is free, and ePals also offers school wide blogs and email accounts.

There are a variety of other services that will connect pen pals across the world, and a Web search for "pen pals" will find many others.

Getting Started with ePals

Go to http://www.epals.com and click on *Join ePals* in the left navigation bar. We recommend you join the ePals "Global Community" of over seven million students and teachers from 191 countries. You are asked to complete a school profile with information about the languages, ages, and number of your students, as well as the number of classrooms that will participate. You are also asked to write a brief description of your school and ePal objectives.

Here is the profile we submitted:

> Our 9th grade "History of the Human Community" (HHC) students will study the history of the Middle East from September to December 2006. They will learn about its religious and historical roots and will also study contemporary conflict in the region. Our students are English speakers between 14 and 15 years old, and many are Jewish (a few are Muslim). We would like to converse with students from Israel as well as from Lebanon, Palestine, and Egypt and learn from their insights and experiences. We have a blog set up where our students will post their thoughts, and we would invite your students to comment. We also have videoconferencing available as well as chat software.

ePal member schools can read each other's profiles and can search for schools by various criteria. Click on *Find Classrooms* in the left navigation bar and search by keywords, area (city/state/country), age, language, or a special category. Keep in mind that some schools from select countries may be more in demand than others. For example, there may be more Western schools in ePals trying to contact Middle Eastern schools than the other way around.

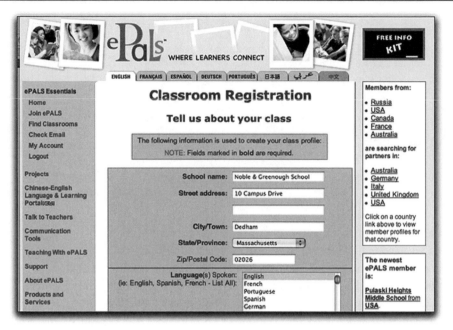

ePals collects information from classrooms looking for pen pals and then publishes that information online so that classrooms from across the globe with similar interests can connect. *Source:* Courtesy of ePals.

We used ePals to put our ninth-grade World History students in touch with teachers and students in Jerusalem and Lebanon during a unit on the Middle East. We searched ePals for participating schools in Middle Eastern countries and sent messages to them inviting collaboration with our students. We also obtained a list of American and international schools in the Middle East and contacted them directly. One school contacted us as a result of our ePals profile and another responded directly to our email. We used a combination of email and blogging to converse with our friends from the Middle East, and we had some logistical problems organizing communication in the different time zones, but overall our students were excited and motivated to hear from students in the regions they were studying. ePals helped make our studies of history and current events more personal and meaningful.

EDUCATIONAL USES OF BLOGGING

One of the most popular new media for communication on the Web is the Web log, or blog. While blogs can become quite sophisticated forms of Web pages, they are all basically chronologically ordered journals where readers can leave comments.

Blogs have many educational uses, and teachers, students, and researchers are increasingly integrating them in the classroom. Blogging provides creative opportunities for active learning activities such as role-playing, debating, and problem solving. Students can use their blogs to discuss, analyze, and reflect on what they are reading and learning.

Topics that deal with controversial subjects, child and teen issues, and current events can be especially meaningful to students and can help elicit active discussion and debate. Students enjoy writing about topics that interest them the most, and teachers can use blogs not only to interact with students beyond the classroom but also to learn more about them.

Breaking Down the Blog

What is a blog anyway? If you are asking that question, we are really glad that you are reading this book and taking some risks learning a new technology.

> **Tech Specs: Getting Started with a Classroom Blog**
>
> **Set-Up Time:** You can have a basic blog up and running in as little as 30 minutes, and you can spend hours customizing your blog with content and features.
>
> **Keep-Up Time:** Writing a blog post as a teacher takes only a few minutes, maybe slightly longer than it takes to send an email.
>
> **In-Class Time:** It takes only a few minutes for a student to post a comment to a teacher's blog or log in to his or her own blog. Writing assignments can be 10-minute reflection pieces or longer class or homework assignments.
>
> **Tech Savvy:** Low. Performing the basic functions of blog—writing posts and leaving comments—is easy to do.

Best Practices in Educational Blogging

Blogging works best in an environment where the teacher is not afraid to act as a facilitator who allows students to learn from each other. Blogging is most effective when students evaluate, discuss, and challenge each other's thinking and come to revise their own understanding of a topic.

Blogging can be used in any number of ways. It can be used to form a reading discussion forum or literature circle, post short current events articles and invite students' thoughts, foster communication among multiple classes, serve as a log of student progress on a research assignment, post photos and homework assignments online, and much more.

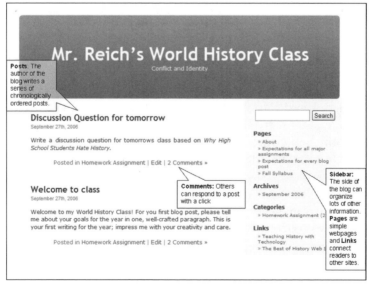

All blogs contain three main elements: posts, comments, and a sidebar.

The key to effective educational blogging is not technological prowess, but rather thoughtful and sustained pedagogical integration.

If blogging is presented as a peripheral activity, with little or no direct connection to your class goals, it will be of limited effectiveness. Likewise, if blogging is a sporadic homework activity, and one without an assessment framework, students may question its importance and utility. So think beyond that first blogging assignment and plan out several regularly scheduled blogging assignments with clear goals and an assessment strategy. Many bloggers—teachers or otherwise—start with a flurry of posts and then stop blogging; plan to post regularly, even if it's just every two weeks. Also, do not underestimate initial student anxiety (and perhaps skepticism) about the process. While many students will likely embrace the innovation that blogging represents—some probably blog themselves—they may be unclear and unsure of how to express themselves in this new academic milieu.

Ten Things to Do with Your Class Blog

1. **Post a homework question**
   a. Each student writes a one-paragraph response.
   b. Read a few before class to see what your students think about the reading.
   c. You can require students to respond not only to the reading, but to each other's responses as well.
2. **Start a discussion**
   a. Pose a question and require that students post at least three contributions to a discussion over the course of a week, or more contributions over the course of a unit.
3. **Invite outsiders to comment on student work**
   a. If you know the author of a book you are reading, have students write feedback and have the author respond.
   b. Have students from another school comment on your students' work.
4. **Have students post discussion questions for tomorrow's class**
   a. This is great when you know you won't have time to plan.
   b. If you know that you've flubbed a class and students are confused, have them post questions about things they don't understand.
5. **Post your lecture notes or a summary of the day's class**
   a. You can even record a podcast and post an audio summary of the day's class on your blog. More on that in Chapter 8, "Student Presentations."
6. **Have students post _their_ notes for the day**
   a. Assign one student per day to be the scribe for the class. This is great for discussion-based classes where you want students to focus on the discussion and not have to worry about taking notes.
7. **Post the daily homework assignment**
8. **Post links to supplementary materials from the Internet**
   a. Author bios or Web sites
   b. Links to book reviews
   c. Links to relevant news articles
9. **Post progress reports on team projects**
   a. Students can post their work to the blog so that others can see what they are doing. They can also comment on each other's work.
   b. If faculty are trying to work as a team or core group, use a blog to communicate with each other about lessons, etc.
10. **Have students create their own blogs for independent study**
    a. We have students post an outline of their week's work before our weekly meeting.

Setting Up a Blog

Three Choices for Blogging Sites

There are many blog creation and hosting services on the Internet. Here are three options that we have experience with and are comfortable recommending to you:

1. http://www.blogger.com

Probably the largest blogging site on the Internet; purchased by Google a few years ago.

Pros: Free. Simple interface. Quick and easy to set up. Good security features. Students who read blogs on their own time will be familiar with the tools and layout.

Cons: Sometimes long load times in posting and managing the blog. You cannot post documents or files to a Blogger page unless you have your own file server somewhere.

2. http://www.edublogs.org

A free blogging site powered by WordPress (another good free blogging tool), with sites set up for educational blogging.

Pros: Free. Simple interface. The ability to create simple Web pages along with your blog for syllabi, course expectations, etc. Constantly improving tools for embedding images, sounds, and files. Justin's choice for classroom blogs.

Cons: It has many great features, but all these extras can make it harder to learn your way around the interface.

3. http://www.typepad.com

A feature-rich subscription service by Six Apart.

Pros: You can upload any type of file—Word documents, PowerPoint presentations, sound files, etc. Lots of template options and easily customized. The ability to create simple Web pages along with your blog for syllabi, course expectations, etc. Easily downloaded from the page. Tom's choice for classroom blogs.

Cons: Somewhat more complicated interface. Subscription-based service. Sometimes down for service.

Getting Started: Blogger

During our workshops we often have teachers blogging in less than ten minutes. It's very easy. For the purposes of this tutorial we will focus on Blogger, Google's popular and free blog creation and hosting service.

Here are some instructions for starting a blog with Blogger:

FEATURED PRODUCT

Blogger Blogs
Web site: http://www.blogger.com
Developer: Google
Cost: Free

Blogger allows anyone who registers for a free Google account to start up a Web log. There are currently no limits on the number of posts you can have or the length of time that your blog will be preserved.

Step 1: Register for a new blog. Go to http://www.blogger.com/. Click *Create Your Blog Now* to get started. Since Blogger is owned by Google, you need to have a Google account to set up a blog. If you have a Gmail account, then sign in using that information. If you need to make one, you can do so when signing up for a Blogger blog. Once you are all set with your Google account, you can choose a title and address for your blog and then click *Continue*. Finally, you'll have a chance to choose a template for your blog. You can change it later if you want to.

Step 2: Create your first post. Once your account and blog are up and running, you'll be taken to the Blogger "Dashboard." This is where you can manage your new blog. The first task is to create your first post. Start by clicking the *New Post* button.

Add a title to your post, such as "Today's Blogging Activity," or the name of the assignment, and then write out the assignment or activity in the big text box.

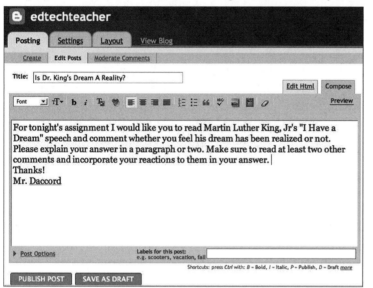

Blogger's simple interface for writing posts looks similar to many basic email editors.
Source: Courtesy of Google.

Below:

Our sample post from the previous image has now been posted to the blog. *Source:* Courtesy of Google.

Step 3: Publish your post. Click on *Publish* to see your post live or *Save as Draft* for later revision. You'll get a message that the post has been published successfully. Then select *View the Blog* to see your work published. Easy, right?

Step 4: Email students your blog URL. Your blog will have a Web address, or URL, associated with it, which will be NameOfYourBlog.blogspot.com. Share it with students so they can visit your blog to read your posts and leave comments.

Step 5: Have students leave you a comment. Your students can now leave comments on your blog that you and your students can read. To leave a comment, click on the *Comments* link underneath the published post. You will be directed to a comments page where you can type your comment and publish it live. So, the next time someone hits the comments link they can read your *Comment* and then leave their own.

> **Note:** *With many blogging tools, blog authors can determine who may read their blog and who may comment. For privacy and security reasons, you may not wish people outside your classroom to see your blog. We discuss privacy and security considerations later in this chapter.*

> **WEBSITE:** If you would like more detailed instructions on how to register and use Blogger, please visit http://www.edtechteacher.org/chapter2.html for some video tutorials.

Blog Types: Single Class Blog, a Blog for Each Student, or Both?

An important consideration is whether you want a **single class blog or a blog for each student in the class**. In the first scenario, you, the teacher, post to your blog and students leave a comment on your post. A single class blog is often quick and easy to create, and you could have a class blog up and running in a very short time. It is also easier to read and review posts and comments on one blog as opposed to many blogs. Students will also tend to read more of each other's work if it is on a single blog versus having to visit multiple blogs.

That being said, students often enjoy having their own blogs, and it may encourage them to write more and take more ownership of their work. Literature teachers, in particular, often want students to have an extended writing space of their own. Moreover, if students each have their own blog then they are *truly blogging,* and not just commenting on someone else's blog. So, it may be worth a few hours at the beginning of the term to create a blog for each and every student.

To help clarify the distinction between these two ways of using blogging in classrooms it can be helpful to think of things this way: in a class blog, teachers post and students comment; with multiple blogs, students post and teachers (and students) comment.

Examples from Real Classroom Blogs

A Simple Blog from a First-Time Blogger

The course below features a teacher blog, but no student blogs. The teacher posts questions, and students then answer using the Comments option.

In this example, the instructor (in this case the head of the Noble and Greenough School, taking his first bold steps into blogging) asks a study question about every week and students respond with a comment. The activity is not so different from a standard study-question exercise, so why use a blog? What are the advantages?

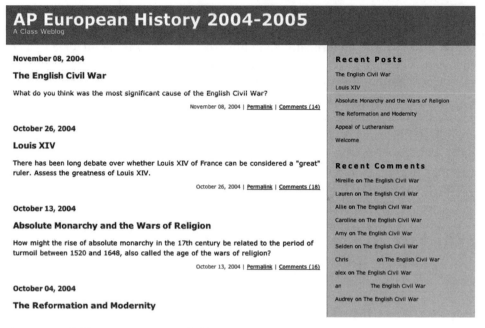

This very simple blog, requiring minimal effort to maintain, gets students involved in a productive conversation through writing.   *Source:* Courtesy of Robert Henderson.

- **When students publish publicly, they tend to do better work.** When they know that not just the teacher, but also all their peers may be perusing their comment, they put a little more care into their work.
- **Blogging creates a permanent record of discussion that everyone can see.** After blogging for several weeks in one class, students began asking if they could cite each other's ideas and language in their own papers. It proved to be a great opportunity for students to engage in a genuine scholarly discussion. For classes with reliable computer access, reading the class blog can be a great warm-up to a class discussion.
- **Blogging can allow exchanges beyond the classroom walls.** Whenever a guest speaker comes to class, students blog about the discussion, and then we invite the speaker to add a comment in response. Blogging also lets parents peek into the work students are doing for class, hopefully stimulating dinner-table discussion. If you teach multiple sections of the same class, blogging can let you create dialogue among sections. Students who collaborate on projects through blogs are more likely to chat with each other about their course work in the halls and by the lockers.

Forty Acres and a Blog: A Blog for Each Student

The course features a teacher blog with student blogs. At the top of the next page is an example of an instructor blog and at the bottom, a student blog. Links to the student blogs are listed on the left, so students can easily navigate between blogs.

Student blogs over time become online portfolios where students can keep a permanent, public record of their work throughout the year. The advantage of individual student blogs is that students may have more ownership over their pages, and it is easier for them to see how they have progressed as writers over the year. It also allows the instructor to have all of the student's writing in one place for final grades or end-of-semester comments.

U.S. History -- Mr. Daccord
Tom Daccord's United States History class at the Noble & Greenough School

CATEGORIES

Current Affairs

Unit 1: Industrial Age

DACCORD U.S.
HISTORY

Brooke

Casey

Daccord U.S. History

Devan

Emily

Hanna

Ian

Julie

Liz

Matt

Mel

Sophie

Stephanie

Tucker

SEPTEMBER 13, 2006

Industrial Age, 1877-1920 (Post #1)

What was the point of today's activity? How does it connect to last night's homework assignment? Please make specific reference to terms/people/concepts from the homework.
Post your 1-2 paragraph answer on your blog.
Thanks

September 13, 2006 at 07:51 AM in Unit 1: Industrial Age | Permalink | Comments (2) | TrackBack (0)

SEPTEMBER 09, 2006

9/11: Are We Safer Five Years Later?

In recent speeches President Bush has claimed that the United States is much safer than 9/11. "Many Americans look at these events," Mr. Bush has said , "and ask the same question: Five years after 9/11, are we safer? The answer is, yes, America is safer. We are safer because we've taken action to protect the homeland." He and others point to air security improvements and revamped intelligence agencies that can share information more freely. Other cited improvements include the expansion of agents assigned to work on counterterrorism.

However, others disagree. For instance, former U.S. Assistant Secretary of Defense Larry Korb says: "What has happened is, particularly with the invasion of Iraq, we have created a lot of al-Qaida wannabees, and there are more people now that are trying to do us harm than there were before we went into Iraq." Senator John Kerry concurs: " [President Bush's] disastrous decisions have made Iraq a fuel depot for terror, fanning the flames of conflict around the world."

What do you remember of 9/11? Do you feel safer now than five years ago? Why or why not?

September 09, 2006 at 08:47 PM in Current Affairs | Permalink | Comments (0) | TrackBack (0)

In Tom's blog, you can see the questions that he has posed to his students. In his student's blog, you can see the response. Both blogs have links to everyone in the class, to facilitate discussion and collaboration.

Brooke (U.S. History)

CATEGORIES

Current Affairs

DACCORD U.S.
HISTORY

Brooke

Casey

Daccord U.S. History

Devan

Emily

Hanna

Ian

Julie

Liz

Matt

Mel

Sophie

Stephanie

Tucker

OCTOBER 06, 2006

What is the proper role of government in American Society?

It is hard to draw a clear line as to where government should interfere with American society and where it should stay out. In my opinion, I believe the government should regulate areas of society where the health of the public is at risk- food and drug regulation especially, and areas where corporations could abuse power because the way that government does these things currently works well. However, I do not agree that the US should feel obligated to spread democracy and capitalism to countries around the world. It is not our responsibility and often times we end up getting ourselves into wars where the other country could have taken ccare of themselves. It is necessary to interevene in this matter sometiems, as it maybe was in Iraq, becuase if the US is in anyway in danger, the government needs to step up and protect its citizens.

October 06, 2006 at 07:06 AM | Permalink | Comments (0) | TrackBack (0)

SEPTEMBER 20, 2006

Ragged Dick

1. Honesty, integrity- Dick refuses to steal, no matter how tempted or hungry he might be
2. Being hardworking and willing to work- this is how Dick gets enough business to support himself
3. Being a good person/friendly- this is how Dick makes friends and connections that help him get more business and sometimes a place to eat, this is also how he meets Frank
4. "honest looking"- without this Dick would not have gotten the chance to make some of these connections
5. Being smart/aware- Dick has to always be on his toes, as was demonstrated with the "dropping" of the wallet. without this quality Dick could have been easily taken advantage of

September 20, 2006 at 07:09 AM | Permalink | Comments (0) | TrackBack (0)

RECENT POSTS

What is the proper role of government in American Society?

Ragged Dick

Ragged Dick

Industrial Age (Post #1)

9/11: Are we safer five years later?

English IV - Ms. Snyder
A blog for Sarah Snyder's English IV classes

November 27, 2006

Creon's character

Assess Creon's character in *Antigone* Scene II through Scene IV. What do his words reveal about him? What do others' words about him reveal about Creon? Use at least two quotations in this paragraph and make sure to sandwich the text with an introduction and unpacking. Please use the correct format with page numbers, quotation marks, and punctuation.

November 27, 2006 at 01:14 PM in **Antigone** | **Permalink** | **Comments (0)** | **TrackBack (0)**

October 16, 2006

Chapter 24 response

There are two things I want you to respond to in your own blog about this chapter. First, do you think Holden's reaction to Mr. Antolini is justified? Please use textual support to augment your argument. Second, please find an important moment/quotation in this chapter and respond to it. Practice using a quotation effectively (sandwiching it and 'unpacking' the words and connecting the quotation to themes or symbols) and correctly (punctuation/page number).

October 16, 2006 at 06:29 AM in **Catcher in the Rye** | **Permalink** | **Comments (0)** | **TrackBack (0)**

October 05, 2006

Quotation response for Tuesday 10/10

Please choose an interesting, telling, powerful, or important quotation in *Catcher in the Rye* from pages 66-104. Analyze this quotation in depth; why is important? What do particular words convey about the characters, themes, or symbols? If the quotation connects to one or more of the paradigms we are using to understand literature, please explain the connection. Make sure the quotation (with page #) is in your analysis. Please use the correct format for weaving in quotations. Have fun!

CATEGORIES

Antigone
Catcher in the Rye
House on Mango Street

ENGLISH IV SNYDER

Audrey
Caitlin
Cassandra
Clark
Dan
Dana
Ed
Eliza
Gene
Gunlee
Ian
Jack
Jesse
Julian
Katherine

Here is another blog where the teacher poses questions in the teacher blog, and then students post responses in their own blogs.   *Source:* Courtesy of Sarah Snyder.

Advanced Features in Blogger

Ⓑ Configure Link List   ? Help

CANCEL   SAVE CHANGES

Title   Important Links
Number of links to show in list: [   ]   *Leave blank to show all links*
Sorting: Don't Sort
New Site URL   http://www.thwt.org
New Site Name   Teaching History With Technology

ADD LINK

Edit Delete   Best of History Web Sites

CANCEL   SAVE CHANGES

Through this window, you can create a list of links for your blog.
Source: Courtesy of Google.

Once you get the hang of basic posts and comments, you will quickly find that nearly everything in Blogger is easily customizable.

Adding Page Elements

Click on the *Layout* button for your blog on the Blogger dashboard, and you'll be taken to a page where you can edit your blog's "Page Elements." These are a wide variety of features that can help you customize your blog and make it more useful for your students.

By clicking the *Add Page Element* button, you will discover a wide range of features that you can add to the sidebar of your blog. For instance, use the "List" feature to include a list of expectations for student posts, or use the "Feed" element to have a running ticker of news clips relevant to your class (there is more on RSS feeds later in the chapter).

Perhaps the most useful feature is the one that allows you to include a list of links. You can link to our Web sites: Best of History Web Sites (www.besthistorysites.net) Teaching English with Technology (www.tewt.org) Teaching History with Technology (www.thwt.org) and Ed Tech Teacher. (www.edtechteacher.org). Equally useful would be linking to your school Web page, other important resources, or if you have every student in your class have a blog, you can create a list of links to all of their blogs. If you create a separate class Web page—and many instructors find that a blog works just fine as a class Web page—then you should link to there from your blog as well (we'll discuss how to make simple Web pages with Google pages in Chapter 8, "Student Presentations").

With a little logistical work, you can set up your blog so that only certain people can view, post, or comment.

Source: Courtesy of Google.

Who Can View Your Blog? Setting Permissions

If you want to keep your blog away from outside eyes, you have several options. Most blog services give you the option of assigning password protection to your blog. Blogger gives you the option of deciding who can view your blog and who can leave a comment on your blog. Just keep in mind that blogging is intrinsically a public activity and cutting your class blog off from the outside world somewhat defeats its purpose.

To set permissions you need to be logged in to your Blogger account. Click on the *Settings* tab and then select the *Permissions* link. You can select *Anybody, Only people I choose,* or *Only blog authors* to view your blog. If you only want your students to view the blog, then choose *Only people I choose.* Invite your students by adding their email addresses in the box provided and then clicking the *Invite* button.

Blogging Logistics . . . Blogistics?

Blog Administrative and Authorship Considerations

At our school we have a centralized system where administrative control of blogs rests in the hands of two Information Technology department members. We create all blogs, train all teachers, and make fundamental design, content, and acceptable-use policy decisions. In some other schools, teachers create and administer blogs on their own and make fundamental design, content, and acceptable-use policy decisions. A centralized system helps ensure some supervision over design, content, and etiquette, but the downside is that it risks stifling teacher initiative and creativity.

WEBSITE: Tom has recorded a podcast on blog administration and authorship considerations at http://www.edtechteacher.org/chapter2.html.

Blog Protocol and Privacy Issues

Students will be posting work to the Internet and must be cognizant of proper Internet protocol, and just plain decency! We tell our students to never publish a personal attack and to never be unduly critical or harsh in tone or content. We encourage students to use the comments option to praise their peer's work, to ask questions, and to point out what they found particularly informative or engaging in a blog post. That being said, we do use blogs as a means of debate and often have students with opposing viewpoints blog on a particular issue. Thus, it is not uncommon for students to criticize each other's arguments via their blogs. However, argumentation should be undertaken in a spirit of constructive criticism and in an effort to sharpen analytical thinking.

You may wish to review student comments before they are actually published. Both the teacher and the student should keep in mind that any malicious or inappropriate content on a school blog may result in disciplinary action for a student, and even a teacher. So the teacher needs to exercise caution. However, the review of all student posts can be a time-consuming and tedious chore for a teacher. Thus, you must gauge the maturity of your students and decide whether expediency is worth the risk of inappropriate public content. Blogger, Edublogs, and Typepad all include options where you can choose to review comments before they are actually posted to the blog.

In Blogger go to *Settings→Comments* and click the *Yes* box next to *Enable Comment Moderation.* Blogger has a helpful tutorial on how this works; just click the question mark icon next to *Enable Comment Moderation.*

Also, avoid publishing student last names. The Web is by nature public and as teachers and administrators we should not reveal the identities of our students online to strangers. Instruct students not to include their last names in posts or comments.

> **WEBSITE:** Visit http://www.edtechteacher.org/chapter2.html to listen to our podcast on blog privacy and security considerations.

Blogging and RSS

> **Tech Specs: Blogging and RSS**
> **Set-Up Time:** Setting up an RSS aggregator and finding your favorite RSS feeds can take an hour or two.
> **Keep-Up Time:** Once you have your RSS aggregator up and running, it takes only a minute or two to add new feeds.
> **In-Class Time:** We mostly use RSS to keep up with the news and developments in education, but with some investment of time, you could get your kids started as well.
> **Tech Savvy:** Medium. Getting started with Really Simple Syndication isn't always so simple.

There are so many different blogs being written by students, teachers, and educators that it can be quite difficult to regularly read your favorites. RSS is a nifty way of receiving new information from online sources you select, like your favorite blogs or Web sites.

RSS is commonly known as "Really Simple Syndication," and through RSS *feeds* you can receive a steady stream of information without directly searching for it.

An RSS feed is a source of information that is regularly updated. By subscribing to RSS feeds, you can get that stream of information delivered to you. For instance, let's say you want to receive every new post that edublogger Will Richardson adds to his Weblogg blog at http://www.weblogg-ed.com/. If you go to his Web site you will see an orange "XML" icon at the top of the page. (At some sites you will see an orange "RSS" icon.) XML is the coding used to send and receive RSS feeds. By placing the orange XML or RSS icon on his or her Web page the author is inviting you to subscribe to this feed. Now you just need a tool to collect these feeds of information.

To collect and read RSS feeds from Web sites, you need what's called an RSS *aggregator.* An aggregator enables you to collect and read RSS feeds in one central location. There are Web-based aggregators, and downloadable software aggregators, so you can choose what's most convenient for you.

There are many potential educational benefits associated with RSS. For instance, a Social Studies class could stay abreast of the latest developments in Iraq. English classes might receive updates on teaching literature from favorite Web sites or collect new poems from poetry blogs.

Collecting and Reading RSS Feeds with Bloglines

A simple and easy way to collect and read RSS feeds is the free Bloglines aggregator at http://bloglines.com/. Bloglines is a Web aggregator that enables you to make your own personalized page tailored to your interests. From within Bloglines, you can choose from millions of live Internet content feeds—including articles, blogs, images, and audio. After you register with Bloglines you can search for and collect the feeds you want to receive. Bloglines constantly checks those feeds for changes or additions and sends new information to your personal Bloglines account.

Step 1. Register with Bloglines. It's free and easy. Go to Bloglines at http://bloglines.com/ and click on the *Sign up now* link. The registration form is short, so you'll be done quickly.

Step 2. Click the *Feed* Tab. Once registered you'll want to add feeds to your account. There are two fundamental ways to do this. One is first to go to a favorite blog or Web page, find the URL of its RSS feed, and then add it to your Bloglines page. The second way is to search within Bloglines for feeds and add them to your page.

Step 3. Click the *Add* button. In this instance we'll assume that you've come across an interesting blog or Web site and want to add its RSS feed to your Bloglines page. To do this, you'll want to copy the URL of the blog's RSS feed and then paste it into the Blog or URL text field you see in Bloglines.

Step 4: Copy and Paste the URL of an RSS feed. To find the RSS feed of a particular blog or Web page, look for a small orange rectangle on the site that says either XML or RSS. It might look something like this: **XML** (If you can't find it, they probably don't offer an RSS feed.) To capture it, *right-click* on a PC (*Ctrl-click* on a Mac) and select *Copy Link.* You can now go back to Bloglines and paste the feed into the Blog or URL text field. Finally, click *Subscribe.* The feed is now added your Bloglines page.

Step 5: Search for feeds using Bloglines; then add them. To search for feeds within Bloglines, use the search function available in the top right corner of the Bloglines page. Toggle the box furthest to the right and select *Search for feeds*. Type in keywords, such as "teaching literature" or "teaching American history," and hit the arrow button to search for feeds.

Search results appear in the form of links to blogs and Web pages. Click on a link and peruse the source to decide if you would like to subscribe to its feed. If so, simply hit the *Back* button in your Web browser and look for the small *Subscribe to feed* link underneath the link to the source. Click it and the feed will be added to your Bloglines page.

Step 6: Read your Bloglines feeds. To read your feeds, make sure you are logged in and that the *Feeds* tab is selected. Simply click on the link that represents the source of the feed you are interested in. By default Bloglines will display the most recent news associated with that feed first. Click on any of the links to read the article post or story. Come back regularly to Bloglines to read new information from your feeds.

If you opt not to use Bloglines, you might download free aggregator software such as NetNewsWire (Mac OS X) or SharpReader. The advantage of Bloglines is that it is a Web-based aggregator, so you have nothing to download and you can access your Bloglines account on any computer connected to the Internet.

One advantage of using RSS for information retrieval is that your aggregator feed is virus free, ad free, and spam free! Additionally, the content is something you want to read because you subscribed to it. To help you sort through thousands of potential RSS feeds try Feedster at http://feedster.com. This search engine uses RSS feeds to discover major happenings in the "blogosphere" in near real time. Technorati at http://technorati.com/ is a great way to search and organize blogs, as well as Internet pictures and video, and provides up-to-the-minute information.

Select Examples of Blogging Activities for the Classroom

Tech Specs: Sample Blogging Exercises
Set-Up Time: Copying or modifying these activities should only take 10–15 minutes once you have your blog up and running.
Keep-Up Time: None.
In-Class Time: Most of these activities are designed for one night or one-half of a class period.
Tech Savvy: Low. Blogging is one of the easiest ways to venture into teaching with technology.

Blogging provides opportunities for active learning techniques such as role-playing, debating, and problem solving. Students can use their blogs to discuss, analyze, and reflect on what they are reading and learning. Blogging tends to heighten student interest and motivate many kids since posts will be "published" and potentially be available to the public at large.

Edublogging can take many forms, and thus these activities are fairly diverse in form and content. Some of these blogging activities may be completed in a single evening, while other will take several classes. Some are stand-alone assignments, while others are part of a broader activity or project.

Discussion Question: "What is the most significant cause of the English Civil War?" (High School)

The following is a straightforward one-night assignment that uses a single blog to help foster debate and analytical thinking. The teacher poses a single question to his blog: "What is the most significant cause of the English Civil War?" Students answer the question via the Comment link located at the bottom of the teacher's post. Students end up answering the question at different points during the evening and are required to read previous student responses before publishing their own. In this way students are prompted to consider the ideas and opinions of their peers before responding to the post. Naturally, the later a student responds to the question, the more he or she will have to read and consider before offering a response. (You might limit a respondent to reading two or three previous comments.) Nonetheless, the teacher insists that each comment include some point or perspective that differs from previous ones. This exercise helps encourage analytical thinking and discussion and provides a great foundation for a verbal debate the next day in class.

See a sample of student comments below:

Comments

The most significant cause of the English Civil War stems directly from Charles I's desire to create a uniform religion (Anglican). By trying to force the "Book of Common Prayer" and bishoprics upon Scotland, Charles was just looking for trouble. Scotland predictably revolted and Charles' stubborn stance against Parliament had to give in. His clear desire to become the absolute ruler of "Britain" instead of using Parliament to simply rule England sparked the English Civil War.

Posted by: <u>Greg</u> | November 8, 2004 03:58 PM

I agree with Greg in that religion was the major cause of the English Civil War. However, I also believe that Charles' personality, and the way he approached certain things was a major factor as well. But back to religion-- when Charles attempted to impose the English Prayer Book on the Presbyterians of Scotland, he had definately gone too far. Charles mounted a campaign against the Scots in 1639, but failed miserably. He then summoned a parliament to raise money for another campaign against the Scots. The parliament was closed in a matter of weeks, because Charles and the council could once again, not agree to terms. The Scots eventually invaded England, and Charles had to buy a truce. But to do this, again, Charles had to turn to Parliament for money. Overall I believe that Charles' arrogance and somewhat stupidity when it came to religion, and, how to manage parliament was the chief cause of the English Civil War.

Posted by: <u>Griffin</u> | November 8, 2004 06:23 PM

I think that the major cause of the English Civil war was the unyielding senses of entitlement of Charles I and of the Puritan gentry of Parliament. The opposing forces would not exist without Charles' desire to embody absolutism (as Griffin and Greg said above) and the gentry's desire to resist. It seems that the more deliberate cause can be attributed to Charles, for in hindsight, we can see that Parliament's efforts to "check" the power of the monarch was more than legitimate.

Posted by: <u>Abby</u> | November 9, 2004 07:37 AM

Recent Comments

Mireille on The English Civil War

Lauren on The English Civil War

Allie on The English Civil War

Caroline on The English Civil War

Amy on The English Civil War

Selden on The English Civil War

Chris ▮▮▮▮ on The English Civil War

alex on The English Civil War

anne ▮▮▮on The English Civil War

Audrey on The English Civil War

Archives

November 2004

October 2004

September 2004

In the example above, you can see how students read each others ideas and react to them.
Source: Courtesy of Robert Henderson.

Discussion Question: Origins of the Cold War (High School)

In this example, blogging is the culminating activity of a one-night Web page reading assignment. The specific purpose of this assignment is to get students to provide a clear opinion on Churchill's "Iron Curtain" speech. These statements then can be used in class the next day as a foundation for a broader discussion on the Origins of the Cold War.

Instructions to Students:

Go to CNN's "The Iron Curtain Special Report" at: http://www.cnn.com/
SPECIALS/cold.war/episodes/02/.

1. Examine Interactive Map: Post-War Europe (Iron Curtain 1946)
2. Click on "Iron Curtain" and read about Poland and West Germany
3. Read PRAVDA: Stalin's "Iron Curtain" Response

After completing the above reading, post an answer to the following question to our class blog:
"Churchill's comments were inflammatory and unnecessary." Do you agree or disagree?
Your posts will serve as the basis of our class discussion tomorrow.

Discussion Question: Life of a Hobo: Interdisciplinary Blogging Activity (Middle School, High School)

This creative writing/historical simulation activity calls on students to research the plight of homeless teenagers during the Great Depression and then create their own fictionalized accounts of a day in the life of a hobo. Students post their stories on their blogs and read each other's work, commenting on other pieces about what they liked about the stories they read and what made them seem authentic. The blogs provide a public forum to present and share student work.

Instructions to Students:

In this assignment you are to write from the perspective of a hobo who is "riding the rails."
Use your knowledge of the period and your creativity to create a story (250–500 words)
about a day in your life as a hobo.
  Here are some questions to help guide your story: How old are you? Where are you from and
why have you left home? Are you traveling alone or with someone? Who? What possessions do
you have? What are your plans? What are your concerns? How are you feeling, physically and
emotionally? What happened to you today? How did it make you feel?

Students were given the links below to help provide background on the life of a hobo:

• Riding the Rails (PBS) http://www.pbs.org/wgbh/amex/rails/
  Part of PBS's American Experience television series, this site focuses on the plight
  of more than a quarter million teenagers living on the road in America.
• Tales from the Rails: http://www.pbs.org/wgbh/amex/rails/sfeature/tales.html
  Weaver Dial: Battling the Bulls
  Leslie E. Paul: I Was a Burden
  Henry Koczu: Going to California
  Norma Darrah: One Weary, Hungry Mile After Another
  Gene Wadsworth: Losing a Brother
  Berkeley Hackett: Feeling Like Tom Sawyer
• New Deal Network http://newdeal.feri.org/index.htm
  The New Deal Network (NDN) features 20,000 items: photographs, speeches,
  letters, documents, and exercises from the New Deal era.
  o   Bumming in California http://newdeal.feri.org/fwp/fwp07.htm
  o   School for Bums http://newdeal.feri.org/voices/voce02.htm

- Breadline: 1929–1939 http://www.pbs.org/wgbh/peoplescentury/episodes/breadline/
  Part of PBS's People's Century television series, this site explores the massive
  unemployment in America during the Depression and offers interviews, a timeline,
  and a teacher's guide.
- Surviving the Dust Bowl http://www.pbs.org/wgbh/amex/dustbowl/
  Part of PBS's American Experience television series, this site examines the region in
  the Southwest renamed the "Dust Bowl" because of a catastrophic eight-year drought.
- Stories from the Great Depression http://www.pbs.org/wgbh/amex/dustbowl/
  sfeature/eyewitness.html%20

The following story was written by a tenth-grade student in response to this
assignment:

THERE'S NO AUNT SARAH

My stomach's empty but it don't hurt and my back's near broke but it don't ache. Can't feel
nothin' right now—not my tired feet that won't stop bleedin' or the on'rous weight of the
dust in my lungs. The physical sufferin' ain't nothin 'pared to the hurt in my heart.

When you've gotta worry 'bout starvin' and freezin' to death you forget to keep track of what
day it is, but I'd estimate today's the 15th of December, year 1932. It took me near three weeks
to get here. "Here" is Lancaster, California. I left home in Kansas when Dadi told me he'd got
word from Aunt Sarah in California. "Aunt Sarah's got a place for you to stay with her and she's
found you a good job in a shop in downtown Lancaster," he said. "You go put your things in the
bag that I've left you upstairs and I'll take you to the train in the morning." I had never met Aunt
Sarah, let alone heard mention of her in our house before the day that Dadi told me I'd to go live
with her. Things were hard for us then. Not just hard for my family but for all the farmin' families in Kansas that depended on the crops. Ever since the topsoil started blowin' 'way nothin'd
wanted to grow. No crops, just dust. It meant no money, empty stomachs, cold bodies.

At 14, I was the third oldest of Mama and Dadi's kids. My brothers Jake, 16, and Tom, 15,
left a few months before I did to find work and s'port themselves on account of Mama and
Dadi could hardly feed themselves. Before Dadi'd told me I'd be leavin' too I'd thought about
gettin' myself a job. I felt awful guilty all the time 'bout bein' another mouth for Mama and
Dadi to fill. It was almost relievin' that I'd be leavin.' My absence'd be improvin' for Mama and
Dadi and my sisters. I kissed Anne-Marie, Sue, and Emily good-bye and went to find Mama
to do the same but Dadi said, "Listen, Sarah, you don't say nothin' to your mother. Good-bye
will break her heart so you just let her be." It broke my heart not gettin' to say bye to her but I
thought Dadi was right so I let her be like he said to. I put a pair of socks, a blouse, skirt and my
doll, Jenny, into the canvas bag that Dadi'd left at the foot of my bed. The next mornin' Dadi
walked me to the train station. He gave me 20 cents, told me which train to take, and left. I like
to think Mama cried when she found out what Dadi'd done the next mornin.

I made quick friends with a hobo 'bout my age named Jim. He warned me 'bout the railroad
bulls and told me where the hobo camps that made the best mulligan stew were on the way from
Kansas to California. I didn't spend more than a day with Jim but he taught me things my life'd
come to rely on later.I spent 'near three weeks ridin' the rails, walkin' on route 66 to get from station to station and stoppin' at hobo camps in between. Pretty much 'came a 'bo myself. Today I
arrived in Lancaster, California. The prospect a' my arrival here's what kept me goin' all the time
I was trav'lin.' Imagine my disapointment 'pon findin' there really wasn't no Aunt Sarah. That
there wasn't no warm place to stay, no good job like Dadi'd promised. I know now that I was a
burden that Dadi made up his mind to get rid of. If the poisnin' mulligan stew I've been livin' off
the past three weeks don't kill me, this feelin' in my heart will.

Here is a comment posted by another student:

"I loved your story! Your use of dialect seemed accurate and enhanced the diary-like tone of the story. I also liked how you conveyed the hobo's feelings of helplessness and sadness. You were able to get a lot of the things we had been talking about in class about hobos in your story . . . the mulligan stew, the hunger, the dreams for a new job, etc. It's so suspenseful, I really want to know what happens next . . . good job!

> **WEBSITE:** These examples and many others can be found at http://www. edtechteacher.org/chapter2.html.

I-Search Literature Project: Reflective Journaling

The I-Search is an independent literature research project where students keep a daily log of their interactions with the works and authors they are researching. Students choose a piece of literature they wish to investigate in depth, read scholarly critiques about the work, and then respond to what they read. Few structured guidelines are provided; students are encouraged to follow whatever theme or topic interests them and discuss their interactions with the literature. The I-Search blog serves as a personal diary of sorts as students record their reflections on the literature they are studying. During the process, students respond to comments made by their teacher, and possibly peers, and use these as the basis for developing a more sophisticated exploration of literature.

Peter Raymond, an English teacher at the Noble and Greenough School, says that the I-Search project he undertakes with high school juniors "encourages a deep personal exploration" with literature within a public context. Student posts "become increasingly sophisticated, personal, and refined" as students develop a comfort with the blogging process and better understand the work in question.

Journal Entry Twelve: Connection Between Mental and Physical Scars

After randomly reading an article in Psychology Toady entitled "The identity dance: the battle between genes and the environment is over. As the dust settles, scientists piece together how DNA and life experience conspire to create personality," I began to think about the physical identity and how it is formed. In the article, scientists have discovered that while we are all born with a certain set of genes, the levels of certain chemicals in our brain which affect our behavior and identity may be altered by experience. A lot of times certain problems we may possess on a genetic scale may be disguised by, for example, a good relationship. The opposite works in the same way--a bad relationship may augment these problems. A Researcher says, ""Maternal nurturing and discipline seem to buffer the effect of the serotonin gene," says Suomi. "If they don't have good mothers, then the [troubled] behavior comes out loud and clear."

I'm not sure if this has anything to do with scars and physical identity, but I'm interested in how a writer may use the idea of a scar itself in connection to identity. By definition, a scar is an area of flesh that has been ripped open and healed again but leaves a mark. I'm interested in how a scar comes from a gaping wound, which may signify an opening into one's personality. A psychological wound, which these psychologist may describe as the absence of a loving mother, may open paths for recessive traits. I think many of the slaves on Sweet Home, and in real life, suffered from these identity crises of having their flesh gouged open, both literally and metaphorically. The wounds they suffered from the plantations gave rise to psychological conditions, explained in this article by the presence of certain harmful genes. These psychological conditions paralleled the physical conditions they also suffered through--for example, bearing the strain of being whipped or beat-up. The scabs that grossly healed over the wounds, creating messy scars also parallel the mental scars left on the minds of the slaves. In the life of a slave, physical and psychological trauma are inexorably related.

Sources Used:

Sinha, Gunjan, The identity dance: the battle between genes and the environment is over. As the dust settles, scientists piece together how DNA and life experience conspire to create personality, "http://findarticles.com/p/articles/mi_m1175/is_2_37/ai_n6006225/pg_3", Psychology Today, March-April, 2004

RECENT POSTS

Journal Entry Twelve: Connection Between Mental and Physical Scars

Journal Entry Eleven: The Relationship Between Physical and Emotional Scars

Journal Entry Ten: Scars As Parts of Identities

Journal Entry Eight & Nine: Slave-Owners' Systems of Power & The Stockholm Syndrome

Journal Entry Six & Seven: Human Superiority Over Animals & Tactics of Slave Owners

Journal Entry Four & Five: The Importance of Establishment and Preservation of Identity

Journal Entry Four: The Formation of One's Undesired Indetity

Journal Entry Two & Three: Biblical Symbolism & Moral Implications of Imposing Condemning Identities

Journal Entry One: Intentional Vs. Unintentional Physical Marks & Their Connected Mental

In reading the titles of this student's journal entries, you can see how his thinking on the topic of identity matures.   *Source:* Courtesy of Peter Raymond.

Role-Playing: What Would You Bring to Walden?

Chris's American Literature 11

Just another WordPress.com weblog

Your Nature Writing Here
March 1st, 2007 by workharder

Please post your piece of writing here. Then, after you've posted, read one or two other posts and just leave one comment for that person. Remember, reference the person whose post you're commenting on.

Posted in | 20 Comments »

What would you bring?
February 24th, 2007 by workharder

Thoreau's Packing List

Following are the 12 items Thoreau took with him when he headed into the woods at Walden Pond in 1854.

* 1 axe
* 2 knives
* 1 fork
* 3 plates
* 1 cup
* 1 spoon
* a jug for oil
* a jug for molasses
* 1 lamp

What would *you* take, if you were headed into the woods to conduct the same kind of experiment Thoreau underwent? You can bring anything you want, no limitations.

Posted in | 30 Comments »

search this site

Pages
» About

Archives
» March 2007
» February 2007

Categories
» Walden (3)

Blogroll
» WordPress.com
» WordPress.org

Meta
» Login
» Valid XHTML
» XFN
» WordPress.com

Here, the teacher asks students to consider and re-write Henry Thoreau's list of the twelve items he brought to Walden Pond. *Source:* Courtesy of Chris Bagg.

This role-playing activity was designed by a teacher who had only been blogging with his students for about two weeks! In this activity, teacher Chris Bagg shows his American Literature students the list of items that Henry David Thoreau brought with him to Walden Pond, and he then asks them to compile their own lists. The student work that emerges is a delightful combination of the insightful and the hilarious.

Faraaz Says:
February 24th, 2007 at 3:03 pm

-a gun
-a bunch of bullets
-a handbook on how to use a gun
-blanket
-knife
-axe
-lantern
-flashlight
-a lot of matches/lighters
-a cooking pot
-plate
-fork,spoon
-glass
-compass
-shovel
-emergency money
-clothes(not too many, 3 pants, 3 shirts)
-garlic salt for squirrel meat

Faraaz's response is humorous, demonstrates a familiarity with the text (garlic salt for squirrel meat), and could start a fine conversation comparing his relationship to the woods with Thoreau's.

WEBSITE: Listen to Tom's comments on some of these blogging activities at http://www.edtechteacher.org/chapter2.html.

PENCIL: If your network is down on a day you planned on having students write blog entries, they can always save their work and post it later when the network is back up. If you are planning a class where students will be reading blog entries, there is not much that you can do if the network goes down, so plan a backup activity.

Edublogging Assessment

It can be a formidable challenge to grade a blog. Blogs are by nature informal and personal and don't always lend themselves easily to a formal grading rubric. Some teachers choose not to grade them directly at all and instead lump them within a class participation grade. Nonetheless, some teachers and organizations have attempted to formalize the blog assessment process. For instance, a team of teachers at San Diego State University has created a simple rubric for assessing blogs, which can be found here: http://edweb .sdsu.edu/courses/edtec296/assignments/blog_rubric.html. A Google search for blog rubrics will lead you to many other possibilities as well.

Your rubric may be quite different, or you may have no rubric at all. The important thing is to provide your students with a clear outline of the grading criteria you will use.

Other Blogging Resources

For more resources on blogs, we have two recommendations. The first is a Web site designed by Bernie Dodge at San Diego State University. In ed-tech circles Mr. Dodge is famous for his development of the "WebQuest" model for Internet-based research activities (See Chapter 4, "Guided Inquiry") and has a wonderfully rich and useful list of resources for blogs as well, which can be found at this URL: http://edweb.sdsu.edu/ courses/edtec700/BL/resources.htm, or by doing a Google search for "Bernie Dodge Resources for Edu-Blogging." His Web site covers a wide range of blogging topics: Protocols, Policies, Etiquette; Blogs by K-12 Students; Blogs by Educators; Blogs About EduBlogging; Example Class and Project Blogs.

CHATTING

Class discussions provide excellent opportunities for people to listen, think, and speak. They have a few problems though. First, only one person can speak at a time. Second, some people are too shy to speak.

Online chatting, using an instant messaging service or chat room, solves these two problems. Chatting is as natural to our students as picking up the phone is to us (for many, chatting is actually more natural). While chatting, students can all talk and listen at once. Many students who are nervous about speaking have no trouble typing their thoughts, so chatting is a terrific way to let shy or quieter students have a more prominent voice in a conversation.

Chats can also be copied, pasted, emailed, printed, and saved. This means that you can evaluate, coach, and grade students on their conversations. You can then give praise to quieter students and encourage them to participate more in class, and you can help students improve their skills, like supporting their arguments with source material. Chatting is like a small group conversation where students have a little bit more time and space to think and where you can give students more one-on-one coaching in a way that you cannot do with small, group discussion exercises.

Once you practice chatting in class, it can be an excellent solution for days when you need to be absent. Just email your students instructions, have a substitute sit in to supervise, and let the kids work the whole period.

Using instant messaging in class looks quite strange to teachers, but it quickly becomes perfectly natural for students. Each year we have a few students who tell us that of all the activities we do in class, this is their favorite.

Sample Assignment for a First In-Class Chat

Instructions to Students:
The leader from each group should invite the other members into a chat. From this point forward NO TALKING, ONLY TYPING.

Each person will then in turn ask one of the discussion questions that you prepared last night for homework. You will be given 15 minutes to discuss. The goal is to discuss questions as deeply and thoroughly as possible. I'd rather read an in-depth examination of two questions than brief discussions of six. GO DEEP!

You will get a 5-point grade for this exercise. While I will raise the standards later, for now the grade will be mostly based on the following:

1. Do you stay on topic?
2. Do you carefully read and respond to each other?
3. Do you ensure that you finish each question before moving on?
4. Do you defend your ideas with quotations from the source material?
5. Do you challenge and question one another?

When you are finished, the leader should copy and paste the chat into an email and send it to TurninReich.

A Sample Chatting Exercise on the Bhagavad-Gita

Pablo [10:11:31 AM]: Why is Arjuna reluctant to fight?
Jess [10:11:54 AM]: **Because he doesn't want to kill all of those people**
Pablo [10:11:55 AM]: Arjuna is reluctant to fight because he believes those people are his family.
Jess [10:12:02 AM]: **and his teachers**
Vinesha [10:12:07 AM]: yeah
Jess [10:12:09 AM]: **and his great uncles**
Vinesha [10:12:22 AM]: his family, he didnt want to kill them
Jess [10:12:29 AM]: **right**
Vinesha [10:12:39 AM]: he felt like he was close to these people
Jess [10:13:12 AM]: **yeah, and he thought it would be cruel and unnecesary to kill them**
Vinesha [10:13:17 AM]: yeah
Jess [10:13:28 AM]: **+, he says he doesnt want a kingdom**
Jess [10:13:30 AM]: **right**
Vinesha [10:13:32 AM]: he became overcome with grief
Pablo [10:14:04 AM]: "Then Arjuna saw in both armies fathers, grandfathers, sons, grandsons; father of wives, uncles, masters;brothers companions, and friends. When Arjuna thus saw his kinsmen face to face i both lines of the battle, he was overcome by grief and despair and thus he spoke with a sinking heart. "
Jess [10:14:20 AM]: **right**
Vinesha [10:14:44 AM]: so that's our conclusion for number 1
Jess [10:14:49 AM]: **then "I have no wish for victory Krishna, nor for a kingdom, nor for its pleasures"**

You might note that these three students made 18 comments with 2 complete textual citations in less than 3 minutes. That's pretty exciting, but what is even more exciting is that at the exact same time four other groups of students were doing the same thing. Our classroom got an awful lot of work done together in a very short amount of time. The next step in the activity would probably be to have the students stop chatting online and to begin a whole group discussion on what they learned from talking to each other.

Basic Guidelines for Chat Groups

1. Have students work in groups of 3–5.
2. Give students clear expectations for grades.
3. Require students to email you their work.
4. Encourage students to challenge each other and to draw from the sources you are using.
5. Make sure students start their chatting exercises with a series of questions to address; often it works best to have a combination of some questions supplied by the teacher and some questions that students have devised on their own.
6. Your school might have a chat function on the school email server (like FirstClass) or class management server (like Moodle). If not, you can have students chat using an instant message service like Meebo (http://www.meebo.com) or in their own private chat rooms with a service called Chatzy (http://www.chatzy.com).

PENCIL: If you can't get online during a class where you have planned a chatting activity, you can always have the students answer questions in small discussion groups instead.

Starting a Chat Room with Chatzy

Tech Specs: Start a Chat Room with Chatzy

Set-Up Time: Plan 20–30 minutes to set up chat rooms for your students in the beginning of the year.

Keep-Up Time: 10–20 minutes to think up chat questions (unless you make students think them up as homework).

In-Class Time: 20 minutes to a whole period.

Tech Savvy: Medium.

Go to http://www.chatzy.com. Click on the link for *Create Virtual Room.*

Fill in the appropriate form windows and you'll soon have your own private chat room with a unique URL. Next, you'll need to click on *Invite People,* where you can fill out a form that will send an email to all of the people you would like to invite to your chat room.

Chatzy[15]

Chatzy is a free private chat service. Fill out the form to create a chat room immediately - only for you and the people you invite!

Why Chatzy is a good alternative to traditional chat sites as well as ICQ, Yahoo, MSN and AOL Messenger:

- Chatzy has no registration steps - your friends can join instantly
- Chatzy is free and has no popup ads
- Chatzy does not require any installation on your computer (= no spyware)
- Chatzy works on any PC, with any language and through corporate firewalls
- Chatzy is simple and easy to use

Frequently Asked Questions

Start Quick Chat   **Create Virtual Room**

The Virtual Room gives you password protection, custom welcome messages and much more. You can send out invitations after you create the chatroom below. Or, if you are running a Web site, link to it and use it as a free hosted chat solution.

Your name/alias:	Justin	Green ▾	❷
Title/subject:	World History Room 1		❷
Welcome message:	Welcome to {title} To join the chat, please identify yourself below.		❷
Room type:	Chat + Messaging (default) ▾		❷
User password:	school		❷
Allow users to:	☑ Send out invitations ☑ View the visitor list ☐ Clear the room		❷
Admin password:	******		❷
Confirm password:	******		❷
Emergency email:	justinreich@yahoo.com		❷

Create my virtual room

When you create a Virtual Room in Chatzy, it exists forever so you can have your students return to it throughout the year.   *Source:* Courtesy of Chatzy.

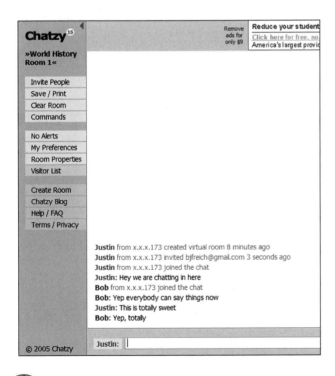

They will receive an email with a link to your chat room. After logging in with the password you selected, your students can begin chatting.

These rooms are persistent, so anytime you want to use them, students can go back to the same Web address. If you made permanent teams in your classrooms, you could easily get this activity up and running with little time investment beyond the initial set-up.

When you create a Virtual Room in Chatzy, it exists forever so you can have your students return to it throughout the year.   *Source:* Courtesy of Chatzy.

WEBSITE: For more ideas on chatting, visit http://www.edtechteacher.org/chapter2.html.

BRINGING THE WORLD INTO YOUR ROOM: SKYPE AND ICHAT

If the perfect guest speaker for your class lives across the country or if you have a class of pen pals across the world, have them join your class by videoconference. There are several newer programs that allow free videoconferencing. If you and your guest are both using recent Apple computers, then iChat is a slick piece of software that allows you to make video calls, even with three or four people. Another great alternative is Skype, which is free to download and works across all different platforms.

Tech Specs: Skype and iChat

Set-Up Time: Downloading and installing Skype is easy—it takes about 10 minutes—and iChat is preinstalled on most new Macs. If you want to set things up so that you can videoconference with your whole class, setting up cameras, microphones and speakers can take a while. A simple audio conference with a small class of students gathered around a computer doesn't take so long.

Keep-Up Time: Setting up a conference with a guest from away can be time-consuming; you need to make sure that they have the necessary equipment and compatible software, and you should practice before you use it in class. For a good guest speaker-though, the rewards are certainly worth the investment.

In-Class Time: Given the amount of time these take to set up, it's worth it to spend an entire class period with the guest.

Tech Savvy: Medium to high. Especially if you are trying to incorporate video, some audiovisual know-how can be quite helpful.

For set-up, you will need:

For the classroom:
- A computer with Skype or iChat
- A projector
- Speakers
- Internet access
- A microphone that students can use to ask questions
- (Optional) A webcam that lets the speaker see the class.

For the guest:
- A computer with Skype or iChat
- A microphone
- Internet access
- (Optional) A webcam so that the class can see the speaker

Tom calling Justin on Skype.   *Source:* Courtesy of Skype.

Skype

FEATURED PRODUCT

Skype Internet Calling
Web site: http://www.skype.com
Developer: Skype, though now owned by eBay
Cost: Free
Skype offers free calls to anyone in the world on the Skype network, and low-cost calls to regular phones across the world. Video calling is also an option.

If both the speaker and the teacher have Skype accounts, then the call will be free. To start a call, you will need to add the other person as a contact in your Skype contacts, which you can do by searching for the person's name or Skype User ID. Once you are on each other's contact lists, starting a call is as easy as clicking the green phone icon near the contact's name. If you both have webcams plugged into your computers, you will also be able to see each other.

PENCIL: These activities depend on a few different pieces of technology working—two sets of computers, speakers, microphones, and the Internet. With a little practice these calls run quite smoothly, but with so many pieces involved, it's best to have a backup plan.

iChat

FEATURED PRODUCT

iChat
Web site: http://www.apple.com/macosx/features/ichat/
Developer: Apple
Cost: Free with Mac OS X
iChat is a chatting software with a beautiful interface that is available only to those with iMacs or MacBooks.

For iChat, you will need to sign in using a Mac account or an AOL account. If you are using Apple OS X Panther (10.3) or Tiger (10.4) you have all the software you need for videoconferencing with iChat. iChat AV automatically detects both external Web cameras and the integrated cameras available on some Macs. You'll want to set up a "Buddy List" with the people you hope to conference with. To initiate a videoconference, double-click on the camera icon next to your guest's name, and you will send out an invitation. Once your guest accepts the invitation and everything connects, you should see each other. Your face will appear in a small box on your guest's computer screen and your guest's picture will appear on your screen. Like Skype, iChat is free.

Some Hints for Better Calls and Videoconferences

In this picture Tom is using iChat to speak to a colleague in Hawaii.

- Be sure that the computer's audio speakers don't point toward the microphone, or you will hear a distracting echo of your own voice.
- Remember that both sides won't be able to see each other perfectly, so you may need to be a little more forceful than usual to interject to make a point or ask questions.
- You don't need to have webcams set up to just have a guest join you by voice, like a conference call.

Skype and iChat are both great tools for bringing the rest of the world into your classroom for dialogue and learning. You also might find that if you have friends or relatives living overseas, the free calling works pretty well for you at home, too. In fact, a lot of what you learn in this book will also be useful in your personal life

 WEBSITE: We have video tutorials for both Skype and iChat at http://www. edtechteacher/chapter2.html.

FINAL THOUGHTS

Classroom conversations used to have two firm boundaries: the clock and the classroom walls. No longer. Using technology we can expand our classroom conversations through time and space. We can foster communication amongst our students and with the outside world from class, from the lab, from the library, and from home. The conversations can start in class, but they can continue long after the bell, and students can contribute anytime during the day or evening. Certainly nothing can replace the impact of face-to-face dialogue, but hopefully this chapter has offered you a number of ideas for how you can add to and extend those conversations.

Chapter 3

Note Taking and Organization

INTRODUCTION

For students who are proficient at keyboarding, taking notes on computers can be much easier than taking notes by hand. Particularly for those with messy handwriting or poor graphomotor skills, typed notes can improve the quality—and the quantity—of note taking. Notes produced on computers can be transformed into papers, study guides, and other assignments more easily than hand written notes can, and if saved in an online environment, digital notes can be accessed from computers at home, in the classroom, and in the library.

Many of the most popular note-taking systems can be replicated using software commonly found in schools. For students using a charting method, like the Cornell system, or an outline method, most word processors can easily create tables, charts, and outlines. For those who prefer using concept maps for notes, software such as Inspiration and FreeMind can create flexible, detailed mind maps.

As your classroom transitions to using computers more extensively, your students will need some help learning how to organize their computer files just like they needed to learn to organize their paper files. We begin this chapter with a discussion of some ideas for online organization and study skills, and then we turn to the best tools and practices for student note taking.

BEYOND THE TRAPPER KEEPER: KEEPING STUDENTS ORGANIZED ONLINE

Find a Place to Save

Before you start having students take notes and write papers online, you will need to have a place for students to store all of that work. Whenever possible, avoid having students save things to a single school computer; these can break, move, crash, or otherwise prevent students from accessing their work. Instead, have students save their work online. Many schools now have some kind of server system where students can save their work and access it at home, in class, and in the computer lab. If you don't have an online service at your school, you might consider requiring your students to create an account with Xdrive or another free online storage system like Gmail (see Chapter 1, "Lectures," for more on these tools). If you work in one of those very rare districts where students have their own laptops, it still might be worth encouraging them to back up their materials somewhere online.

Even if you work in a one-to-one computing environment, you will almost certainly still need your students to have someplace to keep printed class materials, and you will also probably want them to have a notebook for those days where the power is out, the server is down, or handwritten notes will be more useful than typed notes. Just like the much heralded paperless office, the paperless classroom is still, in many cases, a long way off. Even if students are producing most of their notes and papers online, they are still very likely to print things out for editing their drafts or cramming with their study guides. If you will be regularly printing handouts and if they will be regularly printing notes, drafts, and other things, papers can be quickly lost or misplaced if they are crammed in a folder or, heaven forbid, left loose-leaf in the back of a spiral notebook (shudder at the thought).

Consider requiring your students to use a three-ring binder for your class. A three-ring binder is the best vehicle for students to maintain a chronological organization of class materials. If you are dutiful as a teacher about punching holes in all of your handouts and graded papers (and if you keep a few hole punchers accessible in your classroom), students can take some notes on lined paper and intersperse their notes with things they get from you and work they produce. Particularly in courses with cumulative exams at the end of the year, like Advanced Placement classes, spending some time at the beginning of the year helping students develop a system for organizing their materials will pay off generously by the end of the year.

Online Student Portfolios: A System for Saving

Students who work online need training in online study skills, which are somewhat different from other study skills. In addition to training in keyboarding and self-discipline—avoiding games, IMing, Facebook, etc.—they also need to know how to organize themselves online. One of the first skills they'll need to learn is what is formally known as "data asset management," which is basically the practice of organizing online data. Justin recently mentioned to the manager of a small engineering company that he taught students the skills of naming conventions and online organization, and the manager asked if Justin could come teach those skills to the employees at his firm. He worked with brilliant scientists and engineers who spent a lot of time looking for lost files. A few minutes spent helping students organize themselves at the beginning of the year can save time and frustration as the year progresses.

Students basically need two skills to keep their online materials in order: good **folder organization** and intelligent **naming conventions**.

Folder Organization

On the first day of class, as you introduce students to their online server space, you should give them structured instructions on how to name their folders. They should create a main folder for the class, for example "World Religion-Reich," and then sub-folders for the different units: "Judaism," "Christianity," "Islam," "Hinduism," "Buddhism," and so on. Within each of these folders, they should then create at least two more folders: "Homework" and "Classwork." It can be effective to mandate that all students adhere to this minimum level of organization and then also to allow students to create more sophisticated subfolders if that helps them stay organized. Be careful that students don't get too creative, or they may design filing systems so complex that even they can't find their work! The basic main folder and sub-folders should be enough to get most students started.

Below is an example of how a World History student organized her portfolio with her notes and homework for a unit on the history of the Balkans:

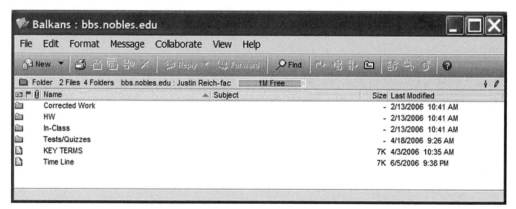

The use of basic folders and sub-folders should keep students' electronic notes and papers well organized and easy to find.

Naming Conventions

Once your students have a good organizational structure to find their files, the next step is ensuring that they name files intelligently. If files are named "Today's Lecture" or "Paper Draft," students will find very quickly that they lose too much time searching for what they are really looking for. The best way for students to keep their files organized is to require them to use simple file-naming conventions.

In the following example, the student's daily homework assignments are given a file name based on the name of the unit, followed by HW and then the homework number, starting with 01. (You need to slip that zero in there, or when the computer alphabetizes the list of files, 11 will come before 2.) So for the Christianity unit, the first assignment is Christianity HW01 and so forth. Students can also add a little extra notation after the standard name, like "outline," so they can remember what each assignment is.

Giving each file and assignment a unique, predictable name makes it very easy to locate your electronic information.

For their in-class notes and writing assignments, students should follow similar conventions. Notes should be saved with the unit name and the date, perhaps something like "Christianity04062008." If students write the date in month-day-year format, then when the computer alphabetizes the files, each unit will be listed in chronological order. Writing assignments with multiple drafts should use some similar convention, like "RomeoandJulietDraft01," "RomeoandJulietDraft02," and so on.

One way to encourage students to use these conventions is to include suggested file names with your assignment sheets or syllabi. Once students are taught these basic principles, they tend to keep using them for their academic career because they are easy and because they work. Of all the computer skills we teach, online organization is one of the ones we are confident students will continue to use for the rest of their working lives.

Checking Student Notes Online

Few teachers would disagree that note taking is an important skill for students to master. Unfortunately, it can be quite time-consuming and challenging for a teacher to collect and review student notes, especially on a regular basis. Simply collecting student's notebooks for a few days could be a tremendous inconvenience to students who rely on a single notebook for one or more courses. And you might be under some pressure to return the notebook as quickly as possible. It can also be pretty difficult for a teacher to decipher students' handwritten notes. Moreover, most teachers simply do not have the time for such an involved review process.

Fortunately, a few email and course-management systems allow teachers to review students' portfolios, enabling you to "collect" their notes without ever separating them from a notebook. With an online student folder, you have access to all of the students' notes for the entire duration of the course. As such, it is an easier and more convenient system for monitoring student note taking than collecting handwritten notes. Also, keep in mind that the students have no idea when you might check their notes or what specific notes you might review! That itself can provide extra incentive for students to take notes carefully and to put them into their online folders in a timely fashion.

TAKING NOTES WITH COMPUTERS

We have the luxury, for some of our courses, of teaching in one-to-one classrooms where every student has access to a laptop. In these classes, students take their daily notes on computers, and in course evaluations, they consistently rate this as one of the uses of computers that they most appreciate. Many students can type more quickly than they can write, and so they find it easier to listen and take notes while they use laptops. Here are some warnings and some tips about having students take notes in the classroom:

1. ***If you let your students use computers and you are not watching their screens, they will be doing something they are not supposed to be doing.*** We regularly have the chance to stroll through schools that are using computers extensively. We often find that while students are supposed to be paying attention in class, they are instead using their computers for chatting, emailing, playing games, checking sports scores, and all manner of other evil things. This is as true in middle school classrooms as it is in graduate schools, by the way. You might decide that you as the teacher need to crack down on this behavior in your classroom, or you might decide these things are just twenty-first century doodling, but either way, don't pretend it's not happening in your class. It is.

    a. **Antidote Number 1: Keep yourself moving.** If you are teaching while your students are at their computers, you need to be constantly circling the room, looking at what students are doing, watching for the telltale signs of illicit programs being quickly minimized. Consider the layout of tables and chairs in your classroom and be sure that you are able to move around the room quickly and unimpeded. If you do this regularly, you'll find that you end up doing a lot of teaching from the back of the room, where you can see everyone's screens. Teaching from the back of the room has the added benefit that you can see the class, the board, and the projection screen from a student perspective. (With a handy pointer device that can be bought at a computer store, it is even possible to control your computer and projector from a distance.) Plus, all that circling and hovering can be great exercise.

    b. **Antidote Number 2: Keep the subject moving.** If the lecture and conversation are moving fast enough and the material is engaging and challenging enough, students won't have time to mess around. Of course, some students might not be able to keep up. Use this one carefully, and think about whether the primary purpose at that moment is for the students to amass information or to reflect upon it to gain understanding. If it's the latter, consider asking the students to lower their laptop screens and focus more acutely on the conversation.

    c. **Antidote Number 3: Hold students accountable.** If you do have problems with students misusing machines, often punishing one or two can have a quieting effect on the rest of the group, at least for a little while. If you do so early in the year, you send a strong message to the students that the computers are to be used for academic purposes and nothing else.

How Closely Should You Monitor Your Students' Online Activities?

There are several "Big Brother" approaches to monitoring student online activity. For starters, there are software programs, like Vision from GenevaLogic (see Chapter 10, "Class Management") or Apple Remote Desktop, that can enable teachers or administrators to watch screen activities on computers. Such an approach, while invasive, can have beneficial educational effects since teachers can see whether a particular student is taking efficient notes or making mistakes. Another Big Brother approach is to read students' emails, if the email platform they use is run by the school. While also invasive, this method can, if used judiciously, be quite effective at deterring improper email activity during class.

Teachers can also monitor Internet activity by checking which Web sites have been visited recently. Ask a student to bring you his or her computer at the end of class to see if he or she has visited any Web sites beyond the ones that students were supposed to use during a particular class. In Internet Explorer, simply select the Go option in the menu bar to see what sites have been visited recently.

The extent to which you monitor your students' online activities is a product of the relationship you have with your students, the institutional policies you are bound to, the culture of the school, and your personal feelings about the distraction that computers represent. Ultimately the best approach is to help students realize that the computers are for their benefit, but they can be used in class only if they are used properly.

2. *Screens create a barrier.* It's subtle, but there is something about the laptop screen that creates a barrier between students and teachers.
   a. **Antidote Number 1: For better discussion, lower the screens.** Whenever you want to just have a discussion with students to flush out an issue, make them lower their screens. If you use laptops, teach your students to "close to a thumb" which means that they don't quite close the laptop, keeping a thumb's width between the keyboard and the screen so that the computer doesn't go into sleep mode. When the conversation ends and you want them to start taking notes again, give them a few minutes to type up a summary of the important points from your conversation before moving on. If you are in a computer lab where students are working with computers, have them shut off the monitors when you want to speak to them.
3. *Be sure that your students' work is easily portable.* It doesn't make sense for students to take notes on computers if they cannot access their files in class, at school, and at home.
   a. **Antidote Number 1: Use online portfolios.** Make sure students have somewhere they can reliably store their notes online. See the section above on Online Student Portfolios.
   b. **Antidote Number 2: Print.** You can have students print their notes at the end of every class, if you have reliable access to fast printers. If you do this regularly, requiring your students to use three-ring binders will make everyone's life easier.

    c.   **Antidote Number 3:** Use a scribe and email. Have just one student take on-line notes to be shared either through email, or on the class Web site or blog, or in print form. See the section below on Scribes.

    d.   **Antidote Number 4:** Use a thumb drive. Some schools mandate that students purchase their own thumb drives, or flash drives, to bring to school. At the very least, you might suggest to your students that they purchase an inexpensive thumb drive to move electronic files quickly from computer to computer. (For more on thumb drives, see Chapter 1, "Lectures")

Once you have students comfortable with taking notes in class, you may find a number of advantages cropping up. Those who are more comfortable typing than writing will find it much easier to listen to lectures and conversations while taking notes. For students with poor handwriting, typed notes can preserve ideas that might be lost amongst scrawls and scribbles. Students can share online notes more easily, which can be helpful when students are sick or absent and can also foster the creation of online study groups. For all students, digital notes are much easier to transform into other useful documents, like essays or study guides, and as an added bonus, when students find notes to be more useful, they are more likely to take better notes.

SOFTWARE TOOLS FOR TAKING NOTES

Using Word Processors for Taking Notes: Microsoft Word, Apple's Appleworks, or Open Office Writing

Word processors are great tools for taking notes, and the current king of word processing, Microsoft Word, is a great choice. Apple's take on the word processor, AppleWorks, is also a fine product, and OpenOffice.org has product called Writing that is basically the same as those two, except it's free, which is a tough price to beat. In this chapter, we'll demonstrate our note-taking ideas in Word, though they could just as easily be done in the other two.

Tech Specs: Note Taking with Word

Set-Up Time: Plan on taking 30 minutes to familiarize yourself with the useful features in Word. If you want to design note-taking templates for your students, plan on another 30–60 minutes.

Keep-Up Time: None.

In-Class Time: If you expect students to take notes on computers, budget a few minutes in the beginning of the period for students to boot up computers and log on, and most importantly plan on a few extra minutes at the end of class for students to save their work.

Tech Savvy: Low.

Microsoft Word
Web site: http://office.microsoft.com/word
Developer: Microsoft
Cost: Comes pre-installed on many computers; otherwise, the Home and Student Edition of Microsoft Office is around $150.
Microsoft Word is the giant of the word processing world. We wrote this book, for instance, using Word.

Tables and the Cornell System

If you read up on the art and science of note taking, you will learn that the challenge for most students is figuring out the difference between larger, more important themes and smaller, more specific details. Students can't write everything down, so they need to learn to sift through class notes to figure out which nuggets they need to store. Many systems, including the Cornell note-taking system, call for students to have a narrow column on the left-hand side of the page for prompts to the important themes and a wider column on the right-hand side for details and evidence. Some include a third column on the right for questions for the instructor or a bottom row for summarizing. We like to ask our students to grade themselves on how well they understand each day's lesson, which is one way for us to evaluate our teaching and for them to be able to yell for help quietly. What all these system have in common is that they require tables, which are easy to create in Word, AppleWorks, or Writing.

Here's an example of a template for note taking:

If you want students to use a table exactly like this, then you can just send them a file with this table in it and tell them to make a new copy for each day of notes. If you want them to be able to design their own tables for note taking, you'll need to teach them a little bit about making tables. This can be a useful skill to learn anyway, as tables are great ways to make comparisons, like between different historical eras or leaders, or to keep track of lots of small bits of information, like the characters in a novel or play.

Giving students a structured template to work with can help them better organize their notes and thoughts during class.   *Source:* Microsoft product screen shot reprinted with permission from Microsoft Corporation.

The simplest way to start making a table is to click on the button on the toolbar that looks like a table and then choose the number of horizontal rows and vertical columns. You can also go to *Table→Insert→Table* to produce the same result.

To create a table, simply click on the table icon in the tool bar and choose your table's dimensions.   *Source:* Microsoft product screen shot reprinted with permission from Microsoft.

To change the height or width of rows or columns, put your cursors on any line, and click and drag to move the line. To combine several boxes, called cells, into a single cell, highlight the cells you want to merge and choose *Table→Merge Cell.* Type some headings in bold on the top or left rows, and you are ready to go. Here's an example of the beginning of an exercise comparing a Shakespeare play with a recent film:

Comparison of Taming of the Shrew and Ten Things I Hate About You	Shakespeare Play	Teen Pop Movie
Character Names	Katarina Bianca Petruchio of Verona	Kat Stratford Bianca Stratford Patrick Verona
Other Similarities	Padua, Italy Bianca can't wed until Kat does	Padua High School Bianca can't date until Kat Does
Shared/Similar Lines		
Summary		

Tables are excellent tools for making comparisons and organizing information.
Source: Microsoft product screen shot reprinted with permission from Microsoft.

WEBSITE: We have some links to sites about note taking at http://www. edtechteacher.org/chapter3.html.

If you take the time to teach your students some of the finer points of structuring their notes, you may find that with computers their notes are not only more plentiful but more meaningful as well.

PENCIL: If the computers are down or not available for the day, all of the tables and charts can be drawn with pencils and paper as well, though the tables in Microsoft Word are probably easier to update and modify. If students have a three-ring binder, it will be easy to keep handwritten notes and printed notes together.

Word and the Outline Method

Many students prefer using outlines to take notes but are not necessarily adept at formatting pages for this system. Microsoft Word has an outline feature that can help students immensely. To access it, go to the menu bar and select *Outline* under the *View* option.

The Outline View relies on "heading styles" and indentations to establish hierarchies of information that can be hidden or expanded. When you select Outline View, Microsoft Word immediately creates a dash at the beginning of the first line. You can use the Outline toolbar to establish a hierarchy for that particular line by selecting Level 1, Level 2, Level 3, and so on. After you type a heading in the first line and hit the *Enter* key, the next line will be at the same level. If the information in the second line is, say, a subtopic, then simply hit the right arrow in the Outline toolbar to indent the line. You'll notice that the first line now has a "+" in front of it, indicating that it is a heading. If you double-click on the "+," the line under it will be hidden. If you double-click it again, the line reappears.

Another nifty feature is the ability to drag and drop items. Simply click and hold the "+" and drag its line, and all the information below it, to wherever you like. Note that you aren't restricted to moving one heading at a time. It is possible to move several contiguous Level 1 paragraphs, with all their subtopics, in the bat of an eyelash.

If students use and stick with the heading system, and are deliberate and consistent about establishing levels of information, they will have a very effective means of organizing and analyzing information in the document. For instance, they could choose simply to view Level 1 information, such as the topic headings. They could then test their knowledge of various subtopics by quickly hiding or revealing them. If their documents are particularly long, hiding subtopics can help them quickly identify central topics.

Non linear Note Taking with Graphic Organizers

Word processors are good for taking notes in outline or chart form, but what about students that don't think in boxes or subjects where relationships are more tangled and interconnected? Teachers have long taught techniques of mind mapping, where students put ideas in bubbles and then draw lines to represent relationships between

---

Evaluating Technology: Is It Better Than a Pencil?

Every piece of technology should be evaluated against the greatest piece of educational technology ever created: the pencil. Pencils can write in multiple fonts and sizes and in bold and italics, and can easily be erased. With a piece of lined paper, the pencil becomes a word processor; with a piece of graph paper, you have a spreadsheet; with a piece of blank paper, you have a graphic organizer or art program; and with a flip chart you have presentation software like PowerPoint. Pencils are inexpensive, rarely crash, and are easy to reboot when they do. If a new technology isn't better than a pencil—if it doesn't pass the pencil test—then you are probably better off not using it.

For a few reasons, some of these graphic organizing software products may not pass the pencil test. Inspiration provides so many different stylistic options for presentations that it's easy to lose sight of the content of the mind map. The files are also large and cumbersome to email, and they don't always print well onto a single page. Finally, the software is very expensive, so if your students can't pony up for the $70 license, then they can't use their Inspiration maps at home. FreeMind avoids the latter problem, though not the former.

There are some neat things that these products can do that we'll show you in this section, and both Inspiration and FreeMind have several excellent classroom applications. But for a quick exercise that students can start in class, take home to work on, and easily store in their notebook, it might be best to just tell them to pull out paper and pencils.

---

bubbles. Some students find this system much more helpful to them than more traditional linear methods, and some students look at the bubbles and can't make any sense of them (teachers also can fit in either of these categories). For those people who like a more visual presentation of their information, mind-mapping software can be very helpful. The most popular of the commercially available programs is probably Inspiration. Another great program is FreeMind, which will both liberate your mind and cost you nothing.

Inspiration Mind Maps

FEATURED PRODUCT

Inspiration
Web site: http://www.inspiration.com
Developer: Inspiration Software
Cost: $70 for an individual license, discounted for groups.
Inspiration is a program designed to help students and teachers make concept maps and graphic organizers. The interface is intuitive, and the software offers an extensive array of features for customizing mind maps and outlines. Many educators around the United States use Inspiration, and so plenty of lesson plans and templates can be found on the Web.

Tech Specs: Inspiration Mind Maps

Set-Up Time: 30–40 minutes to familiarize yourself with the basic features of Inspiration.

Keep-Up Time: Inspiration is a very deep software, and if you use it regularly you may want to budget occasional time to explore the various features.

In-Class Time: Plan at least half a period to teach the basics of Inspiration, and then at least 15–20 minutes every time you want to create a simple mind map. For complex mind maps that summarize entire units, you might need to budget several periods.

Tech Savvy: Medium. Inspiration isn't particularly difficult, but for many it will be unfamiliar.

At the simplest level, graphic organizers allow students to put information in bubbles and then draw lines to represent different relationships between those bubbles. That's the basic idea, anyway, but there are enough options within Inspiration to create much more complicated and sophisticated visual representations of information. For students who don't intuitively understand information in tables, these mind maps, or concept maps, of information can lead to breakthroughs in note taking, studying, and writing.

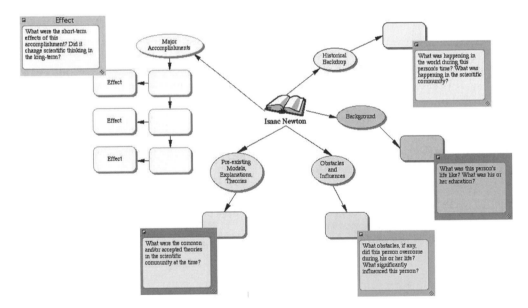

Planning a research project on Isaac Newton is made easier with an Inspiration flow chart.

The simplest way to get started with Inspiration is to use the RapidFire mode. In this mode, as you think up and type new ideas, Inspiration quickly generates a concept map based on those new ideas. The rapidly generated concept map can then be easily redesigned and reorganized to clarify the relationships between ideas.

Four Steps to Getting Started with Inspiration's RapidFire.

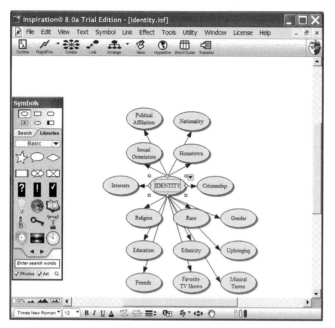

It is very easy to create a whole web of ideas. Just hit the RapidFire lightning bolt icon and you'll be on your way toward your own flow chart.   *Source:* Diagram created in Inspiration® by Inspiration Software®, Inc.

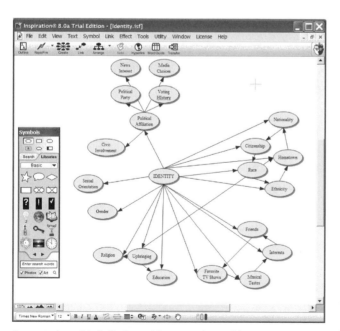

Once you've added all of your ideas, use the *Link* button to organize them and relate them to one another.   *Source:* Diagram created in Inspiration® by Inspiration Software®, Inc.

Step 1: Activate RapidFire mode (sounds like you are an X-Wing pilot, doesn't it!). When you start up Inspiration, you will be greeted by a single blank concept bubble. Write the name of the main topic in this bubble, and then click on the *RapidFire* button on the top toolbar, which looks like a bolt of lightning.

Step 2: Generate related ideas. Start typing everything that you can think of that is related to your main idea. If you hit *Enter* after each new idea, Inspiration's Rapid Fire will generate a new concept bubble for each new idea. Very quickly you can generate an extensive concept map of related ideas.

Step 3: Expand your subtopics. If one of your subtopics deserves to be explored further and expanded, click on that sub-topic and then click on the RapidFire button again. Repeat the process of typing new ideas and hitting Enter after each, and you will create a multi-layered concept map.

Step 4: Reorganize your ideas. Once you have all of those ideas out of your head and onto the graphic organizer, you can move and connect topics using Inspiration's intuitive tools. Click a bubble and you can drag it to somewhere else on your map. Select a group of bubbles and you can move the whole group.

Click on the *Link* button on the toolbar and you can create arrows that show relationships between ideas. Simply click on one bubble and drag the arrow to another bubble. If you want to change the arrows, you can click on one end and drag that end to a different bubble.

By moving concepts and links around the Inspiration map, you and your students can create graphical representations of complex ideas, novels, historical forces, or just about anything else. For the visual learners in your classroom, these concept maps can be extremely effective in helping students understand the relationships between different ideas.

WEBSITE: Visit http://www.edtechteacher.org/chapter3.html for Inspiration ideas, lesson plans, instructions, and templates.

All of those lines and bubbles can be easily rearranged by clicking on different pieces, moving them around, reorienting relationships, and renaming pieces. You can change colors to create different categories of information, use different shapes and symbols for bubbles, and even have the program automatically organize your map into different configurations by clicking the *Arrange* button and choosing a type of organization.

Inspiration Templates

Inspiration also comes with a series of templates for Language Arts, Social Studies, and other subjects, so students can fill these templates in like malleable worksheets rather than develop maps from scratch.

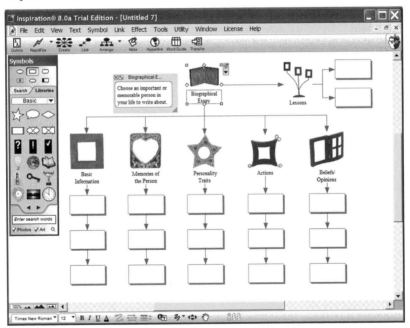

Using Inspiration templates like these can help guide students while still allowing them the freedom to brainstorm.

Source: ©2007 Inspiration Software®, Inc. Diagram created in Inspiration® by Inspiration Software®, Inc. Used with permission.

While Inspiration comes with a variety of pre-designed templates, many teachers throughout the country are using Inspiration, and some have posted custom templates on the Web. Visit http://www.edtechteacher.org/chapter3.html for our ideas and links, or perform a Web search using "Inspiration templates" as one of your search strings.

Problems with Printing: The Downside of Graphic Organizers

Graphic organizers for complex concepts can swell to large proportions quite quickly. If this happens, they can be very difficult to print. You can shrink them so they fit on a single page, but then they're hard to read. You can print them so they fit on multiple pages, which is fine if you are going to post them on a wall, but much less useful if you want them to fit in a student's notebook.

If you are creating a concept map to be displayed in class, this probably isn't much of a problem. If you are using Inspiration or FreeMind for students to use in their note taking, and if students study from printed copies of their notes, then you may want to think carefully about some of the limits of graphic organizers.

Inspiration Jumbles: Organizing Pre-Written Notes

Tech Specs: Inspiration Jumbles

Set-Up Time: 15–30 minutes to design a Jumble.

Keep-Up Time: None.

In-Class Time: 10–20 minutes to complete the Jumble, depending on complexity.

Tech Savvy: Medium. Inspiration isn't particularly difficult, but for many it will be unfamiliar.

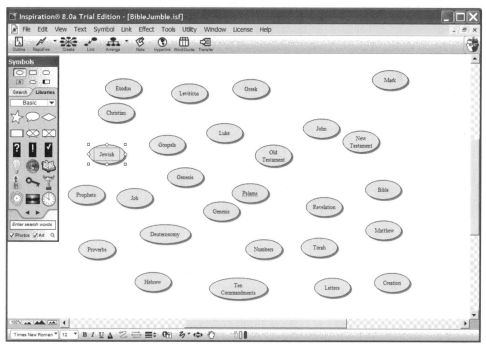

Using Jumbles forces students to think critically and analyze different terms and themes as well as the relationships between them. Inspiration also has helpful tools like a spell checker—note the intentionally misspelled word "Pslams."

Source: Diagram created in Inspiration® by Inspiration Software®, Inc.

Another possible use for Inspiration is to give students teacher-generated concept maps to work with, or in this case, incomplete concept maps. The concept map is all jumbled up, and students need to reorganize the bubbles into a coherent map. These activities don't have exactly one correct answer, though certainly some organizations will be more effective and accurate than others. Jumbles are excellent exercises that can help students work with information sets that have lots of details. They are easy to set up and fun for students to solve. (See below and page 77 for example of before and after Jumbles.).

The best way to design a Jumble is to start by creating your own complete concept map and then going back and erasing all of the links and scrambling all of the concepts. You could also have students create concept maps for certain units one year, and then you could rearrange those maps to be used as Jumbles for next year's students.

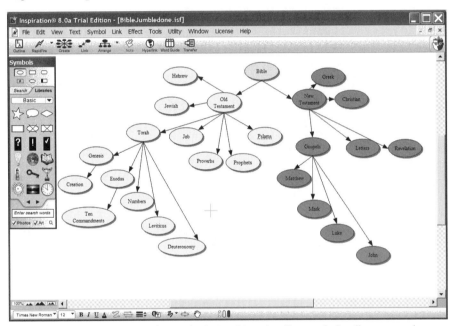

Note that by varying colors and spatial relationships, the diagram helps illustrate and reinforce relationships between the terms.

Source: Diagram created in Inspiration® by Inspiration Software®, Inc.

PENCIL: If you can't get your computers running, you can draw your Jumble on the board and have students reorganize it on paper.

FreeMind: When Less Is More

FEATURED PRODUCT

FreeMind

Web site: http://freemind.sourceforge.net/wiki/index.php/Main_Page
Developer: An open-source project, FreeMind has a team of volunteer developers
Cost: Free

FreeMind is a simple, elegant concept-mapping software that is distributed for free. It perhaps lacks the rich functionality of commercial products, but its interface is simple, clean, and intuitive, and the price can't be beat.

Tech Specs: FreeMind Concept Maps

Set-Up Time: Budget 20–30 minutes to familiarize yourself with FreeMind.

Keep-Up Time: None.

In-Class Time: Plan on 15–20 minutes to teach the basic features of FreeMind, and then students can use it during class as an option for taking notes.

Tech Savvy: Medium. FreeMind is not particularly difficult to use, but it will be unfamiliar to students.

FreeMind is another graphic organizing software that costs nothing and has fewer options than Inspiration, both of which may be good things. With FreeMind you start with a topic, and then you can start creating nodes, which are the equivalent to Inspiration's bubbles. Hit *Enter* to create a same-level node, or hit the *Insert* key to create a sub-level node. By right-clicking on any node, you will find a menu that allows you to change fonts and font colors or add symbols to nodes. You can click and drag nodes to move them around on the map, and FreeMind does a great job of automatically expanding and contracting to keep your ideas from getting too cluttered. If you have too many open nodes, just click on parent nodes and their child nodes will get folded up. Click again to open the parent node up. Many of these functions are similar to Inspiration, but FreeMind has fewer options, which might just get your students to think more about the content and less about the frills and features.

With small file sizes and free software, FreeMind has the major advantage that it is very easy for students to work with its files both at home and in the classroom. If students have trouble keeping themselves organized with day planners or assignment notebooks, organizing themselves with FreeMind would be worth a try.

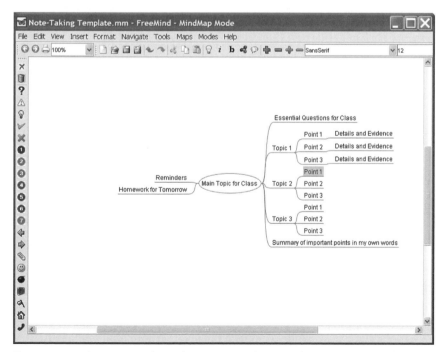

You can expand or contract the nodes in FreeMind to move between viewing all the specific details and viewing just the main headings.

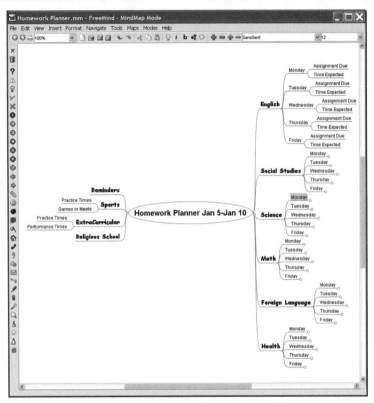

FreeMind can quite easily be used as a student homework planner.

WEBSITE: You can find numerous graphic organizers for the English or Language Arts classroom on the Internet. Here are a few resources to start your search:

- **SCORE** Language Arts

  http://www.sdcoe.k12.ca.us/SCORE/actbank/sorganiz.htm

- **Teach-nology**

  http://www.teach-nology.com/worksheets/graphic/

  Both of these sites feature Language Arts graphic organizers that you can print. Topics include Storyboard, Interaction Outline, Family Tree, and others.

- **WebEnglishTeacher** features an annotated list of graphic organizer sites at

  http://www.webenglishteacher.com/graphic.html.

THE FUTURE OF NOTE TAKING: TABLET PCS IN THE CLASSROOM

Of great interest to educators should be tablet PCs, where the screen of a laptop can swivel around and flop down over the keyboard, so that the screen becomes the top surface of the computer. The screen can then be written on with a special stylus. This has a few great improvements over a laptop. First, it keeps the screen out of the way of conversation. Second, it allows some students to take notes by writing, while others type. Third, it puts you in the technological vanguard . . .

Tablets are equipped with software that can convert handwritten notes to digital text in a searchable format. (The handwriting recognition is generally good, but less effective with technical terms.) Tablets enable underlining, circling, highlighting, and inserting words in ways that are often impossible when projecting a document. They can add a great deal of flexibility and innovation when it comes to classroom presentations and note taking. Furthermore, anything written into a document on a tablet can be saved and sent to students. For instance, you can write on an image, a document, or a PowerPoint slide, save it, and send it to whomever you choose.

Tablets equipped with Livenotes can significantly enhance collaborative note taking (http://sourceforge.net/projects/livenotes/). Livenotes is a software program that, over a wireless network, allows the notes that one person writes to be seen in real- me by others using the same system. In this way, students can exchange notes with each other and build a set of notes that could be used to prepare for a test, a paper, or simply the next day's class.

Tablet PCs remain very expensive compared to regular laptops, so it may be a while before we see them being used widely in schools, but a few independent schools with programs heavily invested in technology have begun to experiment with them. As prices fall and as handwriting recognition software improves, tablets will have a far greater impact on educational technology.

Tablets can help enhance creative note-taking strategies. Here are four possible ideas:

1. **Tablets make it easy for students to make drawings.** In Tom's World History classroom, students are required to graphically represent the Hindu "cycle of life." Specifically, they are asked to draw the voyage of the Hindu "soul" in order to test their understanding of the "cycle of life" concept. With tablets, it is easy for students to draw pictures to represent ideas.
2. **Students can also quickly create their own mind maps.** One class activity for middle school students is to have them visually represent the checks and balances of the three branches in the American political system. Students might do this in small groups. The teacher might select a student to project his group's drawing and ask all students to review it.
3. **The teacher can project a lesson on the board and have students contribute new material, or edit the material presented.** One effective technique to increase student participation is to present a PowerPoint slide show with strategically placed blank slides or empty spaces. The teacher asks students to contribute ideas or questions. With a tablet, the teacher could handwrite ideas directly on the slide while still in presentation mode and then save the slides with the written text and send them to the students.
4. **A related idea would be to present an editorial cartoon or a historic image with an empty box below it and ask students to create a caption or title.** Students could work in small groups to brainstorm ideas for their captions and present them to others for comments and suggestions. Students could even change the cartoon by crossing out or adding elements, symbols, or drawings. Again, anything they write on the image can be saved and sent to others.

TRACKING CLASS PARTICIPATION

One of the hardest grades for teachers to assign is the class participation grade. Taking notes throughout the semester about student's participation is one way teacher's can determine this grade more accurately. During classes where you expect a lively dialogue, consider experimenting with using a graphic organizer to monitor student participation in the classroom. (This technique works especially well with a tablet PC.) Before class, create a bubble for each student in the classroom and put his or her name in the bubble. Arrange them in a circular, semicircular, or horseshoe fashion, and make a bubble for yourself somewhere in the middle of the diagram. During class, draw a line from your bubble to whomever answers a question or otherwise participates in the lesson. This visual representation of class participation can provide you with a quick snapshot of who is participating, how often and the quantity of student-to-student interactions.

To take this visual representation a step further, create a class-participation spreadsheet and enter your daily data into it. If you use an Excel spreadsheet, not only can you tabulate individual and collective student participation easily, but you can also create graphs and charts of your data. Imagine sitting down with a student to discuss their class participation and being able to produce a document with precise statistical data!

CLASS SCRIBE: SHARING CLASS NOTES CREATED BY ONE STUDENT

When a lesson is based on discussion, it can be hard for students to listen to the conversation, prepare their own thoughts, and take notes at the same time. When you have concerns about having the whole class take notes, assign one person to be the scribe for the class. One great advantage of note taking with a computer is that it is quite easy to share a single student's notes with the entire class.

Sometimes the best person to choose to be the scribe is the quieter student who participates in class discussion by actively listening rather than adding much himself or herself. Being the scribe is a great way for this student to make a special contribution to the class discussion.

Tables like these can be helpful tools for keeping track of class discussions. *Source:* Microsoft product screen shot reprinted with permission from Microsoft Corporation.

WEBSITE: This template can be found at http://edtechteacher.org/chapter3.html.

The scribe should take notes using Word, Writer, Inspiration, FreeMind, or some other software tool and should then email the class notes either to the teacher or to the rest of the class. Alternatively, the notes could be posted daily to the class blog (See Chapter 2, "Discussion and Communication," for more on blogs). In general, Word and Writer are easier to use than Inspiration or FreeMind since word processor documents tend to be easier to print, to email, and to read. But if you know that all of your students have FreeMind or another piece of software on their machines, then those can be great options.

You may find it useful to supply all of your scribes with a template so that everyone's notes are somewhat the same, or you may let everyone create notes in personalized ways so that people can see different styles.

TAKING ONE FOR THE TEAM: COLLABORATIVE NOTE TAKING

New and emerging technologies provide some interesting tools for collaborative note taking. For instance, a wiki is a great platform for creating a collaborative set of course notes. Wikis are Web pages that can be collectively edited by a group of people, and we discuss wikis in more detail in Chapter 7, "Writing." While we are on the topic of note taking, we wanted to mention one application for wikis here.

The above is from Tom's United States History course wiki. Tom creates a page for the homework assignments, and then both Tom and his students post class notes and other materials to the page.

The screen shot above is from Tom's United States History class. Students have contributed notes on the Vietnam era in preparation for a unit test. Other students read the notes and can edit or add to them.

Students can contribute to a collaborative set of notes in various ways. One way is to designate a classroom "scribe" for a particular lesson to send his or her notes to the wiki for review. Another option is to have the students work on notes collaboratively during class and then distribute the finished product to everyone else. In any event, students can review the notes after they have been posted and revise them if they feel an important point has been omitted or a central idea from the lesson was misconstrued. Or they might add a graphic, such as a picture or pie chart, that could help illustrate a section of the notes. Some might include links to a helpful Web site that provides additional or supplemental information.

There are also effective ways of using old technologies to enhance collaborative note taking. One simple way of combining student notes typed in Word documents is to insert one file into another. It's easy to do with a PC. First, have students send you or each other the Word document with their notes. With one Word document open, simply select *Insert* from the menu bar and choose *File.* Navigate to the Word files you want and select them. The contents of these documents will appear at the bottom of the document you are in, allowing you and your students to access all of the information at once.

FINAL THOUGHTS

At least since schoolhouses retired their slate tablets, classes have begun with the refrain "Please pull out your notebooks and something to write with." Certainly these tried-and-true note-taking tools are not going to disappear from the educational landscape, but it is exciting to envision the opportunities enabled by classes that begin with "Open up your notebook computer, and let's open the comparative chart that we started yesterday." Notes that are taken on paper have a certain static quality to them, particularly when written in pen, but notes taken on computers can remain alive throughout a course. An English class could begin a comparative chart of all of the novels they read throughout the year, returning to it and updating it regularly. Biology classes can maintain a master taxonomy of life in a list, chart, or diagram. An Ancient History class could create a concept map of important advances in technology and organization for early civilizations. Students who think of something insightful while taking notes in class can copy that idea directly into a new document to start an essay. Students collaborating on creating a study guide can send each other notes to help individuals fill in gaps in their note taking. Especially in education environments that need to prepare students for high-stakes tests, the new possibilities for note taking opened up by computers show much promise for the future.

In all student note taking, whether it involves technology or not, clear and consistent organization is the key. From establishing a simple but effective folder system to establishing hierarchical topics and sub-topics on a page of notes, students need to think deliberately about their goals and how best to achieve them.

Chapter 4

Guided Inquiry

Introduction
Online Scavenger Hunts
Virtual Tours
WebQuests
Google Earth
Select Web Sites for Guided-Inquiry Activities
Final Thoughts

INTRODUCTION

Here's the rub: the Internet is large, and our class periods are short. Therefore, when we bring our students to the World Wide Web in order to take advantage of its resources, we need to provide structure for our activities. Unfortunately, many students simply do not have the information-literacy skills needed to navigate the Web effectively in an open-ended research activity. Teachers often need to direct students to great material and set some boundaries around their exploration of well-chosen sites.

At the same time we need to remember that using the Internet as a huge encyclopedia is not a particularly effective means of incorporating technology into the classroom. While the acquisition of facts and information is a critical first step in the development of a technology-guided project, our broader goal should be to develop our students' critical-thinking skills.

With that in mind, we'll look at four different ways to guide inquiry on the Web: treasure or scavenger hunts, virtual tours, WebQuests, and Google Earth. As we move through this chapter, these various tools will gradually help you move from merely uncovering contextual information to actually using the Internet to help hone critical-thinking skills.

ONLINE SCAVENGER HUNTS

Imagine that you were doing some research last night and you found a Web site that fits perfectly into the unit you are teaching. The site is large, though, with lots of links, and several sections that are not connected to your topic. There are also some pages that are important, but your students might not spend a lot of time with them without your guidance.

One gentle way to guide students toward important information on a Web site is to design a treasure hunt, a type of scavenger hunt, for the site. An online scavenger hunt can be used to introduce students to excellent Web sites while also introducing them to

Tech Specs: Online Scavenger Hunts

Set-up Time: Many can be found on the Web in just a few minutes by searching. Designing your own might take 30–60 minutes to check out new sites and prepare questions.

Keep-up time: You may need to update your exercises each year to eliminate dead links, etc.

In-Class Time: 20–30 minutes to let students explore and then debrief together.

Tech Savvy: Low.

useful information about a curriculum topic. An online scavenger hunt can be an individual or group activity and can be timed or untimed. It typically takes the form of a list of questions that can be answered at a single site or several related Web sites, perhaps with some navigation hints for trickier questions.

A scavenger hunt can be the first step in a scaffolded assignment. For instance, students might hunt through introductory sites on ancient Greece as a first step in the process of evaluating ancient Greek democracy. Keep in mind that ultimately we want to use the Internet to develop students' critical-thinking skills instead of simply as a means of acquiring facts about a topic.

Examples of Web Site Scavenger Hunts

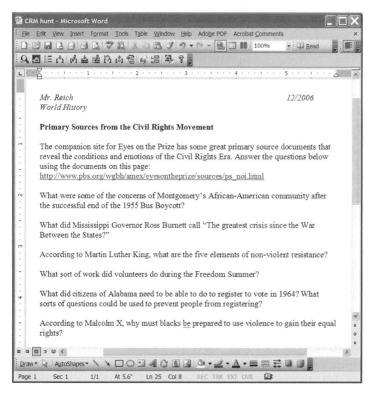

In this first exercise, students are directed to a PBS Web site affiliated with their "Eyes on the Prize" documentary series about the civil rights Movement. This Web page contains a series of primary source documents from the 1950s and 1960s. The simple questions that are posed encourage students to explore the documents in order to find the answers.

Students must answer questions that force them to think critically about the material they find on the Web.

Source: Reprinted with permission from Microsoft Corporation.

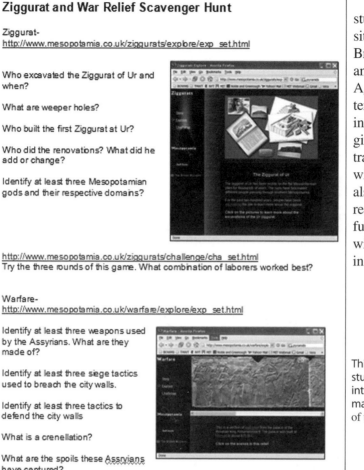

Ziggurat and War Relief Scavenger Hunt

Ziggurat-
http://www.mesopotamia.co.uk/ziggurats/explore/exp_set.html

Who excavated the Ziggurat of Ur and when?

What are weeper holes?

Who built the first Ziggurat at Ur?

Who did the renovations? What did he add or change?

Identify at least three Mesopotamian gods and their respective domains?

http://www.mesopotamia.co.uk/ziggurats/challenge/cha_set.html
Try the three rounds of this game. What combination of laborers worked best?

Warfare-
http://www.mesopotamia.co.uk/warfare/explore/exp_set.html

Identify at least three weapons used by the Assyrians. What are they made of?

Identify at least three siege tactics used to breach the city walls.

Identify at least three tactics to defend the city walls

What is a crenellation?

What are the spoils these Assyrians have captured?

In this next exercise, students explore two Web sites produced by the British Museum about ancient Mesopotamia. Again, the subject matter is inherently interesting, and the questions give students a little extra motivation to explore widely. The questions also ensure that students read pages that are helpful context for ideas that will be introduced later in the unit.

This engaging site draws students in and also introduces them to new materials. *Source:* Courtesy of the British Museum.

WEBSITE: Visit http://www.edtechteacher.org/chapter4.html for more activities and examples.

Designing Online Scavenger Hunts

The easiest way to give students a scavenger hunt is to send one in an email message or as an attached document. You simply need to type a series of questions and then provide your students with the necessary search terms or links to specific Web sites. Send the email or document, and your students can get to work. When they finish, they can email you back the completed scavenger hunt worksheet. You can also post Scavenger Hunts to your class blog (see Chapter 2 for more on blogs), and you could even have students submit their answers as comments.

The key skill for designing online scavenger hunts is creating hyperlinks to Web sites, which is very simple in most word processors and email systems. If you simply type the complete Web address, sometimes called a URL, and then hit *Space Bar* or *Enter,* the Web address will automatically become a hyperlink to that Web site. Most systems follow the convention of formatting hyperlinks with underlined blue text. If you would like regular words to be hyperlinked to certain Web pages, like the *click here* links that can be found on many Web pages, then you will need to learn to hyperlink regular text.

Fortunately, hyperlinking text is also quite simple. In most interfaces for word processors, email software, or blogging software, you will find a little icon with a chain on one of the main toolbars with other editing tools, like buttons for boldface or italics. (In word processors, you can also click on *Insert→Hyperlink.*)

Select a section of text and then click the hyperlink button, and you will bring up an options screen where you can enter the URL that the text should link to. When you close the screen the highlighted text will be usually become bright blue and underlined, and it should link to the appropriate Web page.

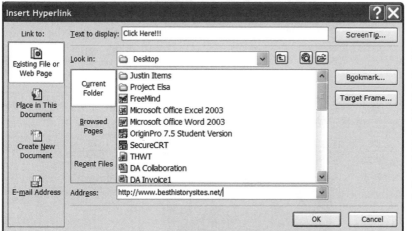

A window like this should appear, enabling you to insert a hyperlink into your text.

Source: Microsoft product screen shot reprinted with permission from Microsoft Corporation.

With this technique you can design an exercise where you have a series of questions followed by links, and the links can even be hints.

Shakespeare Scavenger Hunt

What are the three categories of Shakespeare's plays? <u>Search Here!</u>

Some people believe that Shakespeare did not actually write all of his plays. Who are some of the other possible candidates? <u>Look for the Authorship Debate</u>

Using hyperlinks can be a great way to create a class activity where students are guided to important information on the Web.

More Design Tips

- Some scavenger hunts focus on having students explore a single Web site, but you can also design scavenger hunts where each question directs students to a different page. This might be useful right before a research project, in order to orient students to several different kinds of online sources.
- Another type of scavenger hunt involves simply asking questions and giving students hints, such as well-chosen search terms, and leaving them to search more

generally for the answers. When students are first learning new vocabulary, key words, timeline events, or characters in literature, this might be a more effective, active means of introducing these ideas than simply memorizing the definitions from a worksheet or textbook reading.

- For younger students working on basic reading comprehension, you might ask them questions that solicit simple factual answers. For older students, you can ask questions that challenge them to evaluate a single source or synthesize ideas from several sources.
- If your goal is to have students discover a few specific pieces of information, design a hunt with only a few questions. If you are using a site as an enrichment activity, rather than a core source of information, consider providing far too many questions to be answered in the time allotted, and then let students compete to see who can answer the most questions.
- For these exercises, consider having students work in pairs or small groups. If each group has access to several computers, then one person can be searching the site on her computer while the other student types the answer on her machine.

PENCIL: If the Internet is down, then this activity won't work. If your students can get online, but your email or blog is not working, then you can print out the scavenger hunt worksheet and have students hand it in.

Finding and Editing Scavenger Hunts from the Web

If you conduct a Google search for "online scavenger hunt" or "Internet scavenger hunt" you will find that many teachers before you have created online scavenger hunts and posted them for public use on the Web. Several teachers have created excellent compilations of these scavenger hunts, which can be found online.

If you find something on the Web that you'd like to edit, simply highlight the sections of the scavenger hunt that you want, and then copy and paste the questions and links into a Word document. You'll be able to edit all of the text, and you can even edit the hyperlinks if you right-click (*Control-click* on a Mac) on them and choose *Edit Hyperlink*. You can then post your modified scavenger hunt on your blog or email it to your students. If possible, be sure to ask permission and give the author credit!

Assessment for Scavenger Hunts

Consider one of these three options for assessing your students on their performance with scavenger hunts.

- **No Grade:** Self assessment. After students have had time to complete the hunt, go over the questions together in class. Ask students to correct their own worksheets and send them to you or hand them in for a quick check.
- **Small Homework Grade:** Once students finish, have them email or hand in the worksheets; grade the students on their effort and number of correct answers.
- **Extra Credit:** Reward the student or group that answered the most questions correctly with a little extra credit.

VIRTUAL TOURS

Tech Specs: Virtual Tours
Set-Up Time: 10–15 minutes of searching will yield many good options for virtual tours.
Keep-Up time: None.
In-Class Time: 20–40 minutes to let students explore the tour, depending on the depth of the site.
Tech Savvy: Low.

Field trips are excellent ways to immerse students in physical evidence by visiting museums, historical sites, author residences, or government buildings. Field trips are also expensive, complicated to organize, and draw students away from their other class responsibilities. Fortunately, if you cannot visit an important site in person, you can often visit the site virtually on the Web. While some online virtual tours consist of static two-dimensional images and text, others contain engaging three-dimensional animations and simulations, panoramic video, and more.

Monticello, Thomas Jefferson's home and plantation in Charlottesville, Virginia, offers an excellent example of a virtual tour at http://www.monticello.org/. The site offers two major tours of the house and plantation and several more specialized tours related to domestic life and horticulture. Each section of the tour has a Flash animated visit to a different section of the house and plantation, narrated by the Monticello staff.

Welcome *to the* MONTICELLO EXPLORER

─[EXPLORE]─

Explore *the* PLANTATION
See how Monticello Mountain changed during Jefferson's life with this interactive map of the center of his 5,000-acre plantation in Albemarle County, Virginia.

Explore *the* HOUSE
Navigate a 3-D recreation of Jefferson's architectural masterpiece and discover the objects, people, stories, and details of Monticello.

─[TOUR]─

GENERAL HOUSE TOUR
Journey with Curator Susan R. Stein as she reveals Jefferson through Monticello's rooms, furnishings, and stories.

DOMESTIC LIFE AT MONTICELLO
Discover what life was like for Jefferson, his family, and his enslaved domestic workers with Monticello's Shannon Senior Historian Lucia Stanton.

GARDENS AND GROUNDS
Join Monticello's Director of Gardens and Grounds Peter Hatch for an in-depth look at the unique horticultural world Jefferson created on his beloved mountaintop.

The virtual Monticello exhibit provides a great view into life on Jefferson's plantation.

Source: Monticello/ Thomas Jefferson Foundation, Inc.

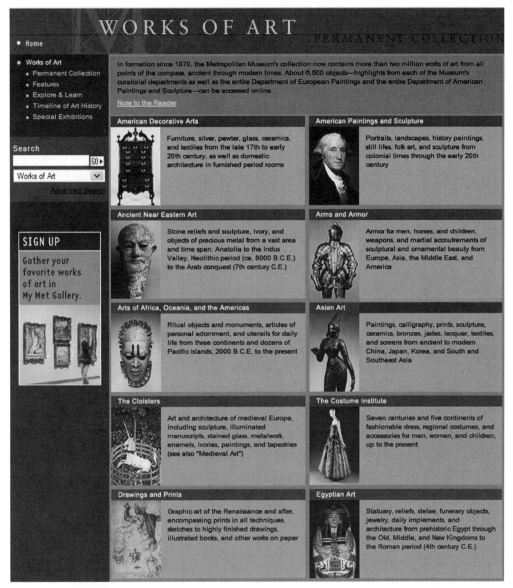

The Metropolitan Museum of Art's Web site offers several structured and educational virtual tours.

The British Broadcasting Corporation has some excellent online virtual tours. BBC History tours are available at http://www.bbc.co.uk/history/interactive/virtual_tours/ and are divided into three major categories: Ancient History, British History, and World Wars. The tours contain panoramas and 3-D models, and several involve historical reconstructions and simulations. The BBC's new Audio and Video service also offers a tour of the trail that links Shakespeare's birthplace of Stratford-on-Avon with the Globe Theatre in London.

Here are some excellent Web sites that offer impressive virtual tours:

• The Metropolitan Museum of Art Timeline of Art History is a chronological, geographical, and thematic exploration of the history of art from around the world:
  http://www.metmuseum.org/explore/index.asp

- Turning the Pages enables visitors to virtually "turn" the pages of manuscripts using touch-screen technology and animation: http://www.bl.uk/onlinegallery/ttp/ttpbooks.html
- The British Museum online features historical reconstructions and 3D animations: http://www.thebritishmuseum.ac.uk/index.html
- Forum Romanum is an award-winning site on ancient Rome: http://www.forumromanum.org/
- Acropolis360 offers a full-screen 360-degree virtual tour of the Acropolis in Athens: http://www.acropolis360.com/
- PBS Nova Online features a virtual tour of ancient Egyptian pyramids: http://www.pbs.org/wgbh/nova/pyramid/
- Virtual Jamestown offers a virtual tour of historic Jamestown: http://www.virtualjamestown.org/jqtvr.html
- ushistory.org offers seven walking tours through historic Philadelphia: http://www.ushistory.org/districts/index.html
- Vatican Museums Online provides virtual tours of the Vatican museums: http://mv.vatican.va/3_EN/pages/MV_Home.html
- The official Web site of the Louvre museum in Paris offers visual tours: http://www.louvre.fr/llv/commun/home_flash.jsp

Virtual tours are excellent vehicles for bringing primary source materials into the classroom, and museums and historical sites are adding more virtual tours to their Web sites.

Some museums have Web sites that are so well structured, you can just let students loose on them and trust that great learning will take place as students explore. If you expect that your students will need a little more guidance, here are some ways to structure student explorations of these tours.

1. Build a scavenger hunt around a virtual tour or a specific museum collection, like this one below:

Egyptian Collection at the Metropolitan Museum of New York Scavenger Hunt

http://www.metmuseum.org/Works_of_Art/department.asp?dep=10

Copy a picture in 10 of 12 the categories below. Beneath each picture, describe a specific detail from the artifact that caught your eye as beautiful or important:

Something to aid the journey to the afterlife	Something for the home	Jewelry for a woman	A pharaoh killing a duck
Something with magical power	Something for a pet, a dead pet	Something for dining	A coffin
A Sphinx	Something with hieroglyphics	A depiction of an animal	A depiction of a god

---

You could also structure a scavenger hunt around the Metropolitan Museum of Art's Web site exhibits.

2. Give students an essay question or a series of short-answer questions to be answered after taking the virtual tour.

3. Have students design their own guided tour of a museum collection organized around a theme, like "Egyptian Objects for the Dead" or "Early American Objects for the Home." Students could post links and their own descriptions on a blog or in Word document.

4. For an advanced class, use a screen-recording program (see Chapter 8, "Student Presentations") to have teams of students record their own guided visit to a museum collection or virtual site.

WEBSITE: Links to a wide variety of Virtual Tours can be found at: http://www.edtechteacher.org/chapter3.html.

WEBQUESTS

> **Tech Specs:** WebQuests
>
> **Set-Up Time:** Searching for a WebQuest, 10–15 minutes; modifying one, another 15–30 minutes; designing your own, 45 minutes to an afternoon.
>
> **Keep-Up Time:** Each time you use a WebQuest, plan on spending 10–20 minutes checking links and updating them.
>
> **In-Class Time:** Many are designed for 3–5 periods, though some are longer or shorter.
>
> **Tech Savvy:** Low to use, medium to design.

WebQuests were pioneered by Bernie Dodge at San Diego State University way back in 1995, but they have matured into one of the most effective frameworks for teaching with technology.

Dodge's two sites for WebQuests, http://www.webquest.org/ and http://www.quest garden.com/, represent a tremendous resource for educators. Over 29,000 teachers have registered on the site and over 14,000 WebQuests are available for teachers to use online. 14,000 WebQuests represent something like 14,000 week-long, free lesson plans for projects built by teachers in all disciplines from around the world.

WebQuests are structured Internet research exercises that lead students to create some kind of educational product. They typically consist of seven standard sections:

1. **Introduction**—an introduction to the essential question or task of the WebQuest.
2. **Task**—a brief description of what the student is expected to do and to produce.
3. **Process**—a step-by-step explanation of the research process and the assessment for the WebQuest.
4. **Resources**—links to Web sites that students will use to conduct their research.
5. **Evaluation**—a rubric evaluating the assessment piece(s) of the WebQuest.
6. **Conclusion**—a parting statement from the WebQuest designer.

Chinua Achebe's THINGS FALL APART: Understanding Context through Expert Interviews

- ■ Introduction
- ■ Task
- ■ Process
- ■ Evaluation
- ■ Conclusion
- ■ Credits

- ■ Teacher Page

by Cherisse Jackson, CSU Monterey Bay

First, learners will research the context categories for this novel. Next, the learners will synthesize their research by creating five-question interviews between a category expert and an interviewer. Finally, the learners will present their research to the rest of the class as they conduct the interview.

Introduction

You will be reading the novel, *Things Fall Apart*, for the next three weeks. Before you begin reading, we're going to use the Web to delve deeply into the novel's context. Being aware of the novel's background will help you understand what you're reading. This Web introduction will keep you from "falling apart" as you make connections with the world of this novel.

This WebQuest is divided up into clear sections.

7. Teacher's Guide—details on how to use the WebQuest and, usually, correlations to state standards.

The genius of the WebQuest model is that it provides simple structure for student inquiry on the Web, guiding them toward important questions and the most useful Web sites. Once you have guided students through one WebQuest, they'll be ready to tackle future ones almost on their own.

WebQuests can be used in almost any discipline. Any time you have an activity where students create a product—a paper, a poem, a PowerPoint, or a play—using guided Internet research, a WebQuest is a great format for presenting and structuring that activity.

Finding WebQuests

A great place to start looking for WebQuests is Dodge's WebQuest portal at http://www.webquest.org/. Click on *Find WebQuests* for three search options.

SDSU WebQuest Search Page

Free Text Search

Since 1996, San Diego State University has maintained a database of example WebQuests. This database is kept up to date and weeded out when a link goes bad (as volunteer time permits). As of this writing, the database contains over 2500 WebQuests. You can search for any string of characters in the Title, Description, Author name or URL.

Search the SDSU Database for [English ∨] language WebQuests with ...

[   ] in the [Title or Description ∨] .

If you type two words in, they'll be treated as a phrase **so in general type in only one word** as a search term unless it's a phrase like *New England*.

[Search SDSU Database]

Curriculum x Grade Level Matrix

Would you like to find WebQuests from the SDSU database for a specific grade and curriculum area? Use the popup fields below and see what comes up. You can bookmark the search results page as well to make it easy to redo the search.

[-- Select Subject -- ∨] [-- Select Grade -- ∨] [Search Matrix]

Google Search

Can't find something in the SDSU WebQuest database? You can search more broadly by going to Google. Type a word or phrase that describes a topic that you'd like to find a WebQuest about and see what you get. *Be aware, though, that the quality of what you find will vary widely, and that many pages that call themselves "WebQuests" are really something else.*

[   ] [Search Google]

The QuestGarden offers three different mechanisms for searching its database of over 14,000 WebQuests.

1. Search the San Diego State University Database. Choose among WebQuests in eight languages and then choose a key word or phrase.
2. Search a Curriculum by Grade Level Matrix. Pick a discipline, then pick a grade level, and you'll get a list of all of the appropriate WebQuests.
3. Put your search term in the Google box and you'll get search results for your term plus WebQuests. You can find WebQuests on just about anything this way; for example, Wisconsin students might want to study up on Cheese Days . . .

WEBSITE: Another way to find great WebQuests is to search the links provided by our site: http://www.thwt.org/webqueststhinkquests.org.

WebQuests can be used for a wide variety of educational purposes.

Evaluating WebQuests

WebQuests vary *greatly* in quality. Many on the Web are made by pre-service teachers, many of the older ones have broken links, and many have resources that are not well chosen or age appropriate. And some are just brilliant.

If you search through the webquest.org search portal, many of the WebQuests that you find will be ranked on a scale from 1 to 50. You can usually depend on WebQuests ranked in the high 40s and 50 to be excellent. Those that are unranked often include the newest WebQuests, so you might check out those as well.

You might also review Tom March's list of recommended WebQuests at http://bestwebquests.com/. March, a former colleague of WebQuest Creator Bernie Dodge, recommends over 40 English and language arts WebQuests, over 50 History and social studies WebQuests, and many more in Math and Science.

50.00 ✳✳ ✳✳ ✳ Add Your Rating	**Angelina's Journey** This webquest incorporates literary and the understanding of oppressed women into the classroom. Learn why everyone in Angelina's life thinks differntly than she. *Submitted Dec 8, 2004 words*	Vanessa Marie Primavera	Grade: 6-8 9-12 College/Adult English/Language Arts Social Studies
49.00 ✳✳ ✳✳ ○ Add Your Rating	**Extreme Sports WebQuest** A virtual field trip across the country to create a magazine article (based on a real project) *Submitted before July, 2003. words*	Rich Werner	Grade: 9-12 Business English/Language Arts Life Skills/Careers Professional Social Studies Technology
49.00 ✳✳ ✳✳ ○ Add Your Rating	**Poetry Quest** Students are often confused by poetry because they are unfamiliar with it. By discovering the types of poetry and breaking poetry and its elements down into manageable and understandable areas, students will be able to identify multiple forms of poetry and express themselves in some of those forms. Students then write a reflective essay about the process. *Submitted Dec 15, 2004 words*	Robert Keim	Grade: 6-8 9-12 English/Language Arts
48.00 ✳✳ ✳✳ ○ Add Your Rating	**How Long Can You Last in France?** In this lesson, groups of five students are given a fictional trip to France and were asked to see how long they can stay abroad with a budget of $10,000. Each member is given a different role with distinct responsibilities.□□ *Submitted before July, 2003. words*	Sarah Blecha, Lisa Camire, Jackie Cimarolli, Katty Heiple, A	Grade: 9-12 English/Language Arts Foreign Language Math Social Studies

WebQuests like these with rankings in the high 40s or 50 serve as excellent classroom activities.

For every WebQuest you consider using, be sure to check all of the links to make sure that they are active and age appropriate.

In the ideal world, you as the teacher should actually try to complete the exercise before you assign it to make sure that the instructions make sense, the sites are well chosen, and the activity is doable in the time frame allotted.

PENCIL: Give students a printed copy of at least the Task, Process, and Evaluation pages of the WebQuest. That way if the Internet goes on the fritz, students can do research in the library with good old-fashioned books, which never have connection issues. They can also start working on their assessments. Even if the assignment is to create a PowerPoint presentation, students can still create paper sketches of their slides.

Modifying WebQuests

WebQuests are usually built in a series of linked Web pages, but there is no need to keep them there. You can copy the WebQuest into a single document or email message for your students, and this gives you the chance to modify the contents of the WebQuest to meet your class's particular needs.

To do this quickly, open a word-processing document, and then open a Web browser with a WebQuest. In the Web browser click *Edit* →*Select All*, and the Web page should be highlighted. Then click *Edit* →*Copy* in the Web browser, switch to your word processor, and click *Edit* →*Paste*. Everything on the Web page should appear in your word processor. It may not be formatted correctly, but you can fix that or not worry about it. Repeat this process for the other pages of the WebQuest, and soon you'll have the whole WebQuest in a single document. It should be easier from there to change any section of the WebQuest—update broken links, add new links, change assignment requirements, or add deadlines specific to your class. Print this document out for your students, and you have your own customized WebQuest.

Too many teachers abandon a WebQuest they like because a link is broken or because the activity takes longer than they'd like. Before you follow suit, forget the technology aspect for a moment. Is it a good lesson idea or activity? Is it interesting? Does it address some content and skill-development needs? Are you excited about trying it out? If you answer yes to any of these, then make the WebQuest work for you.

Remember, you don't have to use the activity exactly as it is drawn up. You can use parts of it. Maybe you like some of the resources, but not others. Perhaps you would like to use part of the task, but not all of it. Perhaps you would like to eliminate one of the steps. That's fine. You can modify the task to suit your needs, and you can edit/eliminate resources as need be. As noted above, you can copy the content of the material off the Web site (just as you copy text in a word processor) and paste it into Word for editing.

And you don't have to know how to create a Web page to make this a technology-based assignment. You can simply print out your modified WebQuest and hand it to the students.

If you want to create a WebQuest online that is available to other teachers around the world, then read on!

> **WEBSITE:** We have a video tutorial overview of WebQuests, including how to do different tasks such as searching for WebQuests, evaluating them and checking their links, and copying them into a Word document to be modified. This can be found at http://www.edtechteacher.org/chapter4.html.

Creating WebQuests in the QuestGarden

You can start creating WebQuests by registering for a free 30-day trial at http://www.questgarden.com/. Once registered, you'll have access to an improved search engine, a listing of the most recent WebQuests, and a cool feature that lets you see where people from around the world are logged into QuestGarden. The most important feature is that you can create your own WebQuest and publish it online without needing to know any programming or HTML skills.

Click on the *Create a New WebQuest* link to get started on your own WebQuest. Once inside the WebQuest creation tool, you will encounter a series of pages with forms for you to fill out, and the whole site can be navigated with the links on the left.

The forms on each page will hold your hand and walk you through the creation process step-by-step.

You will be prompted to provide a title and a description for your new WebQuest.

The creation tool is intended not only for educators, but for pre-service teachers and first-time WebQuesters as well. If you look carefully at the list on the left, you will note that the order for designing the WebQuest is not the final order of publication. For instance, the Evaluation Rubric is created before the Process, and the Introduction is almost the last piece created. The QuestGarden WebQuest generator encourages educators to think carefully about their goals and context first, then get into the specifics of process, and last and least think about polishing the appearance of the WebQuest.

Before you get started, you should skim through all of the different pages to get a sense of how the whole WebQuest is constructed. Each page is filled with suggestions on crafting WebQuests and sprinkled with links to other Web sites with ideas for building WebQuests and using them in the classroom. As you develop your work, you can click the *Preview* button at any time to get a new window with your evolving WebQuest. When you are finally ready for prime time, click on the *Publish* button.

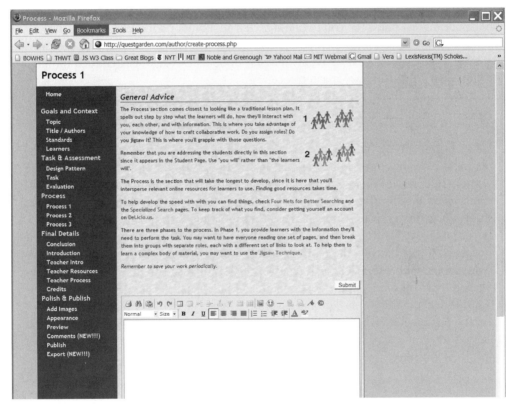

QuestGarden's forms and tutorials make it quite easy to publish your own WebQuest online.

If you have never had the chance to publish something to the Internet, this is a great place to start. It is quite a satisfying feeling to make a little contribution to education that anyone in the world with an Internet link can use in his or her own classroom.

Creating WebQuests in a Word Processor

While publishing WebQuests online is a great service to other educators (unless you publish a crummy one), WebQuests work just as effectively when published in a document. Open Word or another word processor, create a document with the seven standard sections of a WebQuest, and then get to work. When you create the list of links in the Resources section, be sure to completely and accurately type out each Web address (or copy it from your Web browser), and Word will automatically make the URL a link.

To allow students to use your WebQuest, you can print a copy of the document to hand out, but you also should email them the document, or at least the Resources section, so that they can easily follow the links to the Web pages they need for research.

Final Thoughts on WebQuests

If you are just starting to use technology in your classroom, WebQuests might be the best place to start. The structure they provide, for you and your students, means you'll be starting to use computers on a task with clear goals and a clear process. If you select a good WebQuest, you will embark on a student-centered exercise where kids get to do the lion's share of the reading, the writing, the planning, the collaborating, and the learning.

When you get a little more comfortable with WebQuests, the QuestGarden creation tool can be a great place for you to publish your first work on the Web. And if you really want to take WebQuesting to its logical end point, you can start designing exercises so that after a semester or year of WebQuesting, students use the QuestGarden tool to create their own guided-inquiry masterpiece.

A Word about ThinkQuests

A ThinkQuest is an Internet project for students who work in teams to create educational Web sites as part of an annual international competition, sponsored by the Oracle Education Foundation. In 2007 student teams submitted over 500 educational Web sites for the competition. ThinkQuests are published in the ThinkQuest Library, an online resource located at http://thinkquest.org/.

ThinkQuests work this way: Students, ages 9–19, form a "team," and once their teacher "coach" enrolls the team, students work together to create an innovative educational Web site. Each team receives 50 MB of space on the ThinkQuest server and must fill out a short questionnaire. ThinkQuests are judged based on their educational contributions, "global diversity" perspectives, and Web design.

If you select "Visit the Library," you can review previous ThinkQuests. You might show at least one ThinkQuest to your students so that they see what great projects kids their age are creating.

GOOGLE EARTH

FEATURED PRODUCT

Google Earth
Web Site: http://earth.google.com/
Developer: Google
Cost: Free download at http://earth.google.com/download-earth.html. Note: older computers may not be able to run it.

Google Earth is like Google Maps on steroids. Not only is Google the giant of the Internet searching world; it is increasingly offering Web-based software at no charge.

Google Earth is a free program you can download at http://earth.google.com. It features maps and satellite images that you can zoom in on, rotate, and examine in detail. You can even add "layers" of images and other elements to it. It's pretty cool to watch Google Earth in action as it "flies" you across the globe to various destinations and helps you uncover all sorts of useful information about these locations.

Three Steps to Getting Started with Google Earth

Tech Specs: Getting Started with Google Earth

Set-Up Time: Plan on taking 10–15 minutes to familiarize yourself with the basic features of Google Earth.

Keep-Up Time: None.

In-Class Time: If you expect students to work with Google Earth, then download it on the machine they will use. The program is a free download, but it takes time and uses considerable space. So, speak to your IT department first about installing it on school computers and consider having small groups of students work on a few machines. Budget 10 minutes or so for the students to get comfortable with the navigational tools.

Tech Savvy: Medium.

Step 1: Download the Software. The first step is to download the program from http://earth.google.com. Keep in mind that the Google Earth program is a large file, so it may take more than a few minutes to download it to your computer.

Step 2: Open and check out *Search, Places,* **and** *Layers*. When Google Earth opens up, the main window features a large rotating globe accompanied by various tools to help you navigate your "tour." In the left column are three key sections: *Search, Places,*

Google Earth can provide a satellite view of your city, complete with markers for restaurants, coffee shops, and transportation sites.   *Source:* Courtesy of Google.

and *Layers*. Just to the left of each of these three words is a little arrow that you can click on to hide or reveal the information in each section.

In *Places* you'll see the name of the tour you are currently viewing, as well as previous tours you have saved, and controls to both stop the tour in progress and restart it when you're ready. You can save Google Earth files in *My Places* for quick viewing at any time. If you open a new Google Earth file while another one is already open, Google Earth will take you immediately to the new file.

Step 3: Go Home. A good way to get comfortable using Google Earth is to search for your home address. If the search area is not already expanded, click the arrow to the left of the word *Search* to expand it. Now type in your home address and click on the little magnifying glass to the right of the search box. Now the fun begins. The globe in the main window will begin to rotate and zoom to an overhead view of your home.

Three More Steps to Using Google Earth Tools

You can use various tools in the main window to zoom in to your property and view it from different angles. You can rotate the image and even "fly" over your house. Take a minute or two to get comfortable with these navigational tools.

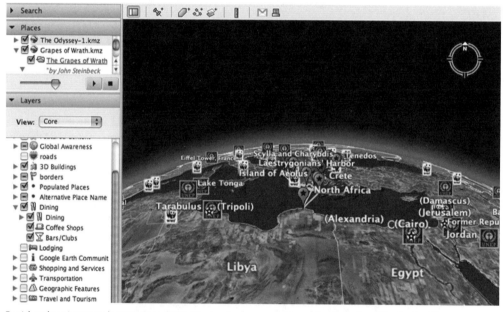

Besides showing your house, Google Earth can show you geographically and politically significant areas worldwide.   *Source:* Courtesy of Google.

Step 4: Throw the World. You'll notice that the cursor becomes a hand icon in the main window. Move the image by simply clicking and holding down on the mouse while you move the hand in any direction. Now repeat the "click and hold" of the mouse, but this time move the mouse very quickly in a single direction and then release it. You are now "throwing" the image in any direction and will move large distances quickly. (The harder you throw the image, the faster it will move across the window.) You can also double-click the hand at any time to zoom in further.

Step 5: Move Around. The directional tools in the top right corner of the main window give you more precise control over your tour. You'll notice two slider tools, one horizontal and the other vertical. To zoom in or out, use the vertical one, and slide the bar up or down. Once you've zoomed in as much as you'd like, use the horizontal slider to get a ground-level view of your property. Move the horizontal slider to the right and the whole image will rotate, giving you a ground-level vantage point. Pretty cool, eh?

At this point you might use the directional tools contained in the circle in the upper right corner. Click and hold on any of the four arrows that point left, right, up, or down and you will move the image in that direction. If you click and hold on the icon in the middle of the four arrows you can move the image in any direction very quickly. Note that you can also click and hold the outer edge of the circle tool to rotate the image 360° in any direction. Finally, you can get the image to face north simply by clicking the "N" at the top of the circle. Are we having fun yet?

Step 6: Add and Remove Layers. Here is where you can use the options in the *Layers* sidebar to locate specific places in your neighborhood. If the *Layers* box is not expanded, simply click the arrow to the left of the word "Layers" to open it. Move the vertical scroll button up or down and select the places that you would like the Google Earth image to highlight. For instance, if you are looking to explore geographical characteristics, then check *Geographic Features* from the list of options. Note that many of these categories can be expanded for an even more precise search. For instance, if you click on the arrow to the left of *US Government,* the folder will open and you'll see you have the option to display *US Congressional Districts*. Many options will be set by default when you open a Google Earth file.

Google Earth Hacks

The real beauty of Google Earth for instructional purposes is the ability to add "layers" of images on top of Google Earth and to include all sorts of information for students to uncover. You can build your own Google Earth file, and we encourage you to do so, but fortunately there are already hundreds of Google Earth files on the Internet that you can download for free. A great place to start is called Google Earth Hacks, found at http://www.gearthhacks.com/.

Google Earth Hacks contains over 20,000 files that can be searched by category or keyword. Click *Advanced Search* in the upper right, and you'll be led to a broad range of Google Earth file categories, such as 3-D Models, Current Events, Past Events, and Historical Place Marks. Click on any of the categories to find an extended list of Google Earth files to download to your computer. Or search a specific topic by typing in a keyword(s) in the search box at the top of the page. For example, a search for "Troy" will lead you to a Google Earth file called "Homer's Troy." To download a file you simply need to click the link called *[Earth]* to the right of *Get File*. (Google Earth files contain a .kmz extension.)

Google Earth in the Classroom

The Troy file contains a map of ancient Troy superimposed on a Google Earth satellite image of its present-day location. The file's creator has added various small icons that can be clicked to reveal information about ancient Troy. If you move your cursor over one of these

3D Models (379) - New three-dimensional models to add to your Earth
--- **3D Cities** (51) - Various smaller cities with some 3d models in them.
--- **Individual 3D Structures** (229) - Noteworthy structures rendered in 3d

Current Events (28) - Locations of events making the news

Image Overlays (1737) - Files with image overlays to enhance your Earth
--- **City/Country Maps** (494) - Overlays with detailed maps for a city or country
--- **Mountains and Volcanos** (82) - Overlays with improved detail for mountains and volcanos
--- **Other Overlays** (345) - Other image overlays that don't fit in any other category.
--- **Real-time Traffic** (27) - Overlays to show real-time traffic on your Earth
--- **War-Related Overlays** (345) - Overlays with information about various wars
--- **Weather: Forecasts** (25) - Image overlays that update automatically to show weather forecasts
--- **Weather: Real-time Conditions** (141) - Overlays that update to show real-time weather conditions
--- **World-wide overlays** (77) - Huge overlays for things like population density, earth-at-night views, etc

Network Links (113) - These items are updated constantly, based on where you are in your Earth.

Outdated Items (445) - These are items that are no longer as useful as they once were (planes that moved, for example), but we're leaving them on the site in case you want to pull them up again.

Past Events (220) - Items that were once in our Current Events category.
--- **Asian Tsunami - December 2004** (9) - Items related to the massive Asian Tsunami in December of 2004.
--- **Hurricane Katrina and Flooding - 2005** (49) - Overlays and placemarks related to Hurricane Katrina (2005) the subsequent flooding.
--- **Hurricane Rita - 2005** (10) - Radar loops and other items related to Hurricane Rita.
--- **Hurricane Wilma - 2005** (9) - Useful items related to Hurricane Rita.
--- **Tour de France 2005** (22) - Locations from the 2005 Tour de France

Sightseeing: Buildings (4639) - Famous or noteworthy buildings
--- **Businesses** (472) - Buildings used by well-known businesses
--- **Famous Homes** (281) - Homes of the rich and famous
--- **Government** (428) - Government and Police buildings
--- **Hotels** (258) - Well known hotels around the world
--- **Malls / Shopping Centers** (256) - Noteworthy malls and large shopping centers
--- **Museums** (370) - Various museums around the world.
--- **Other Famous Buildings** (1342) - Other famous buildings around the world.
--- **Prisons** (144) - Prisons, jails and correctional facilities.
--- **Religious buildings/locations** (475) - Churches, Mosques and other religious buildings from around the world.

Google Earth Hacks provides a broad range of well-organized files you can download and use with Google Earth. *Source:* Courtesy Google Earth Hacks.

icons a location label will pop up. If you double-click on the icon a photograph or image of a location will appear. In this way, the file provides you with a virtual tour of ancient Troy.

Google Earth files often contain much more than just images. Many Google Earth files contain pop-up Wikipedia entries on various locations as well as links to various Web sites and even multimedia files. One of the most impressive Google Earth files is "Crisis in Darfur" from the United States Holocaust Memorial Museum, and it can be downloaded at http://www.ushmm.org/googleearth/. The file contains satellite images of burned-out Darfur villages so that visitors can gain a deeper understanding of the destruction as a result of the civil strife in the area. The file also contains links to Web sites about the crisis in Darfur and even video presentations about the conflict. The file could serve both as a useful introduction to the crisis in Darfur as well as an in-depth analysis of its effects and ramifications.

Google Earth files can also be incorporated into the literature classroom, and Google Lit Trips is an excellent place to start. Google Lit Trips, located at http://www.googlelittrips.org/, contains various Google Earth files that enable visitors to follow the travels of characters from famous novels. For instance, your students could use Google Lit Trips to follow the adventures of Odysseus in *The Odyssey* or the travels of the Joad family in *The Grapes of Wrath*. Google Lit Trips is designed with teachers and students in mind; files are organized by grade level: K–5, 6–8, 9–12, and Higher Ed. A new site, Google Lit Trips does not offer many K–5 and Higher Education files as yet, but new trips are in production.

Source: Courtesy of Google Lit Trips

A Google Earth file can serve as a great introduction to a new topic in your curriculum and can encourage critical thinking as well. Tom has used Google Earth to introduce students to the Vietnam War using a Google Earth file on the Ho Chi Minh Trail found at Google Earth Hacks. Tom flew his students over the Ho Chi Minh Trail and asked them to comment on what they saw. Students picked up on the lack of roadways ("What trail?") and the abundant bushes and trees. They soon realized that it was difficult for American forces to stop the flow of Vietcong and enemy supplies down the Ho Chi Minh Trail because there was no single trail and the Vietcong could hide under the canopy of trees.

Editing a Google Earth File

Tech Specs: Editing a Google Earth File
Set-Up Time: Plan on taking 15 minutes to familiarize yourself with "image overlays" and other editing tools in Google Earth.
Keep-Up Time: None, though it is recommended that you save your edited files.
In-Class Time: Students should first research the location and decide which elements they wish to add to the file. So, budget perhaps 30 minutes for research. Adding overlays and information to a Google Earth file is relatively quick and, depending on how much info students wish to incorporate, could be completed comfortably in 15–30 minutes.
Tech Savvy: Medium.

A great student-centered approach to using Google Earth is to have students add elements to existing Google Earth images. In other words, ask them to construct their own Google Earth file. For example, students could superimpose a map of the Acropolis on top of a satellite image of present-day Athens. They could then create a virtual tour of the ruins, complete with inserted photographs and text. A U.S. History class might create a virtual tour of the first days of the American War of Independence. Literature students might create a virtual tour of colonial Boston as depicted in *Johnny Tremain.*

Step 1: Add Information. To add information to a Google Earth image, simply select *Add →Placemark* from the menu bar, or use the icon shortcuts located above the main window). This will insert a yellow pin at any desired location on the Google Earth image. A description box will open up in which you can give the Placemark a name and include a description. Click *OK* and the information will be included in the file. Simply click on the yellow pin, and the information you added will appear!

Step 2: **Add Pictures.** It's also easy to include an Image Overlay, or picture, on top of a Google Earth image. To do so, click *Add →Image Overlay* from the menu bar. Use the *Browse* button to select an image from your computer to upload. You can specify the transparency of the image by moving the slider between clear and opaque.

Give your image overlay a name and provide a description. At this point you can simply click *OK,* or use the various tabs to provide supplemental geographical information about your image overlay. Save your Google Earth file to *My Places.*

SELECT WEB SITES FOR GUIDED-INQUIRY ACTIVITIES

The following is an annotated list of Web sites that contain guided-inquiry activities, or help you create them. We also recommend that you consult the guided-inquiry homework activities we provide in Chapter 6, "Homework."

Two Tools for Creating Guided-Inquiry Activities

1. The History Lab
http://hlab.tielab.org

The History Lab is a useful tool for creating inquiry activities and lessons using sources found on the Internet. The History Lab provides a free, ready-made template for teachers to include instructions for students, provide external links to primary and secondary sources, and attach documents. To see existing History Labs, select *Search* and then *Select All.* Projects are stored in the database and are available online.

2. TrackStar
http://trackstar.4teachers.org/trackstar/index.jsp

TrackStar is another tool for creating guided-inquiry online lessons and activities. Unlike the History Lab it is not subject specific. With TrackStar you add Web sites, annotate them for your students, and create an interactive lesson called a "Track." You can also adapt one already made by other educators.

Ten Outstanding Guided-Inquiry Web Sites in Humanities

The following Web sites are included for their quality, accuracy, and educational usefulness. These are Web sites that offer engaging educational content and stimulating and useful multimedia technologies and help students examine significant "authentic" materials.

Some of these sites are conducive to extended research-oriented activities and prompt students to become actively engaged in source analysis.

1. **The Digital History Reader: "Why Did Slavery Emerge in Virginia?"**
   http://www.dhr.history.vt.edu
   The Digital History Reader project offers a series of inquiry-based lessons and activities for teaching European and U.S. history. The "United States History" section covers themes and issues from the colonial era to the present. "Why Did Slavery Emerge in Virginia?" is a module that asks students to consider why Virginia's wealthy white settlers decided to enslave Africans. Students are provided with background historical information and an "archive" of documents to consider. As part of the varied tools and resources used for analysis, students employ a Profit/Cost of Labor calculator to gauge the profitability of employing indentured servants rather than buying slaves.

2. **Do History: Martha Ballard**
   http://dohistory.org/
   DoHistory by the Film Study Center at Harvard University is one of the best interactive and guided-inquiry history resources on the Internet. It centers on the 200-year-old diary of a colonial midwife/healer named Martha Ballard and contains numerous original documents, such as diaries, letters, maps, court records, and town records. Students analyze historical documents and wrestle with questions and dilemmas. A key interactive primary source is the searchable twenty-seven-year diary of Martha Ballard. (Visitors can see the actual handwritten notes of midwife Martha Ballard and others.) For grade-appropriate projects and activities click the *If You're Interested In* button and select *Teaching with This Web Site.*

3. **The Metropolitan Museum of Art Timeline of Art History**
   http://www.metmuseum.org/toah/splash.htm
   This impressive interactive timeline from the Metropolitan Museum of Art provides a guided tour of art from around the world. It can be a great framework for guided-inquiry activities that ask students to compare and contrast art from around the globe, at any time in history. The timeline pages are accompanied by world and regional maps, time-period charts, and key events, and include images of art from the museum's collection. The "Just for Fun" section has interactive activities for kids, and "Artist" provides biographical materials on select artists. The "Themes and Cultures" section presents past and present cultures with special features on the Met's collections and exhibitions. Several of these special collections are featured at Best of History Web Sites at http://www.besthistorysites.net.

4. Turning the Pages

http://www.bl.uk/onlinegallery/ttp/ttpbooks.html

"Turning the Pages" is an award-winning interactive site from the British Library that enables visitors to "turn" the pages of historic manuscripts using touch-screen technology and animation. The site provides an excellent opportunity for students to view "authentic" and historic writings, along with accompanying audio, and represents an engaging framework for guided-inquiry activities. Students can view the oldest printed book, as well as Leonardo Da Vinci sketches, Jane Austen's early writings, a Hebrew Prayer Book, the original Alice story from Lewis Carroll, and more.

5. Valley of the Shadow

http://www.vcdh.virginia.edu/teaching/vclassroom/vclasscontents.html

The Valley of the Shadow hosts a wide range of primary sources related to the American Civil War and offers plenty of guided-inquiry lessons and activities. Valley of the Shadow revolves around two communities, one Northern and one Southern, and their experiences of the American Civil War. There are thousands of sources for the period before, during, and after the Civil War, and they include newspapers, letters, diaries, photographs, maps, church records, population census, agricultural census, and military records. Students can explore the conflict and write their own histories, or reconstruct the life stories of women, African Americans, farmers, politicians, soldiers, and families. There are lesson plans for grades 7–12 designed specifically for this Web site.

6. Cold War: From Yalta to Malta

http://www.cnn.com/SPECIALS/cold.war/

This multi-part CNN Web site offers interactive maps, rare video footage, declassified documents, biographies, picture galleries, timelines, interactive activities, a search function, book excerpts, an educator's guide, and more. There are virtual tours, simulation activities, multimedia presentations, and other tools at your disposal. "From Yalta to Malta" is an outstanding educational tools and a teacher could develop an entire teaching unit of guided-inquiry lessons and activities on the Cold War with the resources available at this site.

7. The Sport of Life and Death

http://www.ballgame.org/

The impressive and award-winning Sport of Life and Death bills itself as "an online journey into the ancient spectacle of athletes and gods," and its specific focus is the Mesoamerican ballgame, the oldest organized sport in history. It also provides a revealing glimpse into Mesoamerican culture and provides plenty of opportunities for guided-inquiry activities. The site is much more than a rich multimedia presentation featuring engaging special effects. Its layout and organization are excellent and it contains an abundance of primary and secondary source materials, such as interactive maps, timelines, and Mesoamerican artwork. In all, the site creates a beautiful and engaging blend of images, text, expert commentary, and video.

8. The British Museum
http://www.thebritishmuseum.ac.uk/index.html
The British Museum's various online offerings are excellent. For example, the Ancient Civilizations Web site highlights achievements of select world civilizations and features interactive multimedia tools, historical reconstructions, and 3-D animations. COMPASS is an online database with approximately 5,000 objects from the museum's collections. Children's COMPASS offers a special children's search, activities, and quizzes for use in the classroom. There are plenty of ways for teachers to adopt or construct guided-inquiry activities. The site offers online tours on a variety of subjects as well as other helpful teaching resources and activities.

9. Raid on Deerfield: The Many Stories of 1704
http://www.1704.deerfield.history.museum/
This rich and impressive Web site focuses on the 1704 raid on Deerfield, Massachusetts, and represents the event from the perspectives of varied cultural groups, Mohawk, Abenaki, Huron, French, and English. The Web site is engaging and well organized and provides plenty of opportunities for cross-cultural, guided-inquiry activities. Among the offerings are historical artifacts and documents, essays, voices and songs, historical maps, a timeline, and stories. In all, it is an impressive combination of engaging multimedia features and specific, detailed historical information.

10. The Price of Freedom: Americans at War
http://americanhistory.si.edu/militaryhistory/
This Smithsonian Web site provides students with an opportunity to examine American armed conflict from the Revolutionary War period through the war in Iraq. The site provides a wealth of primary and secondary source information, including art and artifacts from the Smithsonian collection, statistical information, and video clips. Teachers will appreciate a teacher's guide that provides opportunities for guided-inquiry activities. Students can examine historic images and artifacts in great deal thanks to the technology tools available at the site.

 WEBSITE: For more guided inquiry Websites in othe rsubjects visit http://www.edtechteacher.or/chapter4.html

FINAL THOUGHTS

The World Wide Web has so much amazing content for teachers, and each year more is added. Museums are creating new virtual tours, Google Earth enthusiasts are creating new overlays and flyovers, and teachers are posting new WebQuests and Scavenger hunts. Increasingly the problem is not finding great ideas for lessons; it's choosing among all of the options.

The best of these options and the best lesson plans built around guided-inquiry exercises will challenge students not just to read and explore, but to think critically about what they find.

Chapter 5

Open Research

Introduction
"Why Johnny Can't Search": Searching with Key Terms
Google: For Better or Worse, the Number One Student
   Research Tool
Search Directories
Library Catalogues
Grokker Visual Searching
Five Online Collections
Final Thoughts

INTRODUCTION

Thousands of years ago, trying to get information was like dropping a thimble down a well in the hopes of pulling up water. With the advent of the printing press, it became more like dropping a bucket down a well. With the Internet, trying to get information is like drinking from a fire hose. Massive amounts of information are available to students, and simple sources and scholarly sources—junk and gems—are all jumbled together.

In this chapter we'll figure out some basic principles for online searching, and then we'll look at using some specific tools. Mostly we'll focus on searching efficiently, quickly finding the best sources available. Hopefully, this chapter will help you and your students get a nice, cold cup of water from the fire hose.

"WHY JOHNNY CAN'T SEARCH": SEARCHING WITH KEY TERMS

Whatever search engine you or your students use, you will need to use the right **keywords** to unlock the information you want. Use the wrong keywords and you will have a much more difficult time finding information on your topic.

A few years ago, if you looked in the Library of Congress Subject Headings hardcover reference for "Vietnam War," there was absolutely nothing listed for that heading. How could that be? The Library of Congress has plenty of resources on the Vietnam War. That's true, but it had classified the war under the subject heading "Indochina Conflict." The Library of Congress now has a Vietnam War subject heading, but we mention this example because too often students come to us and claim they "can't find anything" on their topic or they "can't find anything good." Often it is because they do not have a search strategy with appropriate keywords. Last year a student told Tom that she was having difficulty finding sources on the Internet about movies in the 1920s. How could that be? Well, the keyword "movies" is not a particularly effective search keyword for information from the 1920s. People in the 1920s simply did not use the term "movies." Had the student done a little background reading on the 1920s in an encyclopedia before turning to Google, she likely would have come up with better keyword terms and phrases, such as "talking pictures," "talkies," or "silent films." The point is that it is a good idea to do some background reading and develop effective search terms *before* turning to a search engine.

Another important search strategy is to move both *horizontally* and *vertically* in the search process. The student in the paragraph above did not think of horizontal, *related terms* to movies, such as "films" or "pictures." With appropriate synonyms her online search could have greatly improved by simply moving *horizontally* in the search process. There are also numerous times during the search process when moving vertically, either up or down, is needed. *Broader terms* (moving up) and *narrower terms* (moving down) can be used effectively to expand or contract a search. For instance, a student who searches for "World War II" will find that these keywords yield many general and broad World War II sites. To narrow the search, the student could add categorizing terms such as names of campaigns, battles, generals, political leaders, and the like, to the "World War II" search terms.

In those instances when search terms are too limiting and search results are too few, a search can be expanded by using broader terms. To illustrate, the three top results in a Google search for "weather underground" have to do with weather and climate, not the radical activist student organization. Adding a broad term such as "1960s" to the keywords "weather underground" leads immediately to sites on the "hippie era" organization.

To help his students think both horizontally and vertically in the search process, Tom draws an inverted triangle on the board and has his students brainstorm related, broader, and narrower terms for various topics. Here is an example using the Vietnam War as a topic:

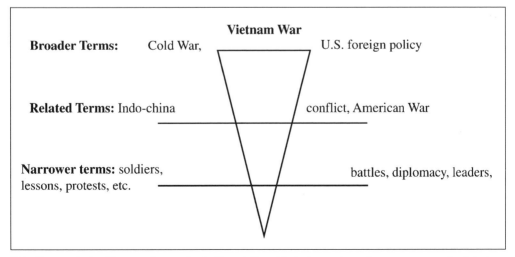

Vietnam War

Broader Terms: Cold War,   U.S. foreign policy

Related Terms: Indo-china   conflict, American War

Narrower terms: soldiers,   battles, diplomacy, leaders,
lessons, protests, etc.

This diagram helps illustrate for students the relationship between broader, narrower, and related search terms.

WEBSITE: A blank version of this diagram is available at the http://www
.edtechteacher.org/chapter5.html Web site. Email it to your students and have them
fill it out online, or print it and copy the blank sheet for them.

PENCIL: If students don't have access to the online version of this document, you can draw the blank version of this diagram on the board and have
students copy the diagram and fill it out.

The Vietnam War is a rich topic, and students, once armed with the right search terms,
will have no problem finding Web resources on it. However, students will have to con-
tinually revise their search strategies horizontally and vertically as they decide how to
focus their research on the Vietnam War.

Remember, a few minutes of careful thought and planning regarding search terms
can save students lots of time when actually searching. Better preparation will yield
better results.

Helping You and Your Students Evaluate Web Sites

As we are all aware, there is plenty of junk on the Web, and it can be difficult at times to
separate the good from the bad. Our students can have an especially difficult time doing
so. Thus, the onus is on us as teachers (and parents) to help them.

With a little prodding, most students are able to identify the common characteristics
of a trustworthy Web site. When Justin starts online research with students, he starts
with a simple activity. On the board he'll write or project a simple table to help students
consider the features of good and bad Web sites:

Qualities of Good Web Sites	**Qualities of Bad Web Sites**

A few minutes later, he'll have the table all filled up something like this:

Qualities of Good Web Sites	**Qualities of Bad Web Sites**
Attractive design	Broken links
Functioning links	Poor design
Well-known sponsor	Difficulty finding the author
"About" page	Unprofessional language
Formal language	

Of all of the features of reliable Web sites, the most important criterion we stress in Web site evaluation is *credibility*. Before we begin to evaluate a Web site's content, we want to know the credentials of the individual or organization that put forward its content. If the authorship is credible, we are more likely to recommend the Web site as well as any Web sites it, in turn, may recommend. For instance, we recommend Web sites from the Library of Congress, National Archive and Records Administration, PBS, and others to students and encourage them to visit the Web sites that these organizations recommend.

It is not enough for teachers and students to simply focus on .edu Web sites or .org Web sites. (We will discuss how to search only on these domains in a bit.) An individual or organization can be affiliated with an educational institution and not be an authority on the content of a particular Web site. Also, an organization does not have to be a non-profit group in the public interest to own a .org domain. For instance, as education technology specialist Alan November points out in his presentations, the Web site http://www.martinlutherking.org appears to be a credible resource on Dr. King's life, but it is actually produced by white supremacists.

As you examine Web sites, identifying authorship is essential in determining credibility. Most reliable sites have an easily accessible "about" or "about this site" section linked from the home page. Find it and read about who created the site. Get students in the habit of doing the same. Not being able to easily determine who created a Web site should stand out as a major red flag as you measure the credibility of a site.

If the authorship of a particular Web site is difficult to determine, you can try using online services that help you find out who registered the Web site. For instance, you can go to: http://www.accesswhois.com/search/. Simply type in the URL of the Web site you want to know more about, and you will be able to get public information regarding who has registered this particular URL. (Mind you, Web site creators can now "unlist" their public information similar to the way many people unlist their phone numbers.)

Once you have discussed these topics with your class, try evaluating some Web sites together. Have students try to find a reliable Web site and an unreliable Web site, project examples of each onto a screen, and then ask them these questions of each Web site:

- Who is the author of this site?
- What is the purpose or goal of the Web site?
- What is the purpose or goal of the individual or organization behind the Web site?
- What are his or her credentials on this topic?
- Does he or she have sufficient credibility to address this subject with authority?
- Is there an organizational or corporate sponsor that may be influencing the content of the site?
- Is there a way to verify the authenticity of the site and its authorship?
- Is there a way to contact the author?
- Has the Web site been recommended by credible organizations?

Satisfactory answers to these questions may not ensure a fault-proof credibility check, but they are a helpful starting point.

THE WIKIPEDIA CONTROVERSY

Beloved by students, reviled by librarians, and vigorously debated in the national media, Wikipedia will brush up against every online search for the foreseeable future. There are a variety of approaches teachers can take toward this new user-created encyclopedia: forbid its use or accept it along with the rest. We recommend more of a middle ground: get to know the strengths and limitations of Wikipedia as a source.

The main problem with Wikipedia is the problem of *credibility*. We have no idea who wrote the article, and in a few high-profile cases, pages on Wikipedia have been intentionally vandalized with false information.

Illustrating this can be pretty fun. Find an important page and click "edit page." Go into the body of the page and type in something false, ludicrous, or the like. Then hover your cursor over the save changes button or click on the show preview button. Sometimes this demonstration will provoke gasps at how easy it is to change Wikipedia. Now if you did make changes, one of Wikipedia's volunteer editors likely would revert the page pretty quickly to get rid of malicious changes.

Alternatively, find a page that you know something about and make an addition. For instance, Justin can almost always find something to add to the Ultimate Frisbee Glossary. Right in class, add to the page. Help Wikipedia that extra little bit.

So, while we should be suspicious of the lack of credibility, we should also recognize the benefits of Wikipedia. First, it's pretty good, and a lot of the information is accurate and can be corroborated by other sources. For very recent topics, it can be tough to beat. (For instance, the page on "leetspeak," an online dialect used by hackers and computer gamers, is thorough and fascinating for students of linguistics.) Another excellent way to use Wikipedia is to read the "talk" pages on controversial topics. At the time of publishing, "Hezbollah" was marked as a controversial entry and the discussion page had a great debate about how to talk about terrorism in a neutral way.

In the final analysis, Wikipedia is probably a safe place to start for most basic searches, although it probably should never be used as a definitive source by itself. But then, probably nothing should be used as a definitive source by itself. It's a good thing the Internet gives us so much to read.

For more help evaluating Web sites, here are three Web sites that we consult in teaching our students this material:

1. **Evaluating Web Sites: Criteria for the Classroom**
   http://www.lesley.edu/library/guides/research/evaluating_web.html
   This is an excellent overview of the topic from Lesley University.

2. **Kathy Schrock's Guide for Educators: Critical Evaluation Surveys**
   http://school.discovery.com/schrockguide/eval.html

   Kathy Schrock is the administrator for technology for the Nauset Public Schools in Massachusetts and the creator of Kathy Schrock's Guide for Educators. She has an excellent series of Web site evaluation guides for students.

3. **Jo Cool or Jo Fool: An Online Game about Savvy Surfing**
http://www.media-awareness.ca/english/special_initiatives/games/jocool_jofool/index.cfm

Jo Cool or Jo Fool is an online activity that helps your students learn about how to surf the Web intelligently. It takes them through 12 Web sites, asking which ones look reliable and secure, and through 20 questions about Internet security and safety. There is also a 50-page pdf guide that informs teachers about how to use the site.

Citing Web Sites

Like any other source, Web sites need to be cited. Unlike just about any other source, it can often be difficult for students to find the information they are supposed to have. There is also the problem that Web sites are diverse types of sources. They can be online books, articles, personal sites, films, audio clips, interviews, poems, or just about anything.

One easy way to get students in the habit of citing properly is to use a **citation generator.** There are many of them on the Web; one good one is KnightCite, which was created by a student at Calvin College in Grand Rapids, Michigan, and can be found at http://www.calvin.edu/library/knightcite/. It allows people to generate citations in MLA, Chicago, and APA styles, it can cite many different types of sources, and it has a clean, simple interface.

FEATURED PRODUCT

KnightCite Citation Generator
Web site: http://www.calvin.edu/library/knightcite/
Developer: Justin Searls, a former student at Calvin College in Grand Rapids, Michigan.
Cost: Free.

KnightCite is a clean, simple citation generator. When you enter publication information about a resource, it will return a citation to you in MLA, APA, or Chicago citation format.

Tech Specs: KnightCite
Set-Up Time: None.
Keep-Up Time: None.
In-Class Time: If you spend 15 minutes running through this citation generator with your students, they should be able to use it independently thereafter.
Tech Savvy: Low.

WEBSITE: There is a video tutorial at http://www.edtechteacher.org/chapter5.html of Justin creating a citation within the KnightCite citation generator.

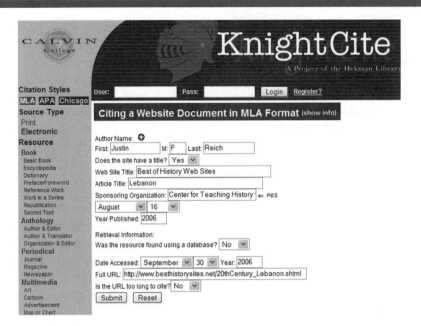

When you get to KnightCite, use the navigation buttons on the left to choose the style of citation and the type of source. Note that KnightCite helps you cite both print and electronic sources. Once you have chosen the style of citation and the source type, then you will need to fill in the appropriate form. In this example, we'll fill in the information needed for citing a Web site.

Some of this information, like the URL, will be very easy to find. Other pieces of information can require hunting. Students should look at the index page (the first page) of a site, view any "About" pages, and look carefully at the tops and bottoms of pages. Sometimes, Web sites won't provide all of this information, which might make you more suspicious about credibility. When you have input all of the information, you can click on the *Submit* button, and it will generate a citation.

Justin Searls's KnightCite is a citation generator that lets you choose from a large number of source types as well as from three different citation styles.   *Source:* Courtesy of Justin Searls and Calvin College.

The citation can then be copied into another document. Citation generators probably should not be used exclusively–students should still learn to cite—but this can get students started with proper citation as they are learning the research process.

Research Journals

Justin learned to write term papers with note cards—one fact per note card (Tom, who is old and Canadian, took his notes on stone tablets). That seems pretty quaint now. Students now can read sources online, take notes online, and write their papers online. The research and writing processes are more integrated than they have ever been before. On the one hand, this efficiency helps make up for some of the time lost searching through millions of online sources, but on the other hand it makes plagiarism far easier for students to commit, even unintentionally.

One way to replace the note cards of yore is to ask students to keep an online research journal. When they find a source, they need to create an entry for that source in their journal. Teachers can give students templates for entries into the research journal, and they need to modify the template for their own researching style and copy it for each source.

STUDENT RESEARCH JOURNAL

Source Short Title:
Source Author:

Full Citation:

Credibility Statement:

Important Information:
Important Page Numbers:
Good Quotations:
Other Notes:

 WEBSITE: Go to http://www.edtechteacher.org/chapter5.html to find this Research Journal in a Word document that you can use or modify for your class.

It is important to stress to students that they should complete the citation as soon as they find a source so that they can find it again, and so they don't have to spend lots of time creating bibliographies at the end of the process.

In the Student Research Journal, it can be quite helpful to ask students to write a "Credibility Statement" for each source. The credibility statement is a sentence that students need to write for Web sites to prove that they have considered whether or not the source is credible. For most published books and journals, such a statement is unnecessary.

If students have a structured place to keep their notes, they are less likely to inadvertently plagiarize by writing something down or copying it without keeping track of where they derived the idea or quotation. For more on dealing with plagiarism, see Chapter 9, "Grading and Assessment."

PENCIL: Even if you cannot have students keep their notes online, still encourage/require them to keep a research journal as they go along.

GOOGLE: FOR BETTER OR WORSE, THE NUMBER ONE STUDENT RESEARCH TOOL

FEATURED PRODUCT

Google
Web site: http://www.google.com/
Developer: Google
Cost: Free

If you don't know what Google is, you need to come out of your cave more often.

Google is currently the Web's most popular search engine, and the primary research tool for most students. Before delving into how to use Google, it is useful to understand a bit about how it works.

Google ranks sites by relevance, popularity, and other variables that Google won't say much about. Relevancy is extremely important, because Google looks for exact matches with the keywords you enter into the search box. The popularity issue is a touch more nebulous. Here is how it works: a link from site A to site B is essentially a "vote" for site B. The more votes site B (or site A) gets, the higher it climbs in Google's ranking of Web pages. If site A is itself a very popular site, then its vote for site B counts more than a vote from a less popular site.

That is a basic explanation of Google's popularity measurement. Just keep in mind (and remind your students) that popularity does not necessarily mean *credibility*. The credibility of a Web site is something that we all have to ascertain.

When used correctly, Google searches can lead you and your students to great resources.
Source: Courtesy of Google.

> **WEBSITE:** Google is great, but we're certainly impressed with Ask.com's recent advances in organizing search results at http://ask.com. We think students can certainly benefit from them. Ask.com's "Ask3D" system organizes and unifies search results in a clearer navigational manner than does Google (at the time of this writing, August 2007). Ask.com provides suggestions for refining your search or for making related searches. It also contains search results in the form of images, news headlines, videos, music clips, and more that you can access without leaving your search page. That being said, the reality is that our students turn to Google more often than not for online search needs, so here we focus our efforts on using that particular tool.

"Active" Google Searches

Basic Google Searches

We don't recommend that you just type in a few keywords in Google and hit Search. In many cases you'll spend plenty of time sifting through unwanted hits. Unfortunately, many Google users do this and do not refine their searches adequately enough. Most would be better served with Google's Advanced Search (discussed in detail later in this chapter).

You can have better success with many basic Google searches if you know a little more about Google syntax. Here are some tips to help you with basic keyword or phrase searches:

- Use quotes to keep words in order and searched as a unit:
  - "March on Washington"
- Instead of a question—"How many years did the American Civil War last?"—put the search in the form of an answer and put an asterisk to represent the missing term.
  - "The American Civil War lasted * years"
- Use OR to find pages that have either one term or the other:
  - "Toni Morrison" OR "Sherman Alexie"
    - This is a useful technique if you want to expand your search.
    - Note that Google automatically includes AND between two or more words.
- Use a minus sign or dash to indicate terms you don't want in your search.
  - Gladiators "Russell Crowe" – movie
    - Any pages with references to Russell Crowe or a Gladiators movie will be omitted.
    - Note: do not put a space after the minus sign.
  - Jackie Robinson -memorabilia -amazon
    - In this example the search will eliminate sites with the word memorabilia as well as Amazon.com products
- Use a plus sign to force Google to include a word, such as "The":
  - +The Crucible
    - Thus you will search "The Crucible" and not simply "crucible."
    - Google does not search for common words such as "the" unless you force it to.
- If you click "Search within results" (at the bottom of the results page) it will search for your keyword(s) within your results page only.

- The *I'm Feeling Lucky* option takes you directly to the first site that would appear at the top of your results if you clicked the regular search button.
- For the definition of a vocabulary term put *define*: in front of it:
  o "define: apathetic"

Keep in mind . . .
- Google has a 32-word limit, though asterisks don't count as words.
- Google treats the first word as the most important (the keywords most important, etc.), so don't put the most important search term at the end of a long list.

Tech Tip: Quickly Search Any Web Page

If you run into Web pages with lots of text and you are losing time searching for a particular keyword(s) on that page, use the Find feature. On a PC press the *Ctrl* and *F* keys together. The Find box will appear. Simply type the keyword(s) you are looking for on that page in the box and select *Find Next*. Mac users: simultaneously press the *Apple* and *F* keys.

If the keyword appears on that page, the Find feature will move you where it is and highlight the word. Keep selecting *Find Next* to find everywhere it appears on the page.

Advanced Google Searches

For serious searching, we use Advanced Search. It helps refine a search along several categories, helps eliminate unwanted sites, and reduces search time. To use an Advanced Search, just click on the link to the right of the search field at http://www.google.com.

Google's Advanced Search helps you refine your search in a variety of useful ways.
Source: Courtesy of Google.

WEBSITE: We have created video tutorials at http://www.edtechteacher.org/chapter5.html that should help you learn how to use Google Advanced Search features.

The following are eight key tips for using Google Advanced Search:

1. **Use the Find results feature to avoid searching for unwanted terms.**
   For instance, if you are searching for materials on Martin Luther, not Martin Luther King Jr., type *king* in the "without the words" text box. In another example, if you don't want movie information on Alexander the Great type *film* and *movie* in the "without the words" text box.

2. **Use the Date feature to find new Web pages.** Don't like running into Web pages that are full of broken links because they haven't been updated in years? Use the "Date" feature on Google's Advanced Search to select Web pages that have been added in the past three months, six months, or year. While this feature does omit old, inactive sites, it can omit established ones as well, so you may want to search both with and without the date feature.

3. **Search exclusively in certain domains, such as .edu or .org.**
   Use this feature to avoid unwanted commercial sites and hone in on educational materials. To do so you can type .edu (or .org) in the Domain text box or just select *Don't* first and type ".com" to eliminate commercial Web pages from your search. If you search "Jesus Christ" in a basic search you'll get links to a set of evangelical and church organizations. If you use the Domain feature and search within the .edu domain, you will get primarily educational materials from institutions of higher learning. Two other useful domains for searching are ".k12.us" for United States public schools and ".ac.uk" for British schools.

4. **Use the File Format option to find a specific type of file on your topic**.
   For instance, if you want to search for only PowerPoint presentations on the Web, then use the File Format pull-down menu and select *Only* and then select *Microsoft PowerPoint.*

5. **Find more relevant sites by searching within titles of Web pages.** If your keywords are buried deep in a Web page, then chances are that page has little to do with your topic. Use the "Occurrences" option and select *in the title of the page* to locate pages that have your keywords in their title. Broaden and narrow your search accordingly. If you get too many results, search in titles only. If you get too few results, search *anywhere in the page.*

6. **If you find a site you like, use "Page-Specific Search" to find others.** If you find one source that you like, enter the URL in the "Similar" window and Google will offer you several other options of pages with similar content. If you are curious about who else likes a particular Web site, see who links to it by entering the URL in the "Links" window. It's a good method to determine if credible organizations are linking to a certain Web site.

7. **Use the SafeSearch feature with children.** When turned on, SafeSearch removes any "adult" content Web sites and images from your search results.

Tip: To search a large site, add its URL to the domain field. For example, Tom often searches the Library of Congress with Google Advanced Search because he finds the Google search engine more effective than the Library of Congress search engine. Put loc.gov in the domain field and search. Tom also searches Amazon.com this way and finds the books he wants faster than with Amazon's search engine!

8. **Use the "Usage Rights" option to find information that you can use, share, or modify, even commercially.** When you select one of these options, Google searches sites with a Creative Commons license, which is a self-registered license that indicates to the public the extent to which your Web site, or information on your Web site, is available for public use. If your goal is to find public-domain materials, then try this option.

If you use Google's Advanced Search regularly, you will save not only minutes daily in your searches, but probably months of your life!

Google Scholar and Google Book Search

Another search tool within the Google toolkit is Google Scholar, found at http://scholar.google.com/. With Google Scholar you can search scholarly publications: articles, books, and citations. If the full text is available online, Google will link you to it. If it is not available online, Google will provide a citation but no link. Google Scholar is helpful for quickly gathering titles of books and articles on selected topics that you could use to search in a library or an electronic database. Google has partnered up with several large academic libraries and plans to put millions of full-text, copyright-free books online in the next few years. You can find these books at http://books.google.com.

 WEBSITE: You are invited to watch our Google Scholar video tutorial at: http://www.edtechteacher.org/chapter5.html.

"Proactive" Google Searches

When most people search, they go to a search engine like Google and type in a few keywords. That's active searching, heading out onto the Web to search out material. In "proactive" search, you don't go after the material; it comes to you. With Google's proactive searching tool, you direct Google to send you news and information on select keywords. When Google finds new information matching your keywords, it presents it to you. It will do so as regularly and for as long as you wish. You can also set up as many proactive searches as you like and modify, eliminate, or edit your searches at any time. If there are topics in the news or on the Web that you regularly follow, a more "proactive" approach can save you much time and effort.

Google News

Sure, http://cnn.com and other online news sites are great. But you can't customize them. Google News, on the other hand, allows you to select the news topics you want to appear on your own customized news page. Google News, found at http://news.google.com, gathers news stories from 4,500 sources, organizes them into categories—including categories that you can create—and updates stories regularly.

In the screenshot at the top of the next page, Tom is editing Google News so that stories on topics *he chooses* will appear on the page. Look at the left of the picture and you will see that "educational technology" is one of the news categories Tom set up.

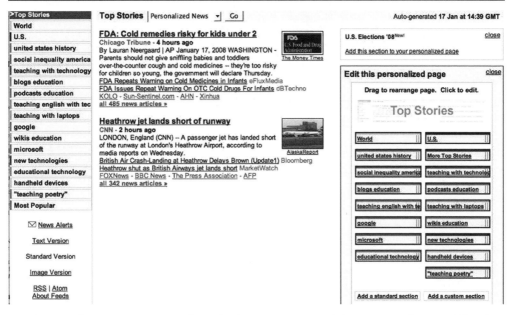

Google News allows you to customize the topics that you want to read about. *Source:* Courtesy of Google.

To create your own customized news page, click on the *Customize This Page* option (upper right of Google News) and then click on *Add a Custom Section*. Then, like Tom did, add a few customized sections: "educational technology," "teaching civil war," and teaching with laptops. You can select how many stories you want per category and then arrange them in whatever order you want the categories to appear. So, each time you return to Google News, the information you want will be there.

Tip: Sign up for a free Google Account and sign in before you go to Google News. That way the Google News page will always be personalized.

Google News Archives

A new feature of Google News is the Google News Archive Search, which enables you to search and explore historical news archives. It is an effective way of searching multiple historical news sources on the same topic. The News Archive Search can present its results either as a list of articles or as a timeline of select time periods. One drawback of the search is that some of the articles it finds require a paid subscription to an archive or service. However, in the *Advanced Search* options you can ask Google to return only articles that cost nothing.

WEBSITE: We have created a video tutorial at http://www.edtechteacher.org/ chapter5.html to help you learn Google News features.

Google Alerts (BETA) — historywebmaster@gmail.com | Settings | FAQ | Sign out

Welcome to Google Alerts

Google Alerts are email updates of the latest relevant Google results (web, news, etc.) based on your choice of query or topic.

Some handy uses of Google Alerts include:

- monitoring a developing news story
- keeping current on a competitor or industry
- getting the latest on a celebrity or event
- keeping tabs on your favorite sports teams

Create an alert with the form on the right.

You can also click here to manage your alerts

Create a Google Alert

Enter the topic you wish to monitor.

Search terms: "crisis in Darfur"
Type: News
How often: once a day
Your email: historywebmaster@gmail.c

Create Alert

Google will not sell or share your email address.

© 2007 Google - Google Home - Google Alerts Help - Terms of Use - Privacy Policy

Google News Alerts are a great example of proactive searching, where instead of searching for material, you select material that you want to come to you. *Source:* Courtesy of Google.

Google News Alerts

Another proactive searching tool is Google's News Alerts, whereby Google will send you news updates via email. Google will notify you of news on topics you select, and you determine how frequently you receive the updates.

To set up these News Alerts, click on the *News Alerts* link on the left-hand sidebar of the Google News page. Enter your search terms, such as "crisis in Darfur" or "terrorism," and then specify the resource type you want, such as news articles, blogs, Web pages, or discussion groups. Next, select how often you would like to receive news alerts (most users will find that once a week is enough). Finally, share your email with Google and click the *Create Alert* button, and the news will start coming to you! You can always unsubscribe or change the settings once you start receiving News Alerts emails.

SEARCH DIRECTORIES

When most students start searching, their instinct is often to head to Google and begin their own explorations, and that is often the wrong first step. On a wide variety of topics, advanced researchers have already searched the Web and separated the wheat from the chaff. Instead of using **search engines**, students should often be starting with **search directories**. Search directories are Web sites where experts or enthusiasts pull together the best resources on the Web on a particular topic.

Let's look at our search directory, the Best of History Web Sites at http://besthistory sites.net/ as an example. In our search directory, we have topics organized on the left and a search engine for our site right in the middle of our page. Within many of the topics, there are sub-topics listed on the left. For each Web site, we have a link and an annotation that explains the strengths and weaknesses of the site.

Remind your students that they probably are not the first people to be researching their particular topic, and they should be on the lookout for directories or bibliographies that previous researchers have compiled. These search directories can usually direct students to useful primary and secondary sources much faster than searching the entire Web through Google.

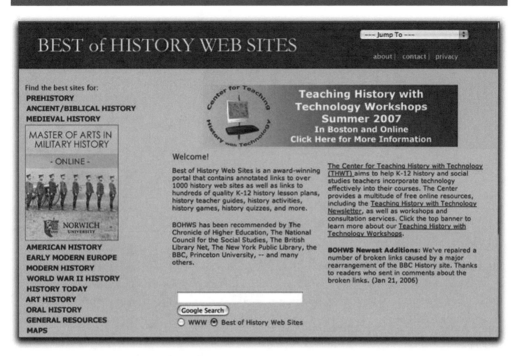

Tom and Justin are webmasters of Best of History Web Sites, an award-winning annotated guide to excellent history resources on the Web.

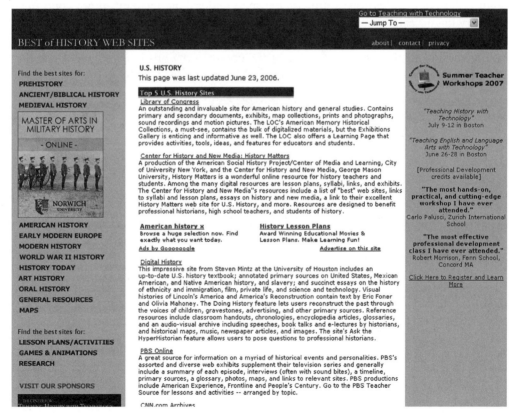

There are several main topics, like U.S. History, which are organized into more specific sub-topics, like South and Slavery.

WEBSITE: Here are some excellent humanities-based subject directories:

- Center for History and New Media
  http://chnm.gmu.edu/
- BBC: History
  http://www.bbc.co.uk/history/
- Web English Teacher
  http://webenglishteacher.com
- BUBL History
  http://www.bubl.ac.uk/
- BUBL Literature and Rhetoric
  http://www.bubl.ac.uk/link/linkbrowse.cfm?menuid=10942
- PBS: Arts and Drama
  http://www.pbs.org/arts/
- PBS: History
  http://www.pbs.org/history/

LIBRARY CATALOGUES

As a medium of data storage, nothing surpasses the book for durability and ease of reading. Long after CDs and DVDs have been scratched or rendered obsolete by new technology, this book will still be sitting on the shelf (at least on our shelf, if not yours).

Every library catalogue is a little bit different, and your reference librarian is the best resource for teaching you and your students how to make the most of your library catalogue. For a general overview of some of the common options in catalogue searching, lets take a look at the Boston Public Library Catalogue Advanced Search:

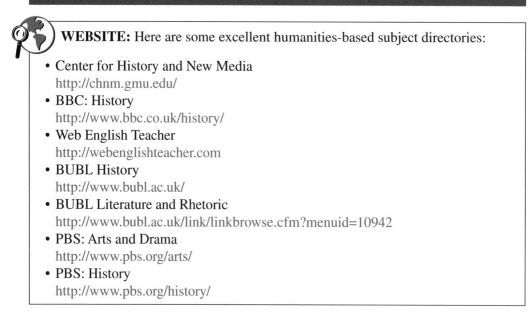

The Boston Public Library, along with many other libraries, has an online catalog with an advanced search function that allows you to search for books and other library resources in many helpful ways.

Source: Courtesy of the Boston Public Library.

Probably the most important choice your students will make is what type of search to perform. If you know that a particular author has written about a topic, then an author search is your best bet. If not, then you can usually search amongst Subjects, Titles, or Keywords Anywhere.

It can be helpful for students to recognize that there is often an inverse relationship between the number of results produced by a search engine and the relevance of those results. Put another way, if you ask the search engine to look in lots of places, it will find lots of stuff, including lots of stuff that you probably don't want. If you ask it to look in fewer places, you will probably find fewer things, but with the right terms those few results will be closer to what you are looking for. So if your search finds too much stuff, tell your search engine to search less. If you find too little stuff, ask your search engine to search more.

The Keyword Anywhere search is the broadest type of search and will produce the most results. When you enter your search term, the search engine will look in all of the titles and subject headings for that term. The Subject Anywhere search will look in all of the subject headings, and the Title Anywhere search will look only in resource titles. To see how these different searches work, let's try a search with the term "Civil Rights."

This broad Keyword Anywhere search produced 6,632 results, including some that are more distantly related to our term, like this biography of Kennedy.

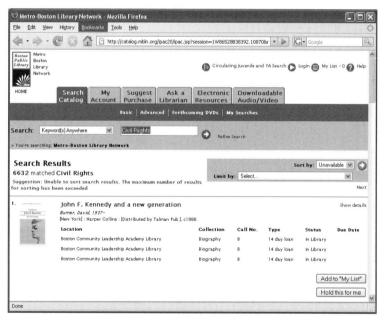

It can be a somewhat daunting task to find the book that you want from the 6,632 matches provided by the Keyword Anywhere search.

Source: Courtesy of the Boston Public Library.

The Subject search produces a somewhat smaller, though still significant, number of results, 5,043. It includes some titles that are certainly relevant to a study of civil rights, such as books written by Martin Luther King, Jr., that do not include the term "civil rights" in the title.

Searching just in Titles has shrunk our list considerably, down to 1,765 titles. We can be confident that many more of these titles are relevant to our research, though of course we will not find some great titles that are right on topic but use a more literary title.

With all these different options, there is no "right way" to search a library catalogue. If students understand the pros and cons of available tools, they are more likely to find relevant and useful results.

Metro-Boston Library Network - Mozilla Firefox

File Edit View History Bookmarks Tools Help

http://catalog.mbln.org/ipac20/ipac.jsp?session=1W86528B38392.108708menu= Google

Boston Public Library
Metro Boston Library Network

HOME   Circulating Juvenile and YA Search   Login   My List – 0   Help

Search Catalog | My Account | Suggest Purchase | Ask a Librarian | Electronic Resources | Downloadable Audio/Video

Basic | Advanced | Forthcoming DVDs | My Searches

Search: Subject Keyword(s)   Civil Rights   Refine Search

» You're searching: Metro-Boston Library Network

Search Results
5238 matched Civil Rights
Suggestion: Unable to sort search results. The maximum number of results for sorting has been exceeded

Sort by: Unavailable
Limit by: Select...
Next

1.   **I have a dream**   Show details
King, Martin Luther, Jr., 1929-1968.
San Francisco, CA : HarperSanFrancisco, c1993.

Location	Collection	Call No.	Type	Status	Due Date
Lee Elementary School Library	Nonfiction	PAPER BACK	14 day loan	In Library	
Hyde Park Education Complex Library	Nonfiction	323.1 KIN	14 day loan	In Library	

Add to "My List"
Hold this for me

2.   **Why we can't wait**   Show details
King, Martin Luther, Jr., 1929-1968.
New York : New American Library, c1964.

Location	Collection	Call No.	Type	Status	Due Date
Boston Latin Academy Library	Nonfiction	323.4 KIN	21 day loan	In Processing – New	
Charlestown High School Library	Nonfiction	305.8 KIN	14 day loan	In Library	
Dorchester Education Complex Library	Nonfiction	323.4 KIN	14 day loan	In Library	
Hyde Park Education Complex Library	Nonfiction	323.4 KIN	14 day loan	In Library	

Done

A Subject search can be helpful as it includes relevant books even if they don't have the keyword in their titles.

Source: Courtesy of the Boston Public Library.

Metro-Boston Library Network - Mozilla Firefox

File Edit View History Bookmarks Tools Help

http://catalog.mbln.org/ipac20/ipac.jsp?session=1W86528B38392.108708menu= Google

Boston Public Library
Metro Boston Library Network

HOME   Circulating Juvenile and YA Search   Login   My List – 0   Help

Search Catalog | My Account | Suggest Purchase | Ask a Librarian | Electronic Resources | Downloadable Audio/Video

Basic | Advanced | Forthcoming DVDs | My Searches

Search: Title Keyword(s)   Civil Rights   Refine Search

» You're searching: Metro-Boston Library Network

Sort by: Select...
Limit by: Select...

Search Results
1795 matched Civil Rights
Next

1.   **The "huddled masses" myth : immigration and civil rights**   Show details
Johnson, Kevin R.
Philadelphia : Temple University Press, 2004.

Location	Collection	Call No.	Type	Status	Due Date
BPL Central - Book Delivery	Nonfiction	KF4819.J64 2004	In Library Use Only	In Library	

Add to "My List"
Hold this for me

2.   **The "Mississippi Burning" civil rights murder conspiracy trial : a headline court case**   Show details
Fireside, Harvey.
Berkeley Heights, N.J. : Enslow Publishers, c2002.

Location	Collection	Call No.	Type	Status	Due Date
BPL Central Library - Copley Square	YA Nonfiction	KF224.M47F57 2002	21 day loan	In Library	
BPL - Dudley	YA Nonfiction	KF224.M47F57 2002	21 day loan	In Library	
BPL - Grove Hall	YA Ethnic	KF224.M47F57 2002	21 day loan	In Library	
BPL - Parker Hill	J Nonfiction	KF224.M47F57 2002	21 day loan	In Library	
BPL - West Roxbury	J Nonfiction	KF224.M47F57 2002	21 day loan	In Library	
Hyde Park Education Complex Library	Nonfiction	345.73 FIR	14 day loan	In Processing – New	

Done

A Title search ensures the relevancy of the returned items, but it may omit useful resources.

Source: Courtesy of the Boston Public Library.

GROKKER VISUAL SEARCHING

Grokker Visual Search Tool
Web site: http://www.grokker.com/
Developer: Groxis, Inc.
Cost: Free

Grokker is a new visual search engine that returns results in maps rather than in lists. Expect to find visual search engines like Grokker popping up in online databases, library catalogues, and anywhere else researchers need to sort through data.

The vast majority of search engines, like Google and most library catalogues, return their information in lists. A new visual system to organize search results is called Grokker, and it is beginning to be an option for some databases and library catalogues. Whether or not you like Grokker will probably depend an awful lot on whether you are a visual learner. For instance, if you prefer to do your brainstorming in concept maps rather than in outline form, then you will probably find Grokker intuitive and helpful. Of course, regardless of whether or not you like visual searching, Grokker is coming and teachers need to know a bit about it.

A free test can be found on http://www.grokker.com/, where Grokker will search through Wikipedia and Yahoo! Content. So let's try one more search of "Civil Rights" and see what we get with Grokker:

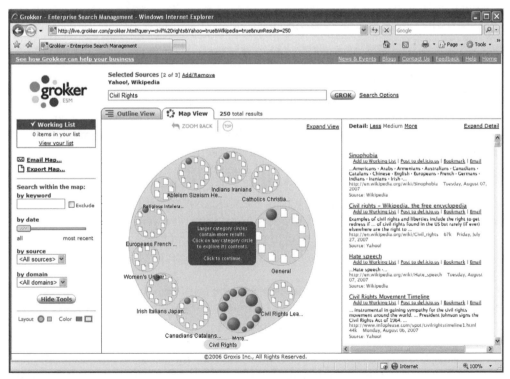

Grokker's visual searches can be useful tools for organizing large amounts of information into more manageable groups. The spheres represent different topics, and the white rectangles are specific documents or Web sites about those topics.   *Source:* Courtesy of Groxis, Inc.

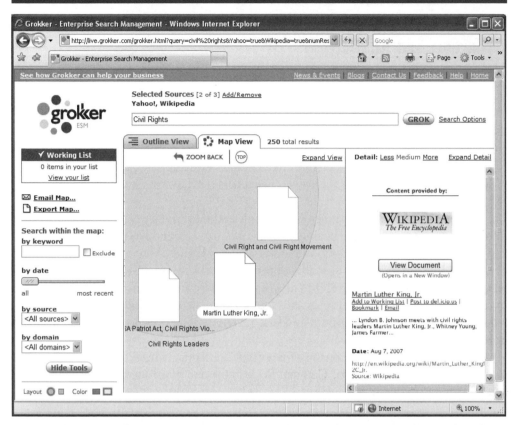

When you find the specific document you want to view, click on it, and Grokker will take you right to it.
Source: Courtesy of Groxis, Inc.

The information from Grokker is clustered in spheres. These top-level spheres contain the broadest topic, and as we search into the spheres, we find more specific topics. The top-level spheres contain more spheres of information, but the bottom-level spheres contain documents. These documents are sources that we can use in our research. For visual learners, or people who are intimidated by finding that their search query produced 10,000 results, this research tool can be more helpful than the standard search engine.

The added benefit of this type of searching is that it helps researchers make connections between different sub-topics. Within the sphere of "Civil Rights" in the example above, there are links to documents about women's suffrage, religious intolerance, ageism, as well as the connections to the civil rights movement that we might expect. These categories may help young researchers divide a topic into sub-topics in their own minds and research.

When you do click down deep enough into the Grokker Web to find a document, the information about the document will be found on the right side of the split screen. Sometimes it will load a preview of the document, but in any case you can click *View Document* and follow the link to the source.

For visual learners, Grokker can be a powerful tool for seeing connections amongst different topics and for making sense of a research query. Given how much more visually-oriented we have become as a culture, it seems likely that Grokker and other visual search engines will play an increasing role in a researcher's tool kit.

FIVE ONLINE COLLECTIONS

This section is an introduction to five commonly used collections of online sources. The goal of this section is to introduce you to some of the resources that are available, to point out some of their most useful tools, and to help you show students how to select the right online collection for their research task.

If your school or local library does not have access to these resources, the best bet is to check with the library of your state capital. Almost every state's capital library lets everyone in the state get a card, and that card almost always provides access to a variety of different online collections. And shouldn't every student get a library card from his or her state capital? With a little digging, almost everyone in America can get free access to a variety of great research tools.

You probably won't have access to the exact same collection that we do, so the point of this section is make three general points about online collections. First, different online collections have different strengths, different target audiences, and different sources. Student researchers should get familiar with the different collections they have access to and figure out which ones are best for which kinds of research. Second, different collections have different search tools, so students will need to learn new tricks to make the most of new collections. Third, each online collection presents information in different ways, so students can find different types of information with different collections. The first step toward helping students get their hands on the source they want is to help students become familiar with the different tools that will get them to their research goals.

LexisNexis

FEATURED PRODUCT

LexisNexis
Web site: Service available through schools and libraries
Developer: Reed Elsevier Inc.
Cost: Available to schools and libraries by subscription

The LexisNexis Scholastic database provides access to legal research, legislation, and census statistics, thought its crown jewel is its extensive collection of news articles from the last thirty years from around the globe.

LexisNexis's most useful resource is its archive of articles dating back to the 1980s from dozens of newspapers from around the country and around the world. The interface is simple and the archive is enormous.

Navigate to the *News→General News* section of the site. Enter either a keyword or an author, and if you want you can narrow down to a particular set of papers or a particular date.

Encourage students to narrow their search by looking in only a few newspapers. To do this, first click on the *Source List* link, which is found just to the right of the *Source* drop down menu. Check off a few papers and then click on *Paste to Search*. You can create some interesting comparisons by selecting different papers. You might ask students to choose one paper from the coast and one from the heartland, or one from a "red state" and another from a "blue state," or one from the United States and another from the United Kingdom.

LexisNexis lets you search a large database of newspaper articles from the 1980s to the present day.

Source: Copyright 2007 LexisNexis, a division of Reed Elsevier Inc. All Rights Reserved. LexisNexis and the Knowledge Burst logo are registered trademarks of Reed Elsevier Properties Inc. and are used with the permission of LexisNexis.

LexisNexis collects news articles published by papers from around the world.

Source: Copyright 2007 LexisNexis, a division of Reed Elsevier Inc. All Rights Reserved. LexisNexis and the Knowledge Burst logo are registered trademarks of Reed Elsevier Properties Inc. and are used with the permission of LexisNexis.

LexisNexis returns results listed by date (most recent first), but you can also ask it to sort by relevance. One great feature of LexisNexis is that it lists the full titles of each search result, and often the titles for newspaper articles are very descriptive. In addition, it tells you how many words are in each article, which can help you avoid pieces that are too long or too short.

If you get too many articles, trying searching for more specific terms within the results using the *Focus* option at the top. By clicking on the relevant buttons, you can also ask LexisNexis to *Print* and *Email* the articles as well.

While Google News is an excellent resource for recently published news, LexisNexis is currently the champion for searches of articles from the last 20 years.

Thomson Gale Powersearch (formerly known as Infotrac)

FEATURED PRODUCT

Powersearch (formerly known as Infotrac)
Web site: Service available through schools and libraries
Developer: Thomson Gale
Cost: Available to schools and libraries by subscription

Powersearch allows you to comb through several enormous databases of newspaper, magazine, and scholarly articles.

The Thomson Gale Databases archive an incredibly wide range of publications from children's magazines to encyclopedias to scholarly journals. It is a vast collection, so Thomas Gale subdivided it into a collection of smaller databases. When you get to the landing page, you'll see the first part of the list. Scroll down and you'll see more, depending on the relationship your library has with Thomson Gale.

Your first step is to choose the databases that you would like to search. Click on the boxes in the left-hand column and then click on *Submit*. When choosing databases, choose the ones most relevant to your topic and age-group. The best general collection for younger researchers (about sixth to ninth grade) is the Student Edition. The best gen-

Thomson Gale provides a number of varied resource-specific databases.   *Source:* Courtesy of Thomson Gale.

eral collections for more advanced researchers are the General Reference Center Gold Collection and the Expanded Academic ASAP. The Infotrac Onefile also has a broad range of resources.

As soon as you get to the first search screen, you will almost always want to choose *More Search Options.* Thomson Gale archives both article abstracts and full-text articles, and most of the time you will want to search full text only so you do not have to track down the article in a library.

With this expanded basic screen, you'll have most of the search options you need to get started. You can choose to search in Subject, Keyword, and Entire Document. In this database, Subject is the narrowest, Keyword is in the middle, and Entire Document finds the words anywhere in all of the documents, so it will return the most results, including the least relevant results.

Your students will almost always want to be sure to click the box that says, "Limit the results to documents with full text."

When Powersearch returns your results, it will break them up by resource type.

Limiting your search to only full-text documents is always a good idea. You can also limit the publication or the time frame that you wish to search. *Source:* Courtesy of Thomson Gale.

Magazines, Academic Journals, Reference sources, News, and Multimedia all have their own separate tabs. Like LexisNexis, Powersearch provides the full title and word count of each article, which are helpful to look at when selecting sources.

To narrow or expand your search you can click on *Expand/Limit*. If you would like to search in other databases with your search term, you can click on *Additional Databases*.

Where LexisNexis shines with newspapers, Thomson Gale's Powersearch provides

an excellent collection of magazines and scholarly journals. With so many archived sources, however, students need to develop their searching skills to find what they need and not be knocked over by this fire hose of information.

You can use the Subject Terms column at the left to refine your search to more specific key terms. *Source:* Courtesy of Thomson Gale.

EBSCOHost Research Databases

EBSCOHost Research Databases
Web site: Service available through schools and libraries
Developer: EBSCO Industries, Inc.
Cost: Available to schools and libraries by subscription

EBSCO has a fine collection of full-text historical sources, and it can be searched using the Grokker visual search engine discussed previously in this chapter.

EBSCOHost's History Reference Center collection focuses on history articles and sources for K–12 students. Once again, clicking the *Linked Full Text* option is key to getting articles that you can read right away. EBSCOHost also has the nice feature that you can limit your search by reading level.

One feature that sets EBSCOHost apart is that it has licensed Grokker's visual searching technology, so you can search the collection using the Grokker interface. Click the visual search tab to use this feature.

EBSCOHost allows you to search for documents and articles with the regular method, which returns a list of results, or with the visual search method of Grokker which returns results grouped by theme or topic. *Source:* Courtesy of EBSCO.

ABC-CLIO

ABC-Clio Social Studies Web Sites

Web site: Service available through schools and libraries
Developer: ABC-CLIO
Cost: Available to schools and libraries by subscription

ABC-CLIO has an excellent collection of databases on historical topics, organized by source type so students can easily distinguish among documents, articles, bibliographies, and other types of sources.

ABC-CLIO has eight different databases of Social Studies Web sites. What distinguishes these databases is that search results are grouped by source type: essays, primary sources, audio, video, and more.

For many research assignments, teachers ask students to write their papers or create their presentations using a wide variety of different source types. This search engine makes that task easier for students, and it helps them see more clearly whether a source is an essay, a primary source, or something else.

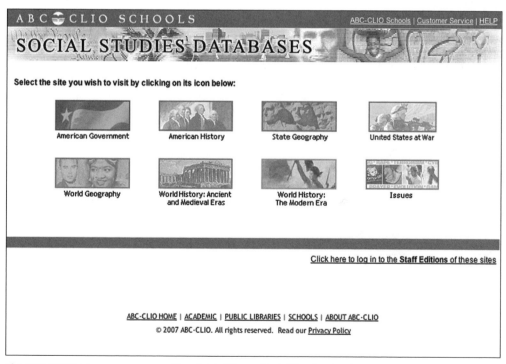

The ABC-CLIO history resource provides eight different Social Studies databases.
Source: Courtesy ABC-CLIO.

ABC-CLIO returns your search results grouped by source type.   *Source:* Courtesy ABC-CLIO.

ProQuest Databases

FEATURED PRODUCT

ProQuest Databases
Web site: Service available through schools and libraries
Developer: ProQuest LLC
Cost: Available to schools and libraries by subscription

ProQuest offers a wide variety of databases useful for both History and Language Arts teachers.

The ProQuest databases are another collection of online tools. The ProQuest Learning: Literature database provides a variety of sources for researching authors and novels

ProQuest's resources include several different databases, each of which contains its own unique and helpful reserves of information. *Source:* Courtesy of ProQuest.

including literary journals, CliffNotes-like study guides, and a wonderful collection of short movies of poets reading their work. The ProQuest Historical Newspapers database provides indexing of the *New York Times* back until 1850 (when it was *the New York Daily Times*). These tools have search engines that are familiar if you have read the previous sections.

The most novel resource, however, is the History Study Center. Like ABC-CLIO, the History Study Center can produce results by source type, but in addition, the History Study Center has over 500 Study Units, where editors have compiled the best of ProQuest's collections on a variety of topics. Take a look at the study unit for "The Rise of Islam" on page 140.

The Study Unit provides a brief introduction and then provides links to a variety of different types of sources (or you can scroll down to see them all). In addition, the editors have chosen a few sources of different types as Highlights, or the best material from the collection.

The ProQuest History Study Center combines some of the best features of a search engine and a search directory. The search engine lets you find documents from the

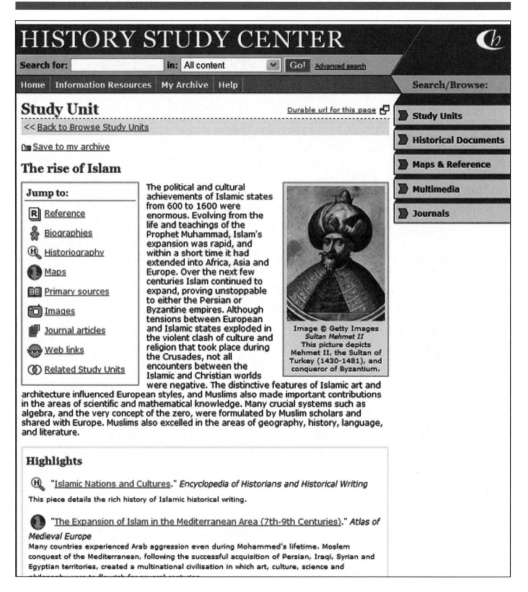

HISTORY STUDY CENTER

Search for: [   ] **in:** [All content ▾] [Go!] Advanced search

Home | Information Resources | My Archive | Help   Search/Browse:

Study Unit   Durable url for this page ⊡

<< Back to Browse Study Units

▸ Study Units

▸ Historical Documents

📂 Save to my archive

▸ Maps & Reference

The rise of Islam

▸ Multimedia

Jump to:

▸ Journals

Ⓡ Reference

🧍 Biographies

Ⓗ Historiography

🌐 Maps

🔲 Primary sources

📷 Images

📰 Journal articles

🌐 Web links

㏇ Related Study Units

The political and cultural achievements of Islamic states from 600 to 1600 were enormous. Evolving from the life and teachings of the Prophet Muhammad, Islam's expansion was rapid, and within a short time it had extended into Africa, Asia and Europe. Over the next few centuries Islam continued to expand, proving unstoppable to either the Persian or Byzantine empires. Although tensions between European and Islamic states exploded in the violent clash of culture and religion that took place during the Crusades, not all encounters between the Islamic and Christian worlds were negative. The distinctive features of Islamic art and architecture influenced European styles, and Muslims also made important contributions in the areas of scientific and mathematical knowledge. Many crucial systems such as algebra, and the very concept of the zero, were formulated by Muslim scholars and shared with Europe. Muslims also excelled in the areas of geography, history, language, and literature.

Image © Getty Images
Sultan Mehmet II
This picture depicts
Mehmet II, the Sultan of
Turkey (1430-1481), and
conqueror of Byzantium.

Highlights

Ⓗ "Islamic Nations and Cultures." *Encyclopedia of Historians and Historical Writing*

This piece details the rich history of Islamic historical writing.

🌐 "The Expansion of Islam in the Mediterranean Area (7th-9th Centuries)." *Atlas of Medieval Europe*

Many countries experienced Arab aggression even during Mohammed's lifetime. Moslem conquest of the Mediterranean, following the successful acquisition of Persian, Iraqi, Syrian and Egyptian territories, created a multinational civilisation in which art, culture, science and

ProQuest Databases, while the Study Units offer researchers materials that editors and scholars have already pulled together.

FINAL THOUGHTS

In looking at the details of these tools and collections, we should not lose track of the big picture, which is that the information available to our students today is *so cool*! Just a few clicks away are videos of Nikki Giovanni reading poetry, the entire *New York Times* from the day each of us was born, a first-hand account of the siege of Constantinople, and great scholarship on every topic under the sun. All of the sources that made us fall in love with our disciplines—sources that we spent hours crawling through stacks to find— can easily fall into a student's lap, or laptop. Helping students be researchers, rather than just information recipients, has never been easier or more exciting.

Chapter 6

Homework

Introduction
Equity and Access
Assiging Online and Computer Homework
What to Do for Homework?
**Examples of Short-Term Online Assignments in the
  Humanities**
Final Thoughts

INTRODUCTION

For many years teachers have been bringing all sorts of exciting things into class—slides, video, audio, additional documents, and other technologies and resources—to enrich the curriculum. But for homework, teachers have still relied on books and textbooks. As the Internet spreads to more homes, schools, libraries, and after-school centers, assigning homework online has become a more realistic option for many schools.

Online homework offers the promise of including a much wider variety of readings and assignments and, for the truly motivated teacher, an opportunity to end the tyranny of the textbook. Online homework can also enable persistent discussion outside the classroom and more collaboration among students after the school bell.

There are some exciting opportunities here, but before we can delve into the possibilities of online homework, we need to think seriously about issues of equity and access.

EQUITY AND ACCESS

Increasingly, educational institutions are building the infrastructure to ensure that students have equitable access to the Internet during free time and in the evenings. Many residential colleges and boarding schools have reached this point, and other school districts around the country are approaching this milestone.

In order to regularly assign homework that requires computers or the Internet, you need to ensure that every single one of your students has access to those tools at home or after school. You can probably safely assign the occasional online assignment to students with access to computers in libraries or school computer labs, as long as you can be confident that students without home access will have enough time to get to those resources. Confidentially polling your students early in the year may be the best way to evaluate how much access your students have to computers, but it may also be helpful to understand access issues from a national perspective.

By the Numbers

The number of homes with Internet access has grown tremendously over the last decade. In just 10 years, the percentage of U.S. adults who use the Internet has gone from just over 30 percent to just over 70 percent. In a Nielsen/NetRatings survey from 2004, 75 percent of American homes had a Web-connected computer, and the majority of those connections were through modems with speeds of 56 kbps or less.[1] Those modem speeds are fast enough for reading simple Web pages and email and sending small documents, but they are too slow to reliably assign online media like streaming video and audio. A Pew Internet and American Life Project report from March 2006 reported that the percentage of American homes with broadband Internet connections—through cable, DSL, or satellite—has risen to 42 percent.[2]

What do these numbers mean? For educators, they mean that there are still plenty of kids out there who don't have reliable access to the Internet. Teachers should also consider that having a single computer in a home may not be enough if parents need it for work and multiple brothers and sisters need it for school. It simply is not fair to assign online homework if students have radically different access to the Internet.

The bottom line is that, for now, colleges, universities, and boarding schools are probably the only institutions that can guarantee easy access to computers for all their students. Still, in many communities there is enough investment in technology for K–12 learners to allow teachers to start experimenting with assigning online homework.

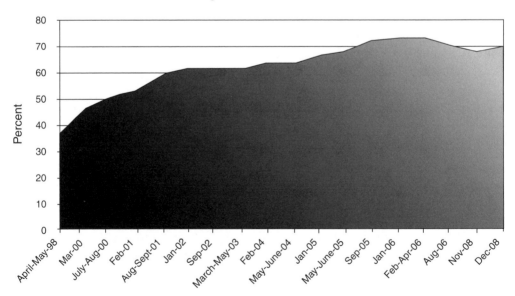

This graph shows the steep increase in Internet use over the past eight years.

Source: Pew Internet and American Life Project Surveys, http://www.pewinternet.org/trends/Internet_Adoption_4.26.07.pdf, accessed 8 Aug 2007.

A Thumbs-Up to Making Computer Work Portable

Students who write on computers need to be able to move their files around among classrooms, labs, libraries, and home. Here we discuss a few great tools for making this possible.

Thumb drives, also called flash drives, are amongst the most important innovations for improving access to computers (for more on thumb drives, see Chapter 1, "Lectures"). For under $15, students can purchase a small hard drive, no bigger than a thumb, which can easily transport document files and even several presentations, music files, or images. This digital notebook can allow students to work in classrooms, computer labs, and libraries and easily transport the same files around. Until computers with Internet access are as ubiquitous as TVs, the safest way to get students to take their files with them is the thumb drive.

Yahoo Mail introduced unlimited mail storage in 2007, thereby giving personal users an opportunity to store a great number of files and attachments. Though Yahoo Mail discourages the use of its service as an online storage depository, or external hard drive, it is possible to store a great number of emails and attached documents. Google's email program, Gmail, followed suit, announcing that it would, sometime in the future, offer "infinity plus one" email storage for its personal users. So, you and your students have two terrific and free online alternatives to store information and files.

Another technology with significant penetration in K–12 populations is the iPod. With a little bit of work modifying preferences, iPods and other portable media players can act as portable hard drives as well. Some schools, like Duke University, have in the past experimented with requiring all incoming students to purchase iPods to be used as storage and media devices. Full instructions for using your iPod as a hard drive can be found on the Apple Web site at http://docs.info.apple.com/article.html?artnum=61131. For other portable players, consult the product documentation.

Homework Title: XXX
> Note: Use *exact* title in subject heading if emailed

Date Due: XXX
Submission Requirements:
> Paper Copy
> Portfolio
> Turninreich-JR

Reading Assignment
Pages Assigned:
Terms:
Reading Notes:
Study Questions:
Special Instructions:
Background Information:
Attached Readings:

Writing Assignment
Question or Writing Prompt:
Expectations:
Expected Length:
Formatting Requirements:
Source Material:
Other relevant due dates:

Grade Value:
> Note: All homework factors into preparation/participation grade.
> One random assignment from the portfolio will be graded bi-weekly.

ASSIGNING ONLINE AND COMPUTER HOMEWORK

Online Homework Templates

In an environment where you can count on students to have reliable Internet access, you can send your homework by email or post it to your blog or class Web page. (For more on blogs, see Chapter 2, "Discussion and Communication"; for more on class Web pages, see Chapter 10, "Class Management.") To make homework assignments easier to write and expectations clearer to students, consider using a template.

Using a uniform template can be an effective way of helping students understand what is required and expected from them in each assignment.

This template is designed to be emailed daily to students. By seeing the same format repeatedly, students become very familiar with the format and with the teacher's expectations. You don't need to use every category for every assignment; simply delete the sections that are irrelevant and fill in the rest.

Greece HW05
    Note: Use *exact* title in subject heading if emailed
Date Due: Thursday
Submission Requirements:
    Portfolio

Reading Assignment
Pages Assigned: Handout from Herodotus, *The Persian Wars*
Study Questions: Answer each in a sentence or two.
1. Why was Pheidippides sent to Sparta?
2. Who are the barbaroi?
3. How were the undermanned Greeks able to defeat the Persians?

Here is an example of a reading-assignment template with study questions included.

Homework Title: MidEast HW04
    Note: Use *exact* title in subject heading if emailed
Date Due: Friday
Submission Requirements:
    Portfolio
    Turninreich-JR

Writing Assignment
Question or Writing Prompt:
For this exercise you will write two paragraphs:
1)   Imagine that you are a Jew living in Israel. How does the conflict around you and the history of that conflict shape and define your identity?
2)   Imagine that you are a Muslim Arab living in Gaza. How does the conflict around you and the history of that conflict shape and define your identity?
Expectations:
1)   Write in formal academic English. No slang, no contractions.
2)   Start each paragraph with a forceful mini-thesis.
3)   Defend the mini-thesis with specific evidence.
5)   Finish your paragraph with a forceful final statement, but do not be repetitive.
Expected Length: These paragraphs should be between 1/2- 3/4 of a page.
Formatting Requirements: 12 point, Times font, 1.5 spacing.
Source Material: You should only use class materials for this exercise. Do not consult any additional sources from the internet.
Grade Value: 20 points

If you explain an assignment verbally in class, in writing on a syllabus, and then again by email, you still probably won't have everyone do the homework correctly, but you sure can get pretty close. Certainly you have a much better chance of helping students do the right work by emailing them rather than by just shouting their assignment at them as they run out the door . . .

The examples on this page are two models for assigning homework using an email template: the first is a reading assignment and the second a writing assignment.

Here is an example of a template for a short writing assignment.

Long-Term Assignments

If your students don't have reliable home access to networked computers, consider assigning one online assignment each week. Give out the task on Monday and let students have until Friday to complete online homework. For the first few weeks, students will probably procrastinate until Thursday night, and some may fail to complete the assignment and bring in excuses about problems with Internet access. With practice and coaching, students will learn to manage their time to complete the assignment punctually. Having well-chosen online assignments that students are excited to complete obviously will help in this regard.

Rotating Responsibility

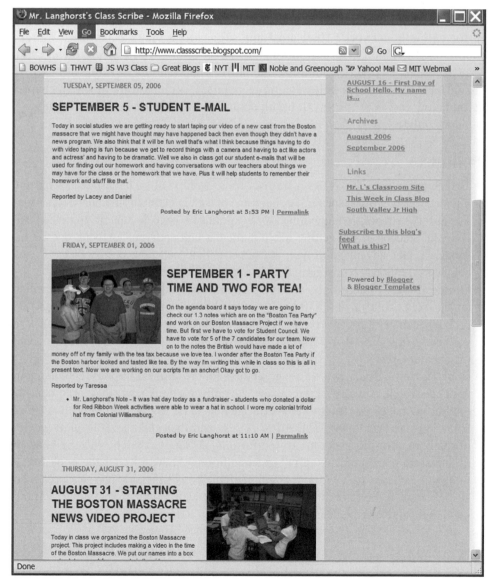

Having a rotating blog can lessen the burden on those for whom accessing the Internet is difficult. It can also help those who struggle to contribute in class and take notes simultaneously.

Source: Image courtesy of Eric Langhorst.

Devise some rotation where students need to complete the online assignment only occasionally. For instance, in the classroom blog shown on the previous page, students take turns contributing class summaries to a blog every few days. Having one or two students act as scribes during class can help with students who miss class due to illness or students who struggle to participate in class and take good notes at the same time.

If you regularly work with teams, especially jigsaw groups, then you can have a fraction of your students responsible for completing an online assignment every few days or weeks. With enough advance notice, students can plan ahead to be sure they have access to computers when they will need them.

WHAT TO DO FOR HOMEWORK?

That was quite a bit about *how* to assign homework online. But *what* can you assign for online homework? Here are some suggestions in six categories: *Reading, Watching and Listening, Researching, Writing, Playing,* and *Collaborating.* Since homework tends to practice many of the skills that students develop in class, you will find many references below to more detailed explanations in other chapters. The list below serves to inspire thinking about the kinds of tasks students can do for homework online.

Reading

- **Text Supplements.** It has never been easier to build your own class reader using the Internet. Reading Shakespeare? Assign some of the Greek myths that inspired his plays. The history textbook getting boring? Assign primary source documents from the period. Are your students really getting into a particular unit and your textbook doesn't have enough to take advantage of their excitement? Find out more on the Web. For some helpful suggestions on searching the Internet, see Chapter 5, "Open Research."
- **Online Books.** Increasingly, anything that has exceeded its copyright is available on the Web. That means if a book is well known and written before 1930, you probably can get it for free on the Internet. Read a little from Plato's *Republic* while you read *Brave New World* or selections from Herodotus's *History* while you study the ancient Greeks.
- **Book Reviews.** Book reviews are great tools for bringing additional scholarship into your classroom. A well-written review can deliver a book's worth of argument with only a few pages of reading. A World History class might read an online excerpt from Thomas Friedman's *The World Is Flat* and then read several online reviews of the book. To find excerpts, try performing a Google search with the book title in quotation marks and "excerpt" as an additional keyword after the book title. To find book reviews, try a Google search with the book title and "reviews" as a search string, or see if the book has a Wikipedia entry with a listing of reviews. For more on Google and Wikipedia, see Chapter 5, "Open Research."

WEBSITE: History teachers should start at the Best of History Web Sites to find great materials from all historical periods to add to their syllabi: http://www .besthistorysites.net/.

The Internet Classics Archive | The Republic by Plato - Mozilla Firefox

File   Edit   View   Go   Bookmarks   Tools   Help

http://classics.mit.edu/Plato/republic.2.i.html   Go   Plato's Republic

BOHWS   THWT   JS W3 Class   Great Blogs   NYT   MIT   Noble and Greenough   Yahoo! Mail

The Republic

By Plato

Written 360 B.C.E

Translated by Benjamin Jowett

Table of Contents

Book I

Socrates - GLAUCON

I went down yesterday to the Piraeus with Glaucon the son of Ariston, that I might offer up my prayers to the goddess; and also because I wanted to see in what manner they would celebrate the festival, which was a new thing. I was delighted with the procession of the inhabitants; but that of the Thracians was equally, if not more, beautiful. When we had finished our prayers and viewed the spectacle, we turned in the direction of the city; and at that instant Polemarchus the son of Cephalus chanced to catch sight of us from a distance as we were starting on our way home, and told his servant to run and bid us wait for him. The servant took hold of me by the cloak behind, and said: Polemarchus desires you to wait.

I turned round, and asked him where his master was.
There he is, said the youth, coming after you, if you will only wait.

Certainly we will, said Glaucon; and in a few minutes Polemarchus appeared, and with him Adeimantus, Glaucon's brother, Niceratus the son of Nicias, and several others who had been at the procession.

Socrates - POLEMARCHUS - GLAUCON - ADEIMANTUS

Polemarchus said to me: I perceive, Socrates, that you and our companion are already on your way to the city.

You are not far wrong, I said.
But do you see, he rejoined, how many we are?

Find: shak   Find Next   Find Previous   Highlight all   Match case

Done

Many great historical works are in the public domain and are available online for free.

Even more exciting are the increasing number of historical book reviews. For instance, the University of Virginia's Electronic Text Center has published selections of book reviews from when *Huckleberry Finn* first came out. (It also has the full text and dozens of illustrations: http://etext.virginia.edu/railton/huckfinn/huchompg.html.)

- **Author Biographies.** Learn more about modern authors from their Web pages or research older authors from online encyclopedias or other Web sites.
- **Magazine and Newspaper Articles.** Most major American and English-language newspaper and magazines have much of their content available online for free. With a little bit of research, you can also find historical articles going back, in some cases, hundreds of years. See Chapter 5, "Open Research," for more ideas on searching through databases with newspaper articles.

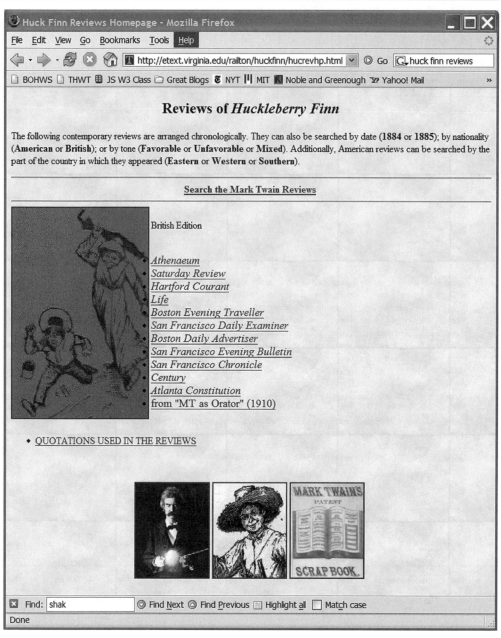

The University of Virginia's Electronic Text Center has an excellent collection of *Huckleberry Finn* book reviews from both from Mark Twain's era and today.   *Source:* Courtesy of the University of Virginia Electronic Text Center.

Watching and Listening

- **Audio and Video News Clips.** Most major media outlets now have news clips available as streaming video. Assign each of your students a current events story and encourage them to find news clips from a few different media sources. National Public Radio also has most of its programs available for listening online or downloading. Many news media outlets are increasingly experimenting with convergence media, where traditional print and photography are supplemented by audio and video, giving readers a chance to see a story from different angles.

- **Primary Source Recordings.** Many poets, authors, musicians, and history makers from the last century can be found speaking online both in audio and video formats. See Chapter 1, "Lectures," for more on finding audio and video.

Primary sources, such as this Beatles clip from the *Ed Sullivan Show*, can help your students get engaged with the material.   *Source:* Courtesy of Google.

- **Animations.** With the advent of the Flash platform for creating animations, increasing numbers of interesting cartoons and animated short films are available on the Internet. *The Big Myth* at http://www.bigmyth.com/ has nine free creation myth animations online and sixteen more for purchase.

  The BBC's Web site for History, http://www.bbc.co.uk/history/, has many different animations to demonstrate everything from troop movements in war to the inner workings of technological innovations.

- **Collaborative Audio Recording.** Students no longer are forced to only listen to audio; they can now create their own. Free online Web sites like VoiceThread.com enable students and others to upload images and leave audio comments for visitors. See Chapter 8, "Student Presentations," for more on making VoiceThreads.

The Big Myth has several interactive animations that include links to class exercises about various creation stories.   *Source:* Courtesy of Distant Train Productions.

- **Virtual Tours.** Many sites offer virtual tours of historic sites and museums. For instance, it is possible to see a panoramic 360-degree view of the Acropolis in ancient Athens as well as to "walk through" some of the most famous museums in the world.

Researching

- If you are skipping around, go back to Chapter 5, "Open Research," for a number of ways to help students do research on the Internet. With practice, students can become finders rather than receivers of information.

Writing

- **Scribing.** As described above in the section on Rotating Responsibility, each student can take turns compiling his or her notes for the day and posting them on the Web. Perhaps have a few students do this each day and encourage students to read the notes and compare how their peers organized the material.

- **Posting.** Post questions or assignments on a class blog and encourage students to post their answers. If a typical night's assignment for your class is to read something and then answer short questions or take notes in writing, have them post that homework to a class blog instead of just scribbling it in their notebooks. (Reading blogs is much, much easier than collecting notebooks.) Another great task is to ask students to post questions about the assignment or the previous day's class for clarification or further discussion. See our discussion on blogs in Chapter 2, "Discussion and Communication," for more ideas.
- **Collaborative Writing.** Wikis are great online tools for collaborative writing. Students can add notes in the goal of building a set of course notes for the year, or they could collaboratively construct a short story, poem, or a vocabulary list. Read more about wikis in Chapter 7, "Writing."
- **Essays and Presentations.** We have two whole chapters on these topics. Check out Chapter 7, "Writing," and Chapter 8, "Student Presentations."

Playing

- In his provocative book entitled *Everything Bad for You Is Good for You,* author Steven Johnson argues that video games hone important cognitive skills.[3] More and more educators agree, and video games are starting to find their way into the classroom. While there is hardly a flood of educational gaming options at the time of this publication, we will probably have much more to say about this in the second edition of this book. Increasingly there are more games, both retail and free, that are directed toward an educational market. *Darfur Is Dying* (http://www.darfurisdying .com/) is a game developed by students from USC in partnership with mtvU that simulates the horrors and difficulties of the genocides in Darfur and is available for free on the Web.

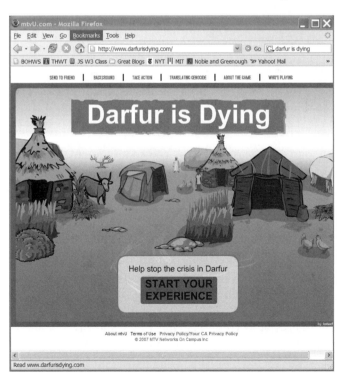

Companies are getting into the act, too, like Knowledge Matters, which publishes a series of historical simulations where students can build an ancient egyptian dynasty or a colony in Early America. (Check it out at http://www.knowledgematters .com/.) You know all those thousands of hours a year that kids spend playing video games? What if they were learning during all those hours?

Online simulation games like *Darfur Is Dying* can immerse students in foreign environments.

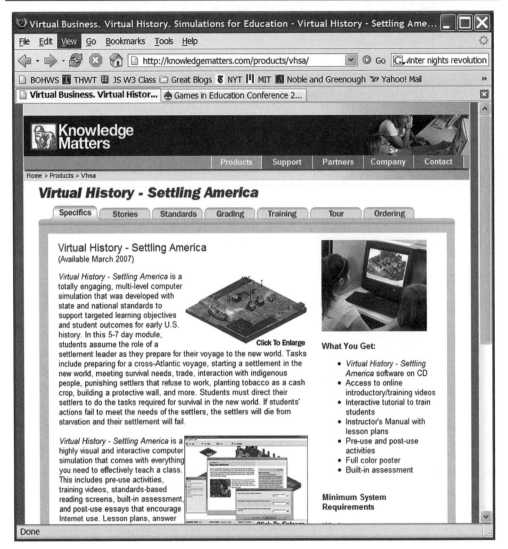

Educational simulations provide an engaging way for students to learn.

Source: Courtesy of Knowledge Matters Inc.

The BBC is an excellent source for varied games. You can find games in many different disciplines and for many different grade levels. For instance, the BBC offers a literacy game for young learners between the ages of four and seven as well as a selection of English, geography, and history games for elementary, middle school, and high school students. The BBC Schools Games site is located at http:// www.bbc.co.uk/schools/games/.

BBC History has its own extended set of history games. They are divided into four major categories: Ancient History, Archaeology, Art History, and World Wars. These are interactive challenges and use animation to engage kids. For example, the Roots of English game prompts students to compose a poem and discover the roots of the words they use. In the Industrial Revolution game, Mock and Brass, students have to balance profits against the cost in lives. There are roughly two dozen games in all. Find them all at http://www.bbc.co.uk/history/interactive/games/.

The BBC has a great variety of games on different subjects and for different grade levels.

Source: Courtesy of the BBC, http://www.bbc.net.uk/history/interactive/games/.

WEBSITE: Our Best of History Web Sites has a page on games and animation at http://www.besthistorysites.net/Multimedia.shtml.

Collaborating

• **Chat or IM Discussions.** Instead of having students write alone about a topic, give them the option to discuss it using a chat room (described in Chapter 2, "Discussion and Communication") or an instant messaging service (you won't need to teach them how to do this). Once they complete their chats, they should copy and paste the dialogue and send it to you in an email or post it to the class blog. These can take the form of discussions, debates, or exercises in generating questions.

- **Peer-Editing.** We discuss this more thoroughly in Chapter 7, "Writing," but once students have written something, have them email it back and forth for comments, suggestions, and polishing.

EXAMPLES OF SHORT-TERM ONLINE ASSIGNMENTS

We define a short-term assignment as one that is to be completed in one or two classes or one or two evenings of homework. The examples below draw heavily from the Internet and prompt students to evaluate varied types of primary and secondary sources. Each assignment's description includes information about the topic, subject, grade level, and resource type, as well as instructions for the assignment and a note for teachers. The idea is to provide you with a wide array of assignments using varied ed-tech tools that you may adopt as your own or that may inspire you to create your own. As you plan your online assignment or activity, remember that not all students may have access to the Internet on any one particular day, so be prepared to be flexible.

1. **Topic: Manifest Destiny**
   Subject: United States History
   Grade Level: High School
   Resource Type: Primary Source Collection
   Teacher's Note: Digital History is a great site for U.S. History teaching resources and includes short excerpts of primary sources that are handy for homework assignments. Digital History organizes the primary sources by topic and includes questions at the end to help students analyze them.
   Instructions for Students: Go to the Manifest Destiny "Classroom handouts" at Digital History: http://www.digitalhistory.uh.edu/historyonline/us17.cfm. Read and answer the questions that follow the primary sources, and email your answers to the TurnInDaccord email account.

2. **Topic: *The Jungle* by Upton Sinclair**
   Subject: American Literature; United States History
   Grade Level: High School
   Resource Type: Primary Source
   Teacher's Note: Many publications over 75 years of age are in the public domain and are available on the Internet. Since *The Jungle* is freely available on the Web, Tom copied sections he wanted the students to read and pasted them into a Microsoft Word document. He then inserted his comments and instructions at select points in the document. In this way Tom guided his students to read selected sections of *The Jungle,* along with his comments, without having to purchase a copy of the book.
   Instructions for Students: Read excerpts from Upton Sinclair's *The Jungle* in the attached Word document. The full text of *The Jungle* is available online at: http://xroads.virginia.edu/~hyper/SINCLAIR/toc.html

THE JUNGLE

BY

UPTON SINCLAIR

`SEARCH`

- __Chapter 1:__ It was four o'clock when the ceremony was over and the carriages began to arrive.
- __Chapter 2:__ Jurgis talked lightly about work, because he was young.
- __Chapter 3:__ In his capacity as delicatessen vender, Jokubas Szedvilas had many acquaintances.
- __Chapter 4:__ Promptly at seven the next morning Jurgis reported for work.
- __Chapter 5:__ They had bought their home.
- __Chapter 6:__ Jurgis and Ona were very much in love; they had waited a long time--
- __Chapter 7:__ All summer long the family toiled, and in the fall they had money enough for Jurgis and Ona to be married....
- __Chapter 8:__ Yet even by this deadly winter the germ of hope was not to be kept from sprouting in their hearts.

Many historical novels and other writings are in the public domain and are available online at no charge. Some include a search feature that makes it easy to locate selected terms and passages in the work.

3. **Topic: Japanese Cooking**
   Subject: Japanese Language Studies
   Grade Level: Middle School, High School, College
   Resource Type: iPods
   Teacher's Note: Tomoko Graham, a creative Japanese language teacher at the Noble and Greenough School in Dedham, Massachusetts, designed a video-based activity that cleverly takes advantage of the iPod's portability. She loaded video of Japanese cooking onto iPods and gave them to students to take home. Students then cooked the meal they watched in the video. The portability of the iPods made it easy for students to move around their own kitchen to grab ingredients and cook the meal while simultaneously watching the video.
   (Two of her students created a hilarious "Iron Chef" parody which you can view at http://edtechteacher.org/chapter6.html.)
   Instructions for Students:
   Watch the Japanese cooking show on your iPod. Pull out ingredients as the chef announces them. Watch as the chef prepares the meal and do as they do! Serve the meal to your parents.

4. **Topic: Kurt Vonnegut Interview**
   Subject: American Literature
   Grade Level: High School, College
   Resource Type: Podcast
   Teacher's Note: National Public Radio is a great source for podcasts on various American and international topics. (For more on Podcasts, see Chapter 8, "Students Presentations.") In this interview from 1986, Kurt Vonnegut talks to NPR about writing, censorship, and the experience of war.

Instructions for Students: Listen to the following NPR interview at: http://www.npr.org/templates/story/story.php?storyId=9567370

Be prepared to discuss Kurt Vonnegut's approach to the writing process and his thoughts on censorship.

5. Topic: Absolute Values

Subject: Math

Grade Level: High School

Resource Type: graphing calculator

Teacher's Note: Doug Guy is a Math teacher at the Noble & Greenough School who makes great use of technology to teach math concepts to students. In this activity, students quickly explore the numerical relationships within a problem, graph the relationship with a graphing calculator, and then translate the written form into symbolic form. Technology allows students to visualize the relationship graphically and numerically, and the connections that students make between the forms leads to the development of analytical skills.

Instructions for Students: A student pilot is practicing take-off and landing skills. The student takes off and climbs at a constant rate of seven hundred feet per minute. When the plane reaches an altitude of 10,500 feet, the student pilot begins the approach for landing at a rate of descent of 700 feet per minute.

Explore the numerical relationship using lists (tables) on your calculator. In the first list enter the values of times in minutes. In the second list enter the corresponding heights after take-off. Initially, height values can be entered by adding 700 to the preceding value.

Next, (as a pattern emerges) enter the height values as the product of the value in list 1 and 700, which leads to the general formula of the product of 700 and the values in list 1 that can be entered in the formula cell. The formula will allow you to explore time values to find the maximum height of the plane.

Once the maximum is determined you should begin to model the descent of the plane. You should determine an appropriate window in which to translate the problem into symbolic form and then graph the function.

Once the symbolic form of the function is analyzed certain questions can be answered. For example, when during the flight is the plane at 8000 feet?

6. Topic: Acropolis 360

Subject: World History

Grade Level: Middle School, High School

Resource Type: Virtual Tour

Teacher's Note: There are many educational virtual tours available on the Internet. Some of these are photo tours, some include audio and video, and some use specialized software like Google Earth (discussed in Chapter 4, "Guided Inquiry"). The following tour uses panoramic images to allow the visitor to tour the ancient Acropolis in Athens, Greece.

Instructions for Students: Go to the following Web page:

Acropolis 360: http://www.virtualbritain.org/

Look underneath the image and make sure that the audio button is on. Turn up the volume loud enough on your computer to hear the audio commentary.

Scroll down and look for *Enter the Tour Here.* Select Broadband or Dialup depending on your connection, and start the tour. Click the numbered links to see a panoramic tour of each location. (Tours appear in a pop-up window, so make sure to allow pop-ups from this site on your browser.)

Use the arrows to navigate forward and backward. You can also zoom in and out of the image. Be prepared to answer the following: What was the purpose of the Acropolis? How do the varied structures and monuments reflect its purpose?

7. **Topic: "9/11: Are We Safer Five Years Later?"**
   Subject: United States History
   Grade Level: High School
   Resource Type: Blog
   Teacher's Note: Tom gave this blogging assignment on the fifth anniversary of the 9/11 attacks, which coincided with the first week of school. Since educational blogs are most effective when students are given opportunities to express their ideas and feelings on topics that interest them, Tom's objective was to engage his students on a current topic on both a personal and academic level. It was also an opportunity to get to know a group of students he had just started teaching. Many students opened up on the blog and revealed deeply personal responses regarding the events of that day.

   Instructions for Students: In recent speeches President Bush has claimed that the United States is much safer now than it was before 9/11. "Many Americans look at these events," Mr. Bush has said, "and ask the same question: Five years after 9/11, are we safer? The answer is, yes, America is safer. We are safer because we've taken action to protect the homeland." [4] He and others point to air security improvements and revamped intelligence agencies that can share information more freely as well as additional agents

U.S. History -- Mr. Daccord
Tom Daccord's United States History class at the Noble & Greenough School

CATEGORIES

Current Affairs

Unit 1: Industrial Age

DACCORD U.S. HISTORY

Brooke

Casey

Daccord U.S. History

Devan

Emily

Hanna

Ian

Julie

Liz

Matt

Mel

Sophie

Stephanie

Tucker

Main | November 2006 »

SEPTEMBER 20, 2006

Ragged Dick & the American Dream

What individual or societal virtues is Horatio Alger trying to advance through his portrayal of Ragged Dick? Which scenes or examples best illustrate these virtues? How?

September 20, 2006 at 07:14 AM | Permalink | Comments (0) | TrackBack (0)

SEPTEMBER 13, 2006

Industrial Age, 1877-1920 (Post #1)

What was the point of today's activity? How does it connect to last night's homework assignment? Please make specific reference to terms/people/concepts from the homework.
Post your 1-2 paragraph answer on your blog.
Thanks

September 13, 2006 at 07:51 AM in Unit 1: Industrial Age | Permalink | Comments (2) | TrackBack (0)

SEPTEMBER 09, 2006

9/11: Are We Safer Five Years Later?

In recent speeches President Bush has claimed that the United States is much safer than 9/11. "Many Americans look at these events," Mr. Bush has said , "and ask the same question: Five years after 9/11, are we safer? The answer is, yes, America is safer. We are safer because we've taken action to protect the homeland." He and others point to air security improvements and revamped

RECENT POSTS

ARCHIVES

April 2007

February 2007

January 2007

December 2006

November 2006

September 2006

This image is from Tom's United States History classroom blog from the 2006–2007 school year. His 9/11 blogging assignment is down the page.

assigned to work on counterterrorism. Others disagree. For instance, former U.S. assistant secretary of defense Larry Korb says: "What has happened is, particularly with the invasion of Iraq, we have created a lot of al-Qaida wannabees, and there are more people now that are trying to do us harm than there were before we went into Iraq."[5] Senator John Kerry concurs: "[President Bush's] disastrous decisions have made Iraq a fuel depot for terror, fanning the flames of conflict around the world."[6]

What do you remember of 9/11? Do you feel safer now than five years ago? Why or why not? Post your answer to your blog.

8. **Topic: Creating a Diamante Poem**
   Subject: Poetry
   Grade Level: Lower School, Middle School
   Resource Type: Online Interactive Tool
   Teacher's Note: This poetry tool is from the outstanding ReadWriteThink Web site at http://readwritethink.org/. The ReadWriteThink Web site is a collaboration of the International Reading Association (IRA), the National Council of Teachers of English (NCTE), and the Verizon Foundation.

   A Diamante poem is in the shape of a diamond and uses specific types of words like adjectives, gerunds, and participles. Students fill out text fields with a topic name and some descriptive terms and the Diamante tool helps shape the students' words into a poem. This tool may really help students who struggle with creating poetic structure.

   Instructions for Students: You will use the online Diamante tool to help you create poetic structure. Go to http://www.readwritethink.org/materials/diamante/ and wait for the Diamante tool to load. Next, click *Get Started* and fill out the identifying information for your poem. Then click the *Continue* button and fill out all the text fields. Diamante will take the words you provide and create a poem in the shape of a diamond.

9. **Topic: "Turning the Pages"—Jane Austen's Early Works**
   Subject: English Literature; World History
   Grade Level: High School
   Resource Type: Multimedia Presentation
   Teacher's Note: Turning the Pages, at http://www.bl.uk/onlinegallery/ttp/ttpbooks .html, is an award-winning site from the British Library that enables visitors to "turn" the pages of historic manuscripts using touch-screen technology and animation. It provides an excellent opportunity for students to view "authentic" and historic primary sources along with accompanying audio. In order to run the program you need to download the free Macromedia Shockwave player, available at http://www.adobe.com/shockwave/download/.

   Instructions for Students: Go to the "Turning the Pages" site from the British Library:

   http://www.bl.uk/onlinegallery/ttp/ttpbooks.html.

   Go to *Jane Austen's Early Work*.

   Once it has launched, click, hold, and drag the mouse to turn the pages. Click on the audio button in the bottom right corner to hear the audio and click the magnify class to zoom in on an image.

   Be prepared to discuss Jane Austen's views on the history of England and how those views may have influenced her writing of *Pride and Prejudice*.

10. **Topic: Toni Morrison Interview**
    Subject: American Literature
    Grade Level: High School
    Resource Type: Online Video Interview
    Teacher's Note: The proliferation of free online video (think YouTube) over the last few years means that there are now many online videos that can be incorporated into your curriculum at no cost. YouTube might be banned at your school because of content or bandwidth concerns, but there are other free alternatives such as Google Video and Yahoo Video. The following video is from Google Video. See Chapter 1, "Lectures," for more discussion of online video.
    Instructions for Students: Since we are reading works by Toni Morrison, the Pulitzer Prize–winning author of *Beloved,* you are to watch a video interview of her conducted by Charlie Rose at:
    http://tinyurl.com/4dkmo.
    (You can also find the video by going to http://video.google.com and using the terms "Toni," "Morrison," and "Beloved" in your search string.)
    Watch the video and be prepared to discuss the biggest influences of Toni Morrison's novels.

11. **Topic: "Industrial Age" Practice Quiz**
    Subject: United States History
    Grade Level: High School
    Resource Type: Online Quiz or Game
    Teacher's Note: Online quizzes and games are a great way to engage students and help them learn course materials. Tom created this online game about Industrial Age America to help his students with fact acquisition before a unit test. He used Quia to create this game and similar ones throughout the school year. For more information about Quia and online games and quizzes in general, go to Chapter 9, "Assessment and Grading."
    Instructions for Students: Go to: http://www.quia.com/cb/85720.html and play the game to review for the unit test. Play solo or challenge a classmate.

12. **Topic: Virtual Tour of Progressive-Era Dwellings**
    Subject: United States History
    Grade Level: Middle School, High School
    Resource Type: Virtual Tour
    Teacher's Note: Here is another integration of an online virtual tour.
    Instructions for Students: Take a virtual tour of two Gilded Age dwellings:

    Virtual tour of the Elms:
    http://www.pbs.org/wgbh/amex/carnegie/sfeature/tour.html
    Virtual tour of New York tenement.
    http://tenement.org/index_virtual.html

    Briefly describe what you see. What do the pictures reveal about living conditions at the turn of the century?

13. Topic: Crisis in Darfur
   Subject: World History; Current Events
   Grade Level: Middle School, High School, College
   Resource Type: Google Earth
   Teacher's Note: "The Crisis in Darfur" from the United States Holocaust Memorial Museum Web site uses Google Earth technology to help visitors understand the genocide unfolding in Darfur, Sudan. You need the free Google Earth program to play "The Crisis in Darfur" file, so be sure to download it on any computer you wish to use. The content is really impressive—even President Bush has commended it—and students can witness burned-out villages and tent cities of displaced people, and can read eyewitness testimony of atrocities. (For more on Google Earth refer to Chapter 4, "Guided Inquiry.")
   Instructions for Students: You will watch a United States Holocaust Memorial Museum special presentation called the "The Crisis in Darfur." Go to: http://www.ushmm.org/googleearth/. Download and install Google Earth via the link provided and then download the "The Crisis in Darfur" layers for Google Earth photographs. Once it has launched, use the tools in the upper right corner to zoom in and out, rotate the images, and get a ground-level perspective. Click the various icons and collect data, read eyewitness testimony, and watch select video clips.
   Be prepared to answer the following questions: What are the most vivid symbols of the destruction in the area? Of the various factors that contribute to the crisis, which are most vividly revealed to you by these photographs and visuals?

14. Topic: Descriptive Paintings
   Subject: Art & French Language Studies
   Grade Level: Middle School, High School
   Resource Type: iPod
   Teacher's Note: Mark Sheeran, a French teacher at the Noble and Greenough School, developed this engaging exercise that combines art and French auditory skills. To begin, students are given color copies of select paintings. After having studied the necessary vocabulary—such as background, foreground, water colors, canvas, and brush strokes—each student records a description of his or her painting in .mp3 format. These individual descriptions are downloaded onto iPods. The teacher then collects all the color copies of the paintings and posts them in a hallway. Next, students walk up and down the hallway, much like they would in an art gallery, and listen to the iPod descriptions. The challenge is to match the description to the painting.
   Instructions for Students: Look at the paintings in the hallway as you listen to various descriptions on your iPod. Match the description you are listening to with the respective painting on the wall and write one or two sentences that add to the existing description.

15. Topic: Debate: Should the U.S. Annex the Philippines?
   Subject: United States History
   Grade Level: High School
   Resource Type: Primary Source Collection
   Teacher's Note: The following assignment is also from the Center for History and New Media site. The activity features selected, short primary sources that offer diverse and interesting opinions on the U.S. States annexation of the Philippines. It might take

a teacher several hours to uncover and assemble the sources conveniently found at this one page.

Instructions for Students: Go to http://historymatters.gmu.edu/d/6613/.

Scroll down the page and read the following brief excerpts:

- U.S. President William McKinley speaking in 1903.
- U.S. Democratic Presidential candidate William Jennings Bryan.
- Samuel Gompers (President, American Federation of Labor)
- Colored Citizens of Boston (the *Boston Post*, July 18, 1899)
- Emilio Aguinaldo (President of the Independent Philippine Republic)
- Clemencia Lopez (an activist in the Philippine Struggle for Independence)

Summarize the major arguments for and against annexation in an outline.

16. Topic: Maps and Battles of World War I

Subject: World History

Grade Level: Middle School, High School

Resource Type: Online Map

Teacher's Note: The Internet is a great source of maps, historic and otherwise. Both PBS and BBC offer helpful maps of historic events at their Web sites. This assignment uses maps from a PBS site on World War I. Online maps are great teaching tools and can be used in homework assignments or class presentations. If you plan to project a series of online maps in class, consider creating a BrowserPoint using the tabbed browsing strategy outlined in Chapter 1, "Lectures."

Instructions for Students: Go to http://www.pbs.org/greatwar/maps/maps_outbreak.html.

Play all the animations and note the following terms:
— Schlieffen plan
— Western Front
— Battles of Verdun and Somme
— Third Battle of Ypres

Then, go to: http://www.pbs.org/wgbh/peoplescentury/episodes/killingfields/.

Read the two Eyewitness interviews. Outline a response to the following question: Why was the "Great War" so horrific?

17. Topic: Oral History of the Holocaust

Subject: United States History

Grade Level: Middle School, High School

Resource Type: Online Oral Histories

Teacher's Note: The Internet is a great source of oral histories on various historical topics. "Telling Their Stories: Oral History of the Holocaust," a video project created by high school students at the Urban School of San Francisco, is perhaps the best student-created oral history project in the country. There are three impressive oral history projects featured at the http://www.tellingstories.org/ site: Holocaust Survivors and Refugees, World War II Camp Liberators, and Japanese-American Internees. We make a point of incorporating student materials in our courses so that students can see what tremendous presentations are created by other kids.

Instructions for Students: Go to the "Telling Their Stories: Oral History Archives Project" at http://www.tellingstories.org/ and watch the interview of Lucille Eichengreen, a German-Polish survivor of the Lódz Ghetto, Auschwitz, Neuengamme, and Bergen-Belsen. Click on the text of the interview to watch video clips of the interview.

Be prepared to discuss the following questions: How did Lucille Eichengreen become aware of anti-Semitism and how did it impact her? Why weren't her parents overly concerned about Hitler's ascendancy to the German chancellorship?

18. Topic: WWII Animations
   Subject: World History
   Grade Level: Middle School, High School
   Resource Type: Online Animated Maps
   Teacher's Note: As pointed out earlier, the Internet can be a great source of maps. You can find plenty of helpful *animated* maps, especially of World War I, at the BBC History Web site. BBC animated maps combine images, text, and animation to create instructive and informative presentations.
   Instructions for Students: Watch the following animations:

   A. Animated Map: Operation Overlord: http://www.bbc.co.uk/history/worldwars/wwtwo/launch_ani_overlord_campaign.shtml
   B. Animated Map: The D-Day Landings: http://www.bbc.co.uk/history/worldwars/wwtwo/launch_ani_d_day.shtml
   C. American Advance Across the Pacific: http://www.pbs.org/wgbh/amex/pacific/maps/maps_02.html

Answer the following questions: What strategy issues did the Allies face and what decisions did they make? How important were America's military contributions? Why did Truman "drop the bomb," and why do historians still debate his decision?

19. Topic: Interactive Timeline of Art History
   Subject: Art History
   Grade Level: High School, College
   Resource Type: Interactive Timeline; Virtual Tour
   Teacher's Note: The are some outstanding interactive timelines on the Internet, and few are better than the Metropolitan Museum of Art's Multimedia Timeline of Art History at http://www.metmuseum.org/toah/splash.htm?HomePageLink=toah_1. (HyperHistory, located at http://www.hyperhistory.com/, is another impressive interactive history timeline.) The Met's Art Timeline of Art History is organized chronologically, geographically, and thematically and includes art from the museum's collection, as well as charts, maps, a list of key events, and other key information. The timeline is a great vehicle to introduce students to art history and to contrast art from different regions and eras.
   Instructions for Students: Go to the Metropolitan Museum of Art's Multimedia Timeline of Art History at http://www.metmuseum.org/toah/splash.htm?HomePageLink=toah_1.
   Click on the timeline bar representing World Regions from 1000 B.C. to A.D. 1000. Next, click on Mexico and examine the artwork presented. Do the same for the Maya Area and Central America. Proceed to the next era, A.D. 1–500.

Be prepared to answer the following question: What similarities or differences do you see, both geographically and chronologically, in the various art pieces?

20. Topic: Research Essay—Step 1
   Subject: United States History
   Grade Level: High School
   Resource Type: Internet Search Engines and Online Databases
   Teacher's Note: Students need to become well versed in both online and print research strategies. The following assignment is the first step in an extended research assignment and helps guide students toward the effective use of online search tools. More specifically, students are prompted to develop an effective list of keywords for searches and to create effective search strings. For more on effective online search strategies consult Chapter 5, "Open Research."

   Instructions for Students: This weekend you will begin the formal process of selecting a topic for your research essay. Your ultimate objective is to craft a formal analytical essay based extensively on primary sources. You will need to develop a historical question to answer. The key to successful research for this project is to adopt a thoughtful and broad-based strategy.

   Here is what you need to do this weekend:

   1. Identify a general topic.
      example: "Cuban Missile Crisis"
   2. Identify what interests you about the topic.
      Example: "I am interested in the EXCOMM discussions and the conflicts between its various members during the meetings. I want to know which member(s) most influenced Kennedy's decision and how. I also want to know which member(s) might have been isolated or even shunned and why. I might then do focused research on an EXCOMM member or two."
   3. Do preliminary background reading (encyclopedia; history Web site; book chapter) and develop an effective keyword and subject search strategy.
      Example keywords: Cuban missile crisis; President John F. Kennedy; (names of EXCOMM members); Fidel Castro; Nikita Khrushchev; blockade/quarantine.
      Example keyword search strings: EXCOMM (and) Cuban missile crisis; EXCOMM (and) President John F. Kennedy; (name of EXCOMM member) (and) EXCOMM; EXCOMM discussions/deliberations/debate/decisions
   4. Search the school library's online catalog online for materials to read.
      Search by title, subject, etc., and use a variety of keywords.
   5. Use Google's Advanced Search function to find education-oriented Web sites on a topic. Also try Google's Book Search to generate a list of scholarly publications.

21. Topic: The Decision to Drop the Atomic Bomb on Hiroshima and Nagasaki
   Subject: United States History
   Grade Level: High School
   Teacher's Note: It would probably take a teacher days to pull together the varied sources and points of view on the decision to drop the atomic bomb that are easily accessible via the "The Decision to Drop the Bomb" WebQuest, located at http://oncampus .richmond.edu/academics/education/projects/webquests/wwii/. (For more information on WebQuests, refer to Chapter 4, "Guided Inquiry.") For this activity Tom and his stu-

dents did not complete the WebQuest in its entirety, nor did they follow the instructions to the letter. Instead, Tom incorporated selected sources available via the WebQuests and modified its instructions and length to better suit his curriculum and schedule.

Instructions for Students: You are going to be studying various perspectives and opinions on the decision to drop the atomic bomb on Hiroshima and Nagasaki. You will read testimonies from individuals and groups representing Harry S. Truman, the American military, the Japanese, and the scientists who worked to develop the bomb. Visit the following pages to get background on the decision:

A. Quotes from some prominent Americans who questioned the atomic bombing of Japan:
   http://www.doug-long.com/quotes.htm

B. President Truman's diary excerpts:
   http://www.doug-long.com/hst.htm

C. Secretary of War Henry Stimson's diary and paper:
   http://www.doug-long.com/stimson.htm

D. A letter from historians to the Smithsonian on the Enola Gay exhibit:
   http://www.doug-long.com/letter.htm

E. Atomic Bomb Decision: Documents on the Decision to Use the Atomic Bombs on Hiroshima and Nagasaki
   http://www.dannen.com/decision/index.html

F. Major Effects of the Atomic Bomb
   http://www.hiroshima-cdas.or.jp/HICARE/en/12/index.html

G. Eye witness accounts of the bombing of Hiroshima:
   http://www.inicom.com/hibakusha/

H. Chronology on the Decision to Bomb Hiroshima and Nagasaki
   http://www.nuclearfiles.org/menu/key-issues/nuclear-weapons/history/pre-cold-war/hiroshima-nagasaki/decision-drop-bomb-chronology.htm

I. Scientific Data of the Nagasaki Atomic Bomb Disaster
   http://www-sdc.med.nagasaki-u.ac.jp/n50/disaster/medical-E.html

J. Gar Alperovitz and the H-Net Hiroshima Debate
   http://www.doug-long.com/debate.htm

22. Topic: Cold War Diplomatic Letter
   Subject: World History; United States History
   Grade Level: High School
   Resource Type: Primary Source
   Teacher's Note: There are plenty of non-English sources available on the Internet. (Google offers a "Translate this Page" link when it includes a non-English Web page in its search results. Click the link to get a basic translation of the page into English.) In this case, CNN has made available a translated diplomatic report from a Soviet Russian official during the early years of the Cold War.

   Instructions for Students: Read the following:

   "Report on the International Situation" http://www.cnn.com/SPECIALS/cold.war/episodes/04/documents/cominform.html. Politburo member and Leningrad party boss Andrei Zhdanov issued this report to the first conference of Cominform, the international communist information bureau.

As a foreign policy advisor to the Truman administration, you will write a 700–900 word letter back to Mr. Zhdanov in which you challenge his analysis of the international situation. You will explain why you disagree with his report and incorporate specific events between 1945 and 1950.

23. **Topic: Martin Luther King Jr. in His Own Words**
    Subject: United States History; American Literature
    Grade Level: High School
    Resource Type: Primary Source Collection
    Teacher's Note: The following assignment is another example of the integration of select online primary sources. The sources are easily available on the Internet and save the teacher the time of having to find and photocopy print materials.
Instructions for Students: Read from the following Web pages:
    A. The Autobiography of Martin Luther King, Jr: Montgomery Movement Begins
        http://www.stanford.edu/group/King/publications/autobiography/chp_7.htm
        At the end of the chapter King says, "The victory was already won," yet the beginning of the boycott was fraught with uncertainty and apprehension. What apprehensions or fears did King experience at the beginning of the movement, and how were they overcome?
    B. Letter from a Birmingham Jail, Martin Luther King, Jr., 1963
        http://coursesa.matrix.msu.edu/~hst306/documents/letter.html
    Answer the following:
    1. Briefly, what is the argument of the "Statement by Alabama Clergymen"?
    2. What reasons does King provide for his decision to support direct action or demonstrations against segregation in Alabama?
    3. What kinds of law does King speak about in this letter, and what is their applicability in terms of political life?
    4. What kind of moderation is King criticizing, and what kind of extremism is he praising?

24. **Topic: Martin Luther King Jr. and Malcolm X**
    Subject: United States History
    Grade Level: Middle School, High School
    Teacher's Note: Here is another example of the integration of video freely available on the Internet.
    Instructions for Students: Watch video of King and Malcolm X (you will need either Quick Time or Real Player to view it):
        http://www.pbs.org/wgbh/amex/mlk/sfeature/sf_video.html
    Answer the following: How are their messages, tone, and philosophies different?

25. **Topic: White House Statements During the Watergate Investigation**
    Subject: United States History
    Grade Level: High School, College
    Resource Type: Primary Source
    Teacher's Note: The following assignment is based on an authentic primary source. The document was scanned and is thus in its original format, complete with handwritten notes in the margins.

Instructions for Students: Go to:

White House Statements During Investigation

http://www.washingtonpost.com/wp-srv/onpolitics/watergate/documents.htm

Read the first ten pages.

Answer the following: How does Nixon defend the presidency? Is he persuasive? Why or why not?

 WEBSITE: To find more about these and other online assignments, visit http://edtechteacher.org/chapter6.html.

FINAL THOUGHTS

As you can see, almost everything we have talked about throughout this book can be adapted into a homework assignment. We hope that as you read this chapter you could feel the shackles—the irons that once bound you assigning textbook readings and worksheets—falling off of your ankles. Now you can assign a cornucopia of readings and activities freely available on the Internet. Not only are these materials free, but also organized collections can save teachers countless hours of searching and collecting. As broadband access improves, so will the opportunities to incorporate online audio and video in our homework assignments. Interactive technologies are improving as well, and it is becoming ever easier to create online quizzes, games, worksheets, and the like. As the Internet becomes a fixture in American homes, the current problems with on-line equity and access hopefully will fade away, and we will enter a new era where the possibilities of homework assignments are not limited by the books we ordered at the beginning of the year.

NOTES

1. US Broadband Penetration Jumps to 45.2%, WebSiteOptimization.com, 16 March 2004, http://www.websiteoptimization.com/bw/0403/, accessed 17 April 2007.

2. John Horrigan, Home Broadband Adoption 2006, Pew Internet & American Life Project, 28 May 2006, http://www.pewinternet.org/PPF/r/184/report_display.asp, accessed 17 April 2007.

3. Steven Johnson, *Everything Bad Is Good For You* (New York: Riverhead Books, 2005).

4. Sheryl Gay Stolberg, "Bush Assures That the Nation Is Safer as Memories Turn to a Day of Destruction," *New York Times,* 7 September 2006, http://www.nytimes.com/2006/09/08/washington/08bush.html?ex=1315368000&en=98aee6ce8b7bb9f7&ei=5088&partner=rssnyt&emc=rss, accessed 8 August 2007.

5. Stolberg, "Bush Assures."

6. Senator John Kerry, "Let America Be America Again," speech delivered September 28, 2006, at Johns Hopkins University School of Advanced International Studies in Washington, D.C., http://www.sais-jhu.edu/centers/cpfr/thinking_archives/09282006.html, accessed 8 August 2007.

Writing

INTRODUCTION

Computers have the potential to make our students much better writers. For sketching out ideas quickly, the pencil may still have an edge, but for crafting carefully refined prose, computers bring a wide array of advantages.

First, for some students, the graphomotor elements of writing—all those fine motor skills needed to produce legible letters—suck up significant portions of brainpower. Pushing buttons lets kids who struggle with forming letters focus on crafting writing.

Editing is also much easier on a computer. For instance, when many students write paragraphs, their best thought often can be found at the end of a paragraph (after they have thought through their ideas in writing), when it probably ought to be at the beginning. Moving that sentence is a difficult change to make with pen and paper, but it's a breeze with a word processor's cut and paste function. With spelling- and grammar-checking tools, students can get instant feedback on their mechanics, and the ease of sending documents back and forth electronically makes editing and peer editing more efficient.

Moreover, software programs like Microsoft Word offer an array of powerful writing tools—some you may not even be aware of—that can help students strengthen their writing. Spend a few minutes with us in this chapter exploring Word's *Tools,* and other software programs, and you will be better equipped to help students write stronger essays and avoid many common writing errors.

STANDARD FORMATTING

Before delving into the writing itself, it's worth spending some time on expectations for how student writing should look. Save yourself some time and eyestrain by requiring a standard formatting for all of the work in your class. If you don't enforce formatting expectations in your classes, your corner cutters will be swelling their margins and line spacing and your nerdlings will cram more words than you ever thought possible in a five page paper. For instance, require your students to submit everything using the following dimensions:

Font: Times New Roman (or choose another serif font—serifs are the little straight lines that embellish some fonts—they enable you read faster, which makes a difference when you have 75 papers to grade)
Size: 12 point
Spacing: 1.5
Margins: Top and bottom: 1", left and right 1.25"
Font Color: Black

For the first few months of class, remind students of these requirements and they will soon become automatic.

Here's a trick if you think a student is trying to stretch a short paper by altering the spacing, margins, or font size: just take a paper that you know is correctly formatted and lay it over the suspect paper. Hold them up to a light, and if they don't line up, then you've got someone trying to pull a fast one on you. Better yet, demonstrate this trick in class (those big fluorescent lights are perfect) with the first set of papers, and you won't get any more sneaky business from your students.

PRE-WRITING AND BRAINSTORMING

Inspiration and FreeMind

We first introduced Inspiration and FreeMind in Chapter 3, "Note Taking and Organization," as tools for helping students take graphical, visual notes. In this section, we'll focus on using these two pieces of software as writing tools.

Inspiration and FreeMind are concept-mapping tools that let students express their ideas in a visual, non-linear medium, which is often just what students need to generate ideas for writing assignments. The mind maps created by these tools can be easily moved, changed, and reconfigured, and Inspiration comes with templates to help students start with some structure to their thinking.

While these are exciting tools, as with every piece of technology, it's worth testing these tools against the pencil test: are they better than a pencil? There are some limitations to these tools, especially in that large concept maps can be big files, difficult to email or share, and difficult to print. In these respects, a pencil and a white sheet of paper might be best. That said, many new tools found on the Internet make collaborative concept-mapping simple and easy to do.

Inspiration

FEATURED PRODUCT

Inspiration
Web site: http://www.inspiration.com/
Developer: Inspiration Software
Cost: $70 for an individual license, discount for groups

Inspiration is a program designed to help students and teachers make concept maps and graphic organizers. The interface is intuitive, and the software offers an extensive array of features for customizing mind maps and outlines. Many educators around the United States use Inspiration, and so plenty of lesson plans and templates can be found on the Web.

Inspiration is a concept-mapping tool that lets students graphically arrange ideas. Ideas are put into bubbles or other symbols, and then the bubbles are linked with arrows. Everything can be moved around and rearranged with simple mouse clicks, so students can generate ideas quickly and then spend more time methodically organizing them. See Chapter 3, "Note Taking and Organization," for an introductory tutorial (page 75).

Brainstorming with Inspiration

For an unstructured approach to brainstorming, students can generate ideas in bubbles and then move those bubbles around into a more orderly format. For instance, to create a standard, introductory five-paragraph essay, students could be asked to identity their three main points from a cloud of ideas, and then figure out which details are most closely associated with each of the three points.

Once students have begun to draw out their ideas, they may be ready to delve into the writing process. If they need more help creating structure from their mind maps, you may want to encourage them to use Inspiration's outline feature.

Tech Specs: Inspiration Brainstorms
Set-Up Time: Give yourself 30 minutes to experiment with the basic features and interface before using it in class.
Keep-Up Time: None.
In-Class Time: Students can create a basic brainstorming mind map in 15–20 minutes, but you could also spend several periods planning and outlining a longer essay.
Tech Savvy: Low to medium. Inspiration has a clean, intuitive interface, but it also has many options that will probably be unfamiliar to many students.

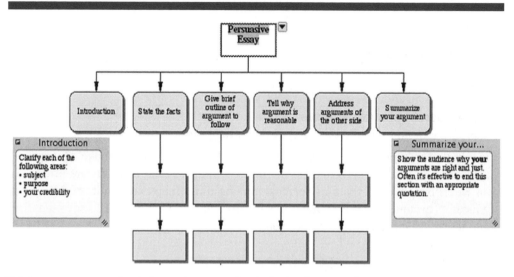

This language arts template helps students organize the basics elements of a persuasive essay.

Source: ©2007 Inspiration Software®, Inc. Diagram created in Inspiration® by Inspiration Software®, Inc. Used with permission.

Inspiration's Outline View

Inspiration allows you to convert your concept map into an outline just by switching the view to Outline Mode, which is done with the *Outline* button in the top left of the toolbar. This will automatically put your map into outline form, which is one step toward writing an essay from your concept map. It's a neat trick, but the concept maps that students generate do not always lend themselves to being easily transformed into an outline. Fortunately, you can move concepts up, down, left, and right in the Outline Mode as well.

The *Topic* and *Subtopic* buttons, found on the toolbar, let you add new concepts while in Outline Mode, and the *Left* and *Right* buttons let you reorder ideas. You can also click and drag concepts up and down on your outline. If you switch back to the diagram mode by clicking the *Diagram* button in the top left of the toolbar, all of these changes will be reflected in your original concept map.

Once satisfied, students can then print their outlines (*File→Print)* or export them by selecting *File→Export* and then choose a format in which they wish to export the outline.

> **WEBSITE:** Watch our video tutorial on brainstorming with Inspiration: http://www.edtechteacher.org/chapter7.html.

Writing with Inspiration Templates

Inspiration also includes numerous templates for different types of writing. In these templates, students are presented with pre-organized models for arranging information, and their job is to insert the specific details. These templates can easily be converted into an outline or exported into a word processor to get students started with their writing. Inspiration gives users many templates to begin with, and many more can be found online with a simple Google search.

Inspiration 7.0 offers fourteen templates for English and Language Arts classrooms and ten templates for Social Studies classrooms. To access these templates, select *File* from the Menu bar, click *Open Template,* and select the *Language Arts* folder. If you are asking students to write a "compare and contrast" essay, then make sure to examine the "Comparative Analysis" template. Use this template to help students compare ideas and themes in a book or piece of literature and hone their comparative analysis skills. If you would like students to focus on historical cause and effect, Inspiration offers a "Cause and Effect" template that can help demonstrate the causes and effects of war, economic trends, political movements, and more. If you wish to help stimulate debate, or just help students see two side of an issue, the "Pro and Con" template prompts students to enter arguments on both sides of a debate and then attempt to resolve the differences.

Tech Specs: Writing with Inspiration Templates

Set-Up Time: It may take you a few minutes to find the right template, but once you have found it, the prep work is done for you.

Keep-Up Time: None needed, though you can search for and find new templates and ideas on the Web.

In-Class Time: With the structures provided by these templates, 20–50 minutes is usually sufficient for students to generate their ideas within the template.

Tech Savvy: Low. Filling in the templates is quite simple, and basic modifications are easy as well.

PENCIL: Though you lose valuable flexibility, printing out the Inspiration templates and having students fill them out by hand could work in a pinch.

WEBSITE: Go to http://www.edtechteacher.org/chapter7.html to get more ideas on using Inspiration in the classroom.

FreeMind: A Free Alternative to Inspiration

FEATURED PRODUCT

FreeMind
Web site: http://freemind.sourceforge.net/wiki/index.php/Main_Page
Developer: As an open-source project, FreeMind has a team of volunteer developers.
Cost: Free

FreeMind is a simple, elegant concept-mapping software that is distributed for free. It perhaps lacks the rich functionality of commercial products, but its interface is simple, clean, and intuitive, and the price can't be beat.

As OpenOffice's Impress is to Microsoft's PowerPoint, FreeMind is a free, open-source alternative to Inspiration. It has far fewer features, but it also has much smaller files and you can put it on unlimited computers at no cost. A basic introduction to FreeMind can be found in Chapter 3, "Note Taking and Organization," but here are a few ideas on using FreeMind to help students prepare to write.

FreeMind Five-Paragraph Essay Templates

Tech Specs: Using FreeMind Templates

Set-Up Time: It should take you only 5 minutes to download the templates from our Web site, http://www.edtechteacher.org/freemind.html, and you could design your own in 20–30 minutes.

Keep-Up Time: Just the time it takes you to email templates.

In-Class Time: Depending on the complexity of the essay, 20 minutes to several periods.

Tech Savvy: Medium. FreeMind isn't particularly difficult, but for many it will be unfamiliar.

While FreeMind does not come with preloaded templates like Inspiration, we have some templates available free at our Web site. In these templates for an introductory, five-paragraph essay, students can replace the generic nodes we have created with ideas for their own essays. If having the whole template open at once is unwieldy, students can collapse everything except the part they are working on.

Once students begin the composing process, they can copy and paste any of the information in their FreeMind nodes to any word processor as they write their essays.

FreeMind maps are somewhat more visual than a regular outline, and somewhat

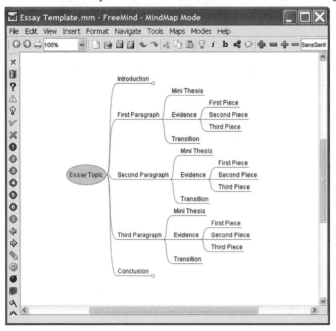

more structured that an Inspiration brainstorm map. Perhaps they are best oriented toward students who need some hand-holding but struggle with the rigidity of a typical outline. FreeMind files are very small, so they can be easily emailed back and forth, and since the software is free, students might be able to work on their outlines for homework as well.

The FreeMind essay templates are easy to use and can help guide students through the thinking process.

WEBSITE: The template on page 172 is available online: http://www.edtechteacher.org/chapter7.html.

FROM PRE-WRITING TO POLISHING: BEST PRACTICES FOR WRITING WITH WORD PROCESSORS

Word processors are some of the most common software programs used in schools, and with every new generation of software, developers are including more tools to help students write. At this point, word processors can help students with every phase of writing, from prewriting to drafting to revising to polishing to responding to instructor comments.

The two word processors most commonly found in schools are Microsoft Word and Apple's Appleworks. For schools where budgets are tight, faculty and technology staff should look seriously at the benefits of OpenOffice.org's Writer, which is an open-source, free writing application with almost all of the functionality of Word and Appleworks.

In this chapter, most of our examples will draw on Microsoft Word, both because it has the most features to help writers develop and because it is the most common word-processing application in schools.

FEATURED PRODUCT

AppleWorks
Web site: http://www.apple.com/appleworks/
Developer: Apple
Cost: $79 from the online Apple store

AppleWorks is a fine word processor, but it also allows you to create spreadsheets, chart and graphs, and illustrations. Unfortunately Apple is no longer working on improving the product.

OpenOffice Writer
Web site: http://www.openoffice.org/product/writer.html
Developer: OpenOffice.org
Cost: Free

Writer is the free alterative to Word created by the OpenOffice volunteer team. It doesn't have every feature that Word or AppleWorks does, but it also doesn't cost a penny. Writer can open and read Microsoft Word documents, so if students are using Word in schools, they can use Writer at home.

Microsoft Word
Web site: http://office.microsoft.com/word
Developer: Microsoft
Cost: Comes pre-installed on many computers; otherwise, the Home and Student Edition of Microsoft Office is around $150.

Microsoft Word is the giant of the word-processing world. We wrote this book, for instance, using Word.

Pre-writing with Word Processors

Tech Specs: Pre-Writing with Word Processors

Set-Up Time: Give yourself 15 minutes to practice using the outline features of your word processor.

Keep-Up Time: None.

In-Class Time: 20 minutes to several periods to complete the outline, depending on the complexity of the topic.

Tech Savvy: Low. Many of your students will already be familiar with these features.

Microsoft Word, Apple's AppleWorks, and OpenOffice Writer all have formatting options that allow students to create outlines. One advantage of creating outlines in a word processor, rather than on paper, is that students can use sections of what they have created in their writing without having to retype anything.

To begin, click *Format* →*Bullets and Numbering* and look at your options (these instructions are the same for Word, AppleWorks, and Writer). Choose the *Outline* tab from the top, and then choose the outline style that you would like to use.

Below are some tips for creating an outline:
- Type your first topic and then hit *Enter*. The next line will automatically be formatted as a topic at the same level.
- To indent the topic to the right and make it a sub-topic, hit the *Tab* key. You can also *right-click* (*control-click* on an Apple) and choose to move things up or down one level.
- At any time you can put the cursor just to the right of the initial letter or number and hit *Tab* to indent the line. If you hit *Delete* right after hitting *Tab,* you can also decrease the indent and move the line to the left.

Word and Writer also have toolbars for modifying outlines. Word's can be found by clicking on *View* →*Toolbars* →*Outlining,* Writer's by clicking *View* →*Toolbars* →*Bullets and Numbering.*

Once students have finished the outline, they can use it as a skeleton for their essays. They should preserve the original essay in one of two ways:

1. Copy the entire outline, and then paste a second copy below the first. Start writing the essay "inside" the second outline by deleting the formatting and expanding words and phrases into complete sentences.
2. Or, click *File* →*Save As* to create a new document with your outline in it. Give the file a new name and start modifying the outline, secure in the knowledge that your original outline is preserved in another file.

Even when students are practicing timed writing at computers for essay tests, encourage your students to spend a few minutes planning and outlining their writing before they dive into the meat of their essay.

Improving Writing Before Typing a Single Word: Setting Word's Grammar Preferences

Tech Specs: Modifying Word's Grammar Preferences

Set-Up Time: It will take you 20 minutes to an hour to familiarize yourself with the grammar preferences and consider which will be most helpful for your students.

Keep-Up Time: Several times a year, it's worth taking some class time to help students update their preferences.

In-Class Time: It will take 15–20 minutes to introduce students to these options and help them customize their preferences.

Tech Savvy: Medium. Most of your students won't be familiar with these options.

It's fairly simple to edit Microsoft Word's preferences to check documents for a whole series of grammatical, spelling, and other types of writing errors. If you are working on a PC, edit preferences by going to *Tools* in the Menu bar and selecting *Options*. If you are using Word 2001 or 2004 on a Mac, click on *Word* in the Menu bar and select *Preferences*.

You'll notice that there are many categories that you can customize to suit your writing requirements. For instance, under the *Spelling and Grammar* tab you can opt to check spelling as you type and have Microsoft Word suggest corrections. Mind you, the more interesting and varied options are found in the *Grammar* section of the *Spelling and Grammar* tab.

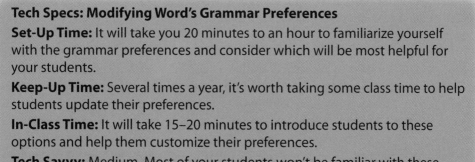

The grammar-checking tools are much more helpful when students are able to take control of the specific options.

Source: Microsoft product screen shot reprinted with permission from Microsoft Corporation.

To take full advantage of Microsoft Word's grammar-checking abilities, make sure the following boxes are selected: *Check grammar as you type, Check grammar with spelling,* and *Show readability statistics.* Word's readability statistics provide the approximate grade level of the writing and the relative ease with which it can be read.

Next to the *Show readability statistics* option is a *Settings* button. Click on it. Choose *Grammar & Style (Formal* in Word for Mac) and you'll notice that you can check a document not only for capitalization, punctuation, and spelling errors, but also for a whole series of writing conventions. Scroll down the list and you'll see that Microsoft Word can check documents for clichés, subject-verb agreement, colloquialisms, contractions, unclear phrasing, wordiness, and much more. Moreover, you can help students learn to place punctuation inside quotation marks (as per the American system) and commas before the last item in a list. After making your choices, click *OK.* You may also have to click a *Recheck this document* button.

You might encourage students who are less-developed writers to select *Grammar* only (*Casual* in Word for Mac), or perhaps suggest they choose only one or two issues for Word to look for. *Grammar* highlights grammar issues only, and not stylistic conventions, making it more appropriate for less-advanced writers. In any event, when students run a spelling and grammar check and are confronted by dozens of potential problems, it can be overwhelming for them, and they may choose to ignore everything. If you instruct students to address a few issues at a time, it can be a more precise and less-intimidating tool and stand a better chance of helping them learn from their mistakes. As students develop as writers and learn to identify and address certain issues, you can encourage them to set Word to check for more grammar conventions. You can also use this feature to individualize your instruction, so different students can be working on different writing conventions at the same time.

Once you have set these options, the next time you check the document with the *Spelling and Grammar* tool (under the *Tools* option in the Menu bar), the document will be much more thoroughly examined.

WEBSITE: Here are three excellent, interactive Web sites that help with grammar and writing conventions:

1. **Online Writing Lab (OWL) at Purdue University** contains hypertext workshops and subject tutorials on writing various types of papers, as well as teacher resources, huge collections of links, PowerPoint presentations about writing, and Web pages that cover all aspects of writing. The Purdue OWL also contains a list of handouts organized by category and a list of interactive practice exercises. Sign up for the free Writing Lab Newsletter for articles and tips: http://owl.english.purdue.edu/.

2. **Guide to Grammar & Writing** is an impressive interactive guide divided into six major categories: Word & Sentence Level; Paragraph Level; Essay & Research Paper Level; Ask Grammar, Quizzes, and Search Devices; Peripheral Devices; and GrammarPoll. There are more than 150 computer-graded quizzes to test knowledge of grammar: http://grammar.ccc.commnet.edu/grammar/.

3. **Rules for Writers: Grammar Exercise** is from the student companion Web site for *Rules for Writers,* fifth edition, by Diane Hacker. It features interactive grammar exercises that correspond to instruction in the book. Hacker is also the author of *A Pocket Style Manual,* and taught English for more than thirty years at Prince George's Community College in Maryland: http://www.dianahacker.com/rules/subpages/gm_menu.asp.

Readability Statistics

When the review is complete, the student will see a series of "Readability Statistics" that indicate the grade level of the writing and the ease with which the essay is read. That information should appear in a pop-up box after you've completed a spelling and grammar check of the document. The Flesch-Kincaid Grade Level score is based on U.S. grade levels; an 8.0 means that the document contains eighth-grade-level writing. The Flesch Reading Ease is rated on a 100-point score; a high score indicates a document that is easier to understand. Both scores are calculated by measuring the average number of words per sentence and the average number of syllables per word, so use the scores as a guideline only.

The Readability Statistics can also provide some averages that lend insight into a writer's habits and tendencies. The Readability Statistics displays both the average number of sentences per paragraph and the average number of words per sentence. You might encourage the student who writes in short, staccato phrases to increase her words per sentence (unless, of course, she is the reincarnation of Hemingway). And you might try and steer the student who includes long, rambling, dirt-road journeys in each paragraph toward trying to reduce her sentences per paragraph. These are certainly crude measurements, but for students with particular tendencies, they might encourage experimentation with new writing styles.

Limitations of Grammar Check

You should also explain to your students that Word's grammar check, while powerful, is not able to catch every error. Consider these examples courtesy of Sandeep Krishnamurthy at the University of Washington (http://faculty.washington.edu/sandeep/check/):

> *Sentences not caught by Microsoft Word's Grammar Check:*
>
> Internets do good job in company name Amazon.
> Internets help marketing big company like Boeing.
> Internets make good brand best like Coca Cola.
> Gates do good marketing job in Microsoft.
> Gates do good marketing jobs out Microsoft.
> Gates build the big brand in Microsoft.
> The Gates is leader of big company in Washington.

Aside from being hilarious, these sentences also suggest that students should not rely on grammar checking to catch all of their grammatical errors.

Working with Word's Spell-Check Tool

The Spell-Check tool can be found under the *Tools* menu in most word processors. Word processors, like AppleWorks and Word, have built-in dictionaries, and the Spell Checker compares words in the document to words in the dictionary.

Some things to remind your students about:

1. Spell checking does NOT replace proofreading. If you use a correctly spelled word incorrectly—like typing "there" when you mean "their"—the Spell Checker won't find that. For instance, the following sentence won't trigger the Spell Checker: "Awl of yore palls want too now if ewe half a reel problem."

2. If the Spell Checker gives you suggestions, don't automatically take the first option from the top of the list. Use a dictionary to help you find the right option.

3. If the Spell Checker doesn't give you any suggestions, use a dictionary to find the correct spelling and then click in the top box of the Spell Checker to manually change the word.

4. The dictionaries in the word processor don't necessarily have every word in them, especially technical or medical terms. If you can confirm that you are spelling a word correctly in a large print or online dictionary, you can tell the Spell Checker to stop highlighting a word by clicking the *Ignore All* option.

5. You can also use the *Add to Dictionary* option so that in the future Word will recognize the highlighted word. This can be very useful for commonly used words like your name, your school name, or your students' names. But be certain you don't do this with a misspelled word!

6. When writing a first draft, the Spell Checker can distract you from getting your good ideas down on paper. Consider disabling the Spell Checker by going to *Tools →Spelling* (sometimes *Tools →Spelling and Grammar*) and clicking *Options* and then unchecking the option *Check spelling as you type.*

WEBSITE: A handout for students that covers this information about writing can be found at http://www.edtechteacher.org/chapter7.html.

Improving Writing with Word Count

Not only is William Strunk's admonishment to "omit needless words" a fine piece of advice, but it also practices what it preaches (unlike the less-well-known "Never use a larger word when a more diminutive one will do)."

The *Word Count* function in Microsoft Word or OpenOffice Writer can help students develop concise prose writing. The function can be found under *Tools →Word Count,* and when selected it displays the number of words, characters, lines, pages, and paragraphs. Students might use this function to be sure that they composed the minimum number of words for an assignment, but it can also be used to help train students to refine their prose.

Lesson Plan for Teaching Concise Writing

Here's a simple writing exercise, spread over three days, for sharpening one's writing:

Day 1: Assign a writing assignment of 280–320 words on any question. Be clear that the complete assignment must fall within the required number of words, and students should use the Word Count tool to be sure they fall within the requirement.

Day 2: In class, explain that the next day's assignment is to edit the first draft down to 180–220 words, without losing any meaning. Again, students should use the Word Count tool to make sure they have exactly the right number of words.

Some hints for students:

1. Look for complete sentences that repeat information and delete them. Make each point once and move on.

2. Look for a series of short sentences that can be combined into a single one. Change *"Beth had superpowers. She could turn invisible. She used these powers*

mostly for good" into "*Beth had the supernatural ability to turn invisible, which she used mostly for good.*"

3. Use possessives instead of prepositional phrases or other long phrases. Write "*Jonas's magical wand*" instead of "*the magical wand of Jonas*" or the mangled "*the magical wand that belonged to Jonas.*"

4. Eliminate unnecessary adverbs, most of which end in -ly. Instead use strong, well-chosen verbs. Use "*Melinda sprinted to the cheeseburger*" instead of "*Melinda ran quickly to the cheeseburger.*"

5. Eliminate passive voice constructions. Write "*Philip saved the drowning poodle*" rather than "*The drowning poodle was saved by Philip.*"

6. Read chapter 13 from Strunk and White's *Elements of Style,* "Omit Needless Words: http://www.bartleby.com/141/strunk5.html#13.

It can actually become a fun game to try to find all the needless words in a sentence, and students recognize the improved sound of the revised language. Find one brave volunteer, and project his or her first draft onto a screen, and then have the entire class come up with suggestions for making the draft less wordy. If you have the ability to project directly onto a white board, you can use colored markers to "edit" the projected image and to help students better see changes.

Day 3: The final task is to get the original draft down to between 140–160 words, or half as long as the original. Keep in mind the words of Blaise Pascal: "The present letter is a very long one, simply because I had no leisure to make it shorter."

Improving Writing with the Find Command

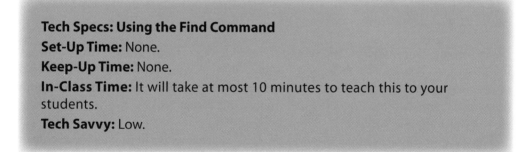

Tech Specs: Using the Find Command
Set-Up Time: None.
Keep-Up Time: None.
In-Class Time: It will take at most 10 minutes to teach this to your students.
Tech Savvy: Low.

One of the best tools for improving student writing is also one of the simplest: the *Find* command. Press *Control-F* (*Apple-F* on Macs), and you will bring up the *Find and Replace* window.

Many teachers keep some sort of list of "no-no" words, "boring" words, or "words that slowly destroy Mr. Reich's soul"—words like "a lot," "good," "I think," and the dreaded "in conclusion." These words are singled out for revision in part because they are so common, and teachers often require that these words be excised and replaced. The *Find* command makes it easy to find these criminal terms. Ask students to put the words in the *Find What* box and then click *Find Next.* The word processor will highlight the offending word, and the student can find an alternative, and then click *Find Next* again to move on to the next offense.

With the Find function, you can search for, and get rid of, mundane words such as "okay."
Source: Microsoft product screen shot reprinted with permission from Microsoft Corporation.

Here are some other elements of weak language to search for:

1. **Weak Verbs:** Have students find and replace "there is," "there was," "there are," and "there were" for more active, lively verbs.
2. **Adverbs:** When using the *Find* command, you don't have to search for whole words. Enter "ly" and you can find most adverbs and then eliminate unnecessary ones.
3. **First and Second Person:** In essays where "I" and "you" are inappropriate, these can be found and revised.
4. **Commonly Misused Homonyms:** If you know a student has trouble with "there," "their'" and "they're," use *Find* to search them out, as the Spell Check tool may not catch the problem.

For students who repeatedly make the same error, the *Find* command can be a powerful tool for improving their writing.

Saving Files

It can be quite frustrating to deal with different file types from different word processing programs. Fortunately, there is a file type that all word-processors read: the rich text format, or .rtf. To save files in this type, choose *File →Save As* and then look for a dropdown menu that says *Save As Type.* Choose this format and require your students to choose this format as well.

The .rtf files are smaller and more secure than .doc and other files, which can contain viruses.

Peer Editing with Word Processors

Tech Specs: Peer Editing with Word Processors

Set-Up Time: Expect to spend a few minutes modifying some of our example rubrics to meet your needs.

Keep-Up Time: None.

In-Class Time: Budget 20 minutes to a whole period to let students peer edit. If you can count on students having access to email at home, you can also have them exchange papers for peer editing for homework.

Tech Savvy: Low.

Educators know that the best way to learn something is to teach it. One of the best ways to learn to write, therefore, is to edit other people's writing.

Creating a classroom environment that fosters honest, supportive communication is a key prerequisite to good peer editing. Students need to feel like their peers will provide helpful criticism without harsh tones or unkind words. In face-to-face settings, students are likely to be too gentle with their peers, while in online settings, students will often critique more vigorously and sometimes too harshly. Students need to be coached to provide specific feedback that identifies problems and offers encouragement.

Students need guidance on how to provide feedback, so teachers should provide students with either peer-editing worksheets or copies of the grading rubric that the teacher plans on using. If the rubrics are built only of numbers to be circled, then they should be modified to include space to write specific suggestions.

All of this can be done electronically. Teachers can email rubrics or worksheets to their students, students can email their papers back and forth or transfer them with thumb drives, and students can email their revisions back to the author and the teacher.

A very simple peer-editing rubric to help guide students in editing might include just a space to compliment the author and spaces to offer specific criticisms and suggestions. Here is an example:

Peer Editing Rubrics:

Your Name:_____

Author's Name:_____

Title of Work:_____

Provide three specific compliments for the author:

1.

2.

3.

Provide three specific suggestions to improve the paper:

1.

2.

3.

Provide three specific constructive criticisms about the work:

1.

2.

3.

Tom's Essay-Writing Checklist

Tom's Essay-Writing Checklist is designed to help students write more purposeful and cohesive essays and eliminate common writing errors. The idea is to focus students on addressing their essay topics in a direct, clear, and persuasive manner and to ensure that students include relevant, well-chosen, and clearly explained examples and illustrations.

The Checklist reminds students of the importance of the thesis statement and that the introduction should be clear and lively and provide concise but necessary context. As for the body paragraphs, the Checklist guides students to create clear and direct topic sentences that help support the thesis statement. It places emphasis on the incorporation of relevant and persuasive supporting evidence and encourages students to anticipate and neutralize opposing arguments. The Checklist also guides students to craft effective restatements of their thesis statements and major points of their essays, as well as provide final forceful assertions of the importance of their essays.

Essay-Writing Checklist _____

Introduction

❏ The introduction includes an opening sentence that grabs the reader's attention.

❏ The writer does a satisfactory (and brief) job of informing the reader of the topic (who?, what?, where?, when?, why?, how?).

❏ The introduction has a clear, direct, and arguable thesis statement that answers the question and offers a decisive opinion.

Comments:

Body

❏ All the paragraphs in the body have clear topic sentences that relate directly to the topic of the essay and help support the thesis statement.

❏ The evidence in each body paragraph supports the topic sentence in that paragraph and, thus, supports the thesis statement.

❏ The evidence includes material from primary sources that has been clearly identified and has been either quoted or paraphrased.

❏ All the body paragraphs have a "punch" or tie-in sentence that reinforces the paragraph's main idea and supports the thesis statement. (The body paragraphs may also, but are not required to, contain a transitional sentence.)

❏ Evidence, events, or issues that may strongly contradict the writer's thesis statement and arguments have not been ignored in the body, but have been effectively counter attacked or neutralized.

Comments:

Conclusion

- ❑ The conclusion includes a restatement of the thesis statement and the major points in the body.
- ❑ The conclusion makes a connection to a broader theme or related topic that is relevant and underlines the importance of the essay.
- ❑ The writer has made a final, forceful attempt to persuade you of the correctness of his or her thesis statement and the importance of the topic in general.

Comments:

Spelling and Grammar

You have checked for the following common errors :
- ❑ Their/there/they're
- ❑ To/too/two; lose/ loose
- ❑ Its/it's; then/than
- ❑ Your/ you're; a lot
- ❑ Were/where/we're
- ❑ Missing or incorrect capitalization
- ❑ Incorrect pronoun reference—one, he/she, they, your, etc. (Canada = it; Canadians = they)
- ❑ Comma splices, run-on sentences (join independent clauses by semi-colon or split into two sentences)
- ❑ Inconsistent tense (was, is, will be); history essays are usually in the past tense
- ❑ Apostrophes for possessives (Tom's house, the city's leader)

Comments:

Name of author of essay _____   Your name_____

My "buddy" has provided me with a completed rough draft that I have reviewed and edited. I provided comments and suggestions to improve the essay. (Your signature) _____

Tom's Essay-Writing Checklist helps peer editors identify basic conventions of structured and persuasive writing.

Justin's Essay Rubrics

These rubrics are designed to allow the teacher and students to comment extensively on student writing without needing to spend inordinate time doing so. Students are evaluated in seven categories, and the most common comments that might be applied to a student's paper are provided for each of those seven categories. Thus the reviewer, whether a teacher or student, just needs to highlight the appropriate comments. Space is also available in the rubric to provide comments specific to the essay.

This example is a rubric modified for evaluating an essay on the civil rights movement.

CIVIL RIGHTS MOVEMENT ESSAY RUBRIC

Name:	Getting Started 1	Approaching Standard 2	Meets Standards 3	Exceeds Standard 4
Overall	Essay disorganized, unclear, or not persuasive. Thesis not defended. Topic poorly explained.	Essay argues thesis. Incomplete support from evidence. Some confusing lines of argumentation. Essay describes rather than explains.	**Thesis argued with specific evidence and clear argumentation. Interesting interpretation of source material. Essay explains the efficacy of nonviolence.**	Thesis persuasively argued with specific evidence, elegant argumentation, and original interpretation of source material.

Comments:
-you use great evidence
-polish up your thesis so it is clear and explains exactly what you will be arguing
-you explore and tie in the Christian religion very well

| **Introduction** | Topic unclear. Main points of essay unclear. **Thesis unclear.** | **Topic introduced. Some main points of essay introduced.** Thesis describes rather than explains. | Clear and decisive thesis that explains a causal (cause-and-effect) relationship. Main points of essay introduced. | Thesis and main points elegantly introduced. Thesis particularly original or insightful. Introduction grabs readers attention. |

Comments:
I am not quite sure what your thesis is. Both the first and last sentence of the paragraph introduce some main points, but it is hard to distinguish what you are going to talk about in your body paragraphs. Introduce nonviolence in the civil rights movement, explain your main points, and then have your thesis be the last sentence of your intro.

| **Body Paragraphs** | Paragraphs disorganized or insufficient. | Some body paragraphs begin with a topic sentence and present one idea cohesively. | **Body paragraphs have topic sentences, present one idea clearly, and are linked with transitional sentences.** | Each paragraph reads with the clarity of a mini-essay, and the paragraphs seamlessly transition from one to the next. |

Comments:
-good topic sentences
-good use of examples and good explanation of examples

| **Conclusion** | Main argument restated with recycled language. | **Central argument restated in similar language.** | Central argument restated with different language. Broader significance of arguments explored. | Central argument persuasively reexamined using the developed evidence. Broader significance of essay explained. |

Comments:
-you have not finished this paragraph, but just make sure you bring up a new point in your conclusion

| **Analysis** | Essay is focused on narration and summary rather than analysis and interpretation. | Essay in some parts is driven by analysis rather than narration. Some parts of argument refer back to thesis. Connections are limited. | Essay is driven by analysis rather than narration. Analysis serves to support and reinforce thesis. Connections are made amongst paragraphs. | **Essay showcases a sophisticated and/or original interpretation of historical events. Disparate historical elements are synthesized.** |

Comments:
-you use historical examples very well; they support the point you are trying to make very well
-your paragraphs are all connected in a way and you do a great job transitioning into new paragraphs

| **Evidence** | Minimal evidence presented. Citation incorrect; evidence presented without citation or works cited missing. | General evidence supports thesis. Significance of some evidence unclear. Missing some types of sources. | Specific evidence supports the thesis. Significance of evidence is clear. Evidence is gathered from multiple sources. | **Significant, specific evidence persuasively supports the thesis. Clear indications of original interpretation of sources.** |

Comments:
-you use a lot of different evidence...quotes from people, historical examples, etc.
-you explain your examples and how they relate back to and support the point you are making

| **Grammar, Style, and Proofreading** | Grammar and usage obstruct the paper's meaning. | Grammar errors are distracting to the reader. Several errors. | **Only one or two grammatical errors. Paper reads easily.** | Paper is free of grammatical errors. Paper reads easily and style supports the argument. |

Comments:
-grammar is great
-writing gets a little choppy and hard to understand at some times

This rubric that Justin gives to his students for peer editing is the very same rubric he'll use to grade this paper.

PENCIL: If you do a lot of peer editing throughout the year, keep a stash of blank, generic rubrics in your classroom. That way if you plan to use computers for peer editing but something goes wrong, you'll have a ready backup.

WEBSITE: These rubrics and several others can be downloaded and modified at http://www.edtechteacher.org/chapter7.html.

Simple Word Processing Tools for Peer Editing

Three tools that are very useful for inserting comments in an essay include the **bold** typeface, the change font color function, and the highlight function.

Boldface type can be inserted by hitting *Control-B* (*Apple-B* on Macs) before typing or by clicking the large, dark **B** button on the top toolbar. This is probably the easiest way of interjecting a comment into someone else's writing.

The font color can be changed in the *Format →Font* menu or by using the font color dropdown menu in the *Formatting* toolbar. The highlighter can typically be found right next to the font color tool. These tools work as well as inserting bold type, but they require more clicking with the mouse.

Peer editors should recommend changes with these tools rather than directly changing or revising the original wording of the paper. That way, authors can evaluate the comments of their editors before making any changes.

If this entire process takes place electronically, with students emailing papers back and forth, editors are much more likely to be harsher critics. It's much tougher to deliver criticism with the person sitting right next to you. Depending on the dynamics in your classroom, this can be for good or for ill. Coach students to be sure that they are giving helpful, specific, and critical feedback and also providing support and encouragement.

Peer Editing with Track Changes

A more complex editing function built into Word is the Track Changes system. This system lets you edit and make changes directly in the document without permanently modifying the original document. It is especially useful when several people are reviewing the same document.

To start the function, click on *Tools →Track Changes*. A new toolbar will appear with one button automatically depressed: the *Track Changes* button. (You may have to go to *View →Toolbars →Reviewing* to see this toolbar.) When this button is pressed, new text added will be underlined and in red (red is the default color, though you can choose others in the *Preferences* menu). Any text that is deleted or modified will appear in a bubble to the right of the document. Pressing the *Insert Comment* button will allow you to type comments that appear in the right margin and are connected to a specific area in the document by a dotted line (in older versions of Word, these comments will appear at the bottom of the page).

Reviewers use these tools to edit and make commentary inside a document, and when they save the document, the edits and comments are preserved. The author can open the document, and then use the same tools to accept or reject the changes. The buttons with arrows in the toolbar move the cursor to the next or previous change, and the check button and the *X* button accept and reject the proposed changes.

These buttons allow the writer to move through the changes of the editor and accept or reject the changes.

Source: Microsoft product screen shot reprinted with permission from Microsoft Corporation.

It's a slick interface and popular in the workplace, but it does require that all students have access to Microsoft Word. It's also a little more time-consuming to teach than teaching students to insert commentary with the bold key.

WEBSITE: For a video tutorial about using Microsoft Word's Track Changes function, go to http://www.edtechteacher.org/chapter7.html.

Peer Editing or Workshopping with Blogs

Blogs, with their built-in comment functions, are natural places for certain kinds of peer editing. Word processors are better environments for editing long pieces or getting into the nitty-gritty of spelling, grammar, and sentence structure. But for making a document available to many people who can offer more holistic comments, blogs are a terrific environment. Blogs can create conditions similar to a writers' workshop rather than the one-to-one author and editor relationship. (For a fuller explanation of blogs, refer to Chapter 2, "Discussion and Communication.")

If you have a system where each student has his or her own blog, then you can assign students to post their writing assignments to their blogs and then visit the blogs of their peers and comment on their work.

If you have just one class blog, it might be best to take turns posting student writing to the blog, where each week (or a few times a week) one student-author gets to receive extensive feedback from the rest of the class. Conversations about writing naturally evolve from this model, where the students comment both on the posted writing and on the feedback of others. Dialogue and debate can emerge about how best to improve the featured piece of writing.

Students who would be terrified to share their work in class can be much bolder with the distance provided by the Internet. Similarly students who might never comment on another student's writing in class might feel safer posting a comment on a blog.

BEYOND THE ESSAY: USING WORD PROCESSORS TO DEVISE NEW ASSESSMENTS

When the idea of a stack of 75 papers on the same topic starts to seem a little daunting, here are some great ways to get students writing without you having to read the same old essay over and over again.

Editing with a Twist

Tech Specs: Editing with a Twist
Set-Up Time: 30–60 minutes to create a new writing assignment or modify an old one.
Keep-Up Time: None.
In-Class Time: It will take perhaps 10 minutes to explain the assignment during the first class and then a full period for students to edit in the second class.
Tech Savvy: Low.

In this exercise, students prepare a piece of writing with the expectation that they will have one class period in the computer lab to refine their work. When they arrive, give them a surprise that requires them to alter their writing as they revise.

Example: Sermon in Birmingham

In this assignment, students who have studied Christianity and the civil rights movement are asked to compose a sermon to be delivered on September 15, 1963, right in the heart of the Birmingham campaign and two weeks after the March on Washington.

Instructions to students:

1. Write a two-page sermon, drawing on the New Testament readings we have read for homework and in class. The sermon will be delivered on September 16, 1963, in Birmingham. This is several weeks after the successful March on Washington, and right in the middle of the heroic and brutal Birmingham Campaign for Civil Rights. Your sermon should use Christianity to inspire, console, and motivate your congregation.
2. Please use Times New Roman 12 point font with 1.5 spacing.
3. Save it to the school server or your thumb drive. If you use a program other than Word or Appleworks, you should copy and paste the text into an email or a document.
4. At the beginning of class I will give you instructions, and then I'll give you about 30 minutes to revise the sermon.

When students arrive in class—with a digital copy of their two-page sermon—they get set up at their computers and then receive this information:

> After successfully presenting your sermon at the morning service, you retire to your quarters to rest before the 11:00 service. At 10:30, one of the church members rushes in and tells you that something horrible has happened: the 16th Street Baptist Church in Birmingham has been bombed; four little girls at Sunday school have been killed.
>
> As an important leader in your community, it will be your job to console people, and to help them understand how these deaths fit into the struggle for civil rights.
>
> The second service starts in half an hour. You probably don't have time to write a whole new sermon. Your challenge, then, is to adapt what you have written to take into account this shattering loss of innocent lives.
>
> Good luck; your congregation is depending on you.

Students are also given an excerpt from "Six Dead After Church Bombing," an article from September 16, 1963, by United Press International, which can be found here: http://www.washingtonpost.com/wp-srv/national/longterm/churches/archives1.htm.

Students are then evaluated on their ability to revise their sermon to mourn the loss of life, to motivate their congregations to press on with the civil rights movement, and to support their assertions with evidence from the New Testament.

The editing tools available in word processors enable students to revise their writing based on new information without necessarily starting from scratch, making engaging "twist" exercises like this one possible.

Writing Newspapers or Magazines

Tech Specs: Designing Historical Newspapers or Magazines

Set-Up Time: Plan on spending at least 30 minutes familiarizing yourself with some of the formatting tools that might help students make a newsletter. It will probably take another 30–60 minutes to create an appropriate assignment, but you can find several newspaper-type projects on the Web.

Keep-Up Time: None.

Classroom Time: Anywhere from three periods to several weeks.

Tech Savvy: Low to medium.

A newspaper or magazine can be a terrific collaborative project, combining writing, editing, design, and teamwork into a single assignment.

A newspaper layout can be easily created in word processors using two tools: the *Text Box* and *Columns*.

Text boxes are inaptly named; you can put images and other things in them as well.

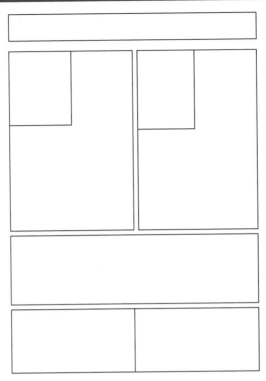

The *text box* is a useful tool for creating simple layout and design, and each box can be filled with text or even an image.
Source: Microsoft product screen shot reprinted with permission from Microsoft Corporation.

They simply act as placeholders. To draw a text box, click on *Insert* → *Text Box* and then click and drag the mouse to draw a box on the document. Once the box is drawn, you can click and drag on the corners of a text box to enlarge or shrink it.

A long rectangular text box along the top of a page can be a newspaper banner. A short vertical text box in the lower left-hand corner can be a table of contents. The front page can contain several different small text boxes with story leads and then the rest of the articles in text boxes on subsequent pages. Students can jazz up their newsletters with digital photographs or images from the Web that are copied and pasted into text boxes. With a little formatting work, your students can create a slick-looking newspaper in short order.

Another tool that can be helpful is the *Column* tool. Click on *Format* →*Columns* to reveal a window of options for formatting with Columns. Using this tool, a page can easily be broken up into two or three columns like a newsletter. This is simpler than formatting with text boxes, though the boxes have more flexibility. You can also combine these tools, inserting text boxes onto pages formatted with columns.

PENCIL: If you don't have enough computers to go around, or you can't use them every day of this project, your students can still make progress on their articles. They can mock up a layout for the newspaper with pencils and paper, and they can also peer edit printed copies of each other's articles.

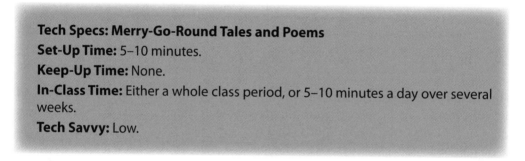

Using columns can help easily create the appearance of a newspaper or periodicals.

Source: Microsoft product screen shot reprinted with permission from Microsoft Corporation.

Merry-Go-Round Tales

Tech Specs: Merry-Go-Round Tales and Poems
Set-Up Time: 5–10 minutes.
Keep-Up Time: None.
In-Class Time: Either a whole class period, or 5–10 minutes a day over several weeks.
Tech Savvy: Low.

When you need a break from the regular routine, try this very silly writing exercise.

Ask each of your students to begin a story with 1–2 sentences in an email editor or word processor. Give them 2–3 minutes, and then have them email those introductions to a classmate; it can help to create a rotation. Everyone should then get another 2–3 minutes to write another 1–2 sentences.

The writers should then change the font color of the first few sentences to white font on a white background, rendering the original text invisible. Students should once again email around their stories. When the next student receives the emailed story, he or she should again add a few sentences and turn the previous sentences to white font on white background. In this way, the story progresses, though each student can see only the previous few lines and not the entire story.

This activity can be modified in a few ways. It works just as well with poems as with prose. If you are in a computer lab and don't want to futz with email, you can have the students change seats instead of sending the files. You can also set up this activity to take place over several days or weeks, with students adding 1–2 sentences for homework each night, or as a warm-up to class. However you choose to run the exercise, be sure to read a few aloud in class or post all of them to your class blogs. A few are guaranteed to be hilarious.

Writing to Others: Letters to the Editor, Editorials, and Communicating with Other Real People

As mentioned in Chapter 2, "Discussion and Communication," great writing projects can include letters to newspaper editors, to writers, to professors, and to anyone else with email, which is just about everyone. Have students direct their thoughts to people in the wider world rather than just you, the teacher.

WRITING COLLABORATIVELY WITH WIKIS

A wiki is essentially an encyclopedic Web site that anyone can edit, making it the perfect tool to enable teams and classes to write together. Wikis can be in-house sites meant to serve a limited number of editors or wide-open sites where almost anyone can contribute. The most famous example of a wiki is Wikipedia, an online encyclopedia whose articles are edited by volunteers and whose content is subject to change by nearly anyone. Wikipedia is one of the most popular reference sites on the Web, with around 60 million hits per day. (See Chapter 5, "Open Research," for our take on Wikipedia.) The term "wiki" comes from a Hawaiian word meaning quick.

WEB 2.0 OR THE READ/WRITE WEB:

Much ink has been spilled heralding innovations known collectively as Web 2.0 or the "Read/Write Web" that allow users to contribute to the sprawling Web. *Time* magazine's decision to make "You" the 2006 Person of the Year—if you added content to the Web—marked the ascendance of a series of Web-based tools that allows people to do that easily. Blogs and wikis are the most frequently mentioned tools with educational applications in the Read/Write Web, though Bernie Dodge's WebQuest creation tool fits well into this category. Flickr, a photo-sharing Web site, and YouTube, a video-sharing Web site, are two other popular vehicles for ordinary citizens to add to the Web. Social-networking sites, like Facebook and MySpace, represent another avenue for people to make their mark on the global Internet.

What should educators make of all this? Well, if the best way to learn how to write is to write, then young people have many more venues in which to share their thoughts through writing, with audiences as intimate as their circle of friends and as wide as the rest of the world. There are some safety concerns related to online predators and other wackos, but a few commonsense reminders (like Don't Post Personal Information on the Web) can steer kids clear of much danger. If educators can use the hype and excitement of these tools to get students to do more writing and communicating, then Web 2.0 can be a significant step forward for educators who use technology in their classrooms.

Why Wiki?

Wikis are a pretty exciting technology for classroom teachers, and these are just some of the reasons why:

- Students, teachers, and even parents can collaborate to gather, edit, and present information on a wiki.

- A wiki can be used to build a classroom dictionary of terms in a subject area. For example, students could build a list of historical or literary definitions for a course.
- Students can also use a wiki as a class notes page that serves as a study guide for tests. Each student could contribute a set of notes and add comments to existing notes.
- Another idea is to break kids up into small groups for a project or activity and have them paste their work on a wiki. One could then invite other student groups to comment.
- Wikis are a great medium for peer editing and workshopping papers, poems, and other forms of writing, since multiple people can contribute thoughts to the same document.
- Wikis can also be used to enhance professional collaboration. For example, teachers in a department or district could build a curriculum unit together or simply post their lessons and assignments.
- A teacher can post words for students to expand into definitions.
- Students can research new topics and contribute their findings.
- Students can use the wiki to prepare for a final exam, like an AP test. Students can each be given responsibilities for a given set of topics.
- A wiki can be used as a portfolio showing development of a project.
- Teams of teachers who instruct core courses can develop and edit curricula together.

A wiki is a great option if you want to create a space where students can collaborate on a project or series of projects and with the increasing and immense popularity of Wikipedia, students and teachers are becoming increasingly familiar with the look and navigation style of wikis.

Anatomy of a Wiki

Wikis can be designed with a wide variety of templates, but most wikis have three basic sections: a *navigation sidebar* on the left, *page-editing tabs* on the top, and information in the body of the page.

A well-designed navigation sidebar will have links to important sections of the wiki or, perhaps, for larger wikis like Wikipedia, a search function.

The page editing tabs typically have one tab for the article of the page, one tab for discussion concerning the contents of the page, one tab for history of who has edited the page and when, and one tab for directly editing the page.

The body of the page can contain text, internal links to other sections of the wiki, external links to anything else on the Web, and images and other media. Editing a wiki page does not require knowledge of HTML or other programming languages.

Four Wiki Examples

Tom Daccord's U.S. History Wiki

For Tom's U.S. History class wiki, students took turns posting their homework assignments using a variety of formats, including Inspiration concept maps (see Chapter 3, "Note Taking and Organization"). Tom also provides links to other resources, like study guides and online quizzes (see Chapter 9, "Assessment and Grading") that he has created.

Tom uses his classroom wiki to create a set of collaborative notes for students to consult when writing essays or preparing for tests. Students can create their notes using Microsoft Word or another program and then paste them into the classroom wiki. Tom organizes the wiki by setting up sections and pages to which the students will post. He

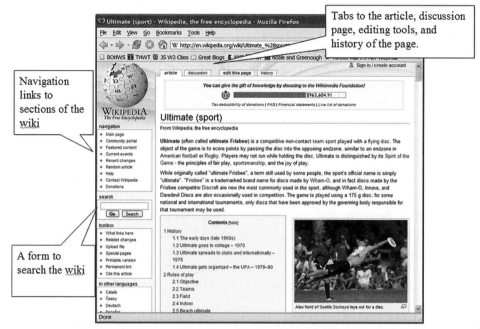

Tabs to the article, discussion page, editing tools, and history of the page.

Navigation links to sections of the wiki

A form to search the wiki

Well-designed wikis are easy to navigate and intuitive to use.

also includes his own notes as well as images and other types of illustrative content. One of the advantages of the wiki is that students have a shared set of notes that they consult and edit as needed. It encourages collective student ownership of the material and creates an archive of notes that could potentially be of service to other classes or even to other schools. To see Tom's wiki, go to http://nobilis.nobles.edu/tcl/doku.php, follow the link to *Courses*, and then choose his 2006–2007 U.S. History course.

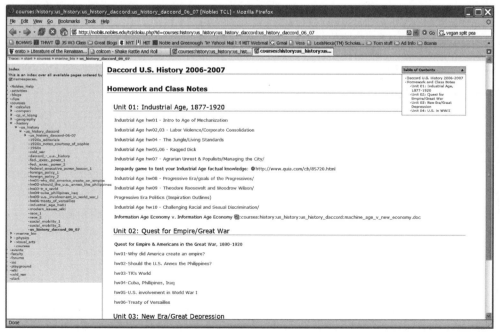

Organized by unit and then by assignment, Tom's wiki provides an interactive database for his students.

Dr. Reich's Chemistry Wiki

http://reich-chemistry.wikispaces.com/

Dr. Blair Jesse Ellyn Reich is a chemistry teacher at Natick High School in Natick, Massachusetts, who has created a fabulous instructional wiki. Students in his various classes consult the wiki for weekly assignments, projects, notes, ideas, labs, and instructional videos. Dr. Reich's engaging "Video Labs" and "Video Lectures" are quite popular and are watched by many more people than just his students!

Dan McDowell's AP World History Wiki

http://www.ahistoryteacher.com/~ahistory/apwhreview/index.php?title=AP_World_History_Review_Wiki

To be inspired by usefulness and simplicity, visit this gem of a review page by Dan McDowell's class in San Diego. McDowell organized his students into groups to review for the World History AP exam and created a simple, well-organized, streamlined wiki project.

The pages are written by students and have simple formatting, basic text, and a few images. This is a great model for a teacher embarking on a first wiki project.

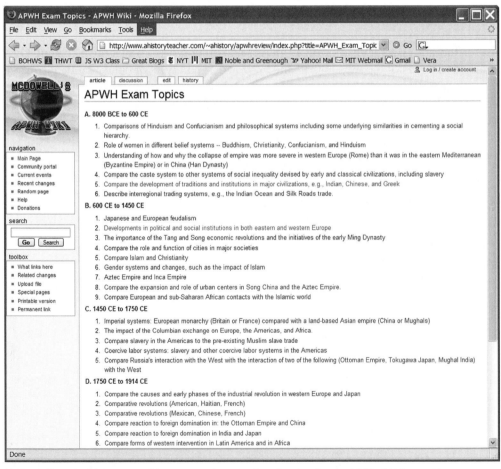

McDowell used wikis to create this great, student-produced review for the AP World History test.
Source: Courtesy of Dan McDowell.

Flat Classroom Project

http://flatclassroomproject.wikispaces.com/

This more sophisticated project shows off more of the advanced possibilities of wikis. In this project, students in Georgia and Bangladesh worked together to research and explore topics from Thomas Friedman's book *The World Is Flat*. Each article was co-designed by students on two continents and includes texts, images, tables of contents, and videos that were produced by students, uploaded to Google video, and then embedded in the wiki.

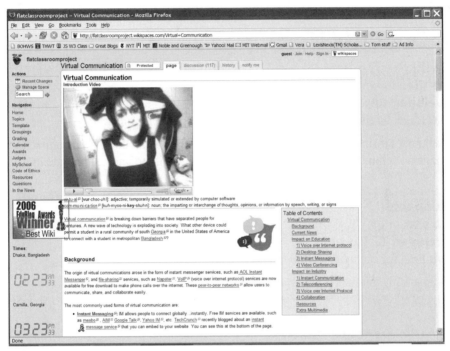

The Flat Classroom Project wiki, produced by students on opposite sides of the globe, shows the unifying potential of classroom wikis.   *Source:* Courtesy of Vicki Davis and Julie Lindsay.

Visit this site and be sure to look at the discussion pages, where you can follow the conversations that students shared from across the world as they created this wiki.

Your First Wiki Project

Tech Specs: Getting Started with Wikis

Set-Up Time: Plan on investing at least an afternoon in learning about wikis and designing your own.

Keep-Up Time: If you use it regularly, you will need to budget at least an hour a week to monitor and update your wiki.

In-Class Time: Depends on how you use it.

Tech Savvy: Medium to high. Wikis are still very new to most people, so there is some unfamiliarity. They are not the simplest tools, but they are very powerful. Most people will find it quite possible to design and manage a basic wiki.

Choosing a Wiki Host

The easiest way to get started with wikis is to choose a wiki provider that will host your Web sites, offer basic templates, and have a simple interface. Right now, http://www .pbwiki.com/ and http://www.wikispaces.com/ are two good choices. Simple wikis with PBwiki are currently free, with premium pages costing $10 a month. Wikispaces is offering free wikis to the first 100,000 educators to sign up, and they have 25,000 left, so you might still get in there after this goes to print. Otherwise, plans start at $5 a month.

FEATURED PRODUCTS

PBwiki
Web site: http://www.pbwiki.com/
Developer: PBwiki
Cost: Basic wikis are free, and premium wikis are $10/month.

PBwiki uses a simple, Web-based interface so that you can design, customize, and manage an online wiki that your students can contribute to and collaborate in.

Wikispaces
Web site: http://www.wikispaces.com/
Developer: Tangient LLC
Cost: Free for the next 25,000 teachers who sign up

Wikispaces is another popular and functional Web-based wiki-creation tool.

Ten Steps to Starting a PBwiki

Step 1: Register for a Wiki. Getting started with PBwiki is quite simple. Choose a site name, which will be the Web address, and submit your email.

Step 2: Confirm Your Wiki. A second page will be loaded that announces that PBwiki has sent you a confirmation email, and it includes a little movie introducing you to PBwiki.

Step 3: Choose a Password and Settings. Open up your email, find the email from PBwiki, and open the link to a confirmation page. Answer the basic questions, and be sure to choose to use the new WYSIWYG editor. WYSIWYG stands for What You See Is What You Get and is pronounced something like wizzy-wig. In general, things that are WYSIWYG are simple and good.

When you choose your password, remember that you will need to share this password with your colleagues or students to enable them to edit the wiki.

Click the *Take me to my wiki* button to get started.

Step 4: View Your New Wiki. The text you see on your home page is given to you by PBwiki, but you will want to soon delete the "Welcome to your PBwiki" message and replace that with your own text.

You can start making changes or adding new pages by clicking the *Edit Page* and *New Page* buttons at the top and bottom of the page. If you ever get lost, click the *Home* button or the name of your wiki to return to your home page.

When you get to your new wiki, you will see a home page similar to this one.
Source: Courtesy of PBwiki.

Step 5: Explore the Sidebar. You will notice that the PBwiki does not include the left hand navigation bar common to Wikipedia and most wikis. Instead, it has a sidebar box on the right-hand side of each page that has QuickStart links for creating new pages, a Recent Activity tab to see who has been changing your page, and a sidebar with a small *Edit* button in the corner.

If you click the sidebar *Edit* button, you can replace the introductory text with your own text. The sidebar should include links to the most important pages on your wiki and any other basic information students or colleagues need to understand how to navigate your page.

Before editing the sidebar, let's create a new page so we have something to link to!

Step 6: Create a New Page. From the front page of your wiki, click the *New Page* button to create a new page. PBWiki has three handy templates for educators, so perhaps start by choosing a classroom page. The templates are previewed on the right. Type the name of the page in the form on the top left and your new page will blossom into existence.

Step 7: Edit your New Page. When you choose a template, you will be taken to a page editor pre-loaded with sample information that you should replace.

If you look at the buttons at the top of the page, you will see commands that should be familiar to you from word processors.

You can use boldface type, italics, bullets, numbers, different font colors, and background colors, and you can make all sorts of other changes.

The editing bar toward the top of the page provides you with many different options for formatting your page. In this example Justin is modifying a template.   *Source:* Courtesy of PBWiki.

Step 8: Create a Link. Several of the buttons will bring up additional menus that will guide you through the creation of advanced features, like adding links, photos, or other features.

To add a link, click the *Add Link* button and then follow the instructions on the menus. Creating internal links is particularly easy; just choose the name of the page from the dropdown menu.

Step 9: Rename your Wiki. Click on the *Settings* button from your front page to get to the settings menu. The first option lets you rename your wiki. Other options let you change or add different features to your wiki, like setting up passwords, creating different templates, and so on.

Step 10: Share your Password. Once you give someone a password to the wiki, they'll be able to change any part of it. You'll need to be clear with your students that they must follow the school's acceptable use policy (AUP) and your classroom guidelines for using the wiki.

If anyone does cause any serious damage to a page, you as the administrator can use the history button on the bottom of each page to look at earlier versions (as well as the name of the miscreant) and can revert back to those versions. No one can really permanently damage your wiki.

And that's it! If you can create a new page, add links, and edit your wiki's name, that's really all you need to be able to do to start compiling a wiki project. The PBwiki tools have a great depth of editing features, so you can learn to do much more if you choose to. But if you just want to create a space for students to collaborate on writing projects—peer editing, exam reviews, or research—then those basic tools are all you really need!

FINAL THOUGHTS

Of all the things we have discussed in this chapter, some of the tools for evaluating writing—the Find command, the grammar-checking preferences, the readability statistics, the Word Count command—are especially exciting because of the way they change the relationships among students, teachers, and writing. In the past, students wrote, and teachers identified the mistakes. Students would go back and correct them; rinse and repeat.

The new tools discussed above empower student to evaluate their own writing. They can now mine a fair amount of data about their writing without the help of their teachers. With a better ability to evaluate themselves, we can focus more on teaching them how to fix one example of a particular error, rather than spending our time identifying the same errors throughout an essay. Ideally, students who understand their writing better will be better equipped to improve their writing.

All new technologies have a variety of positive and negative effects, and they always come with a group of prophets decrying the doom of the future. When it comes to computers and writing, the naysayers lament that all good habits of spelling, convention, and decency will come crumbling down once everyone is emailing and instant messaging. Perhaps. But students are also doing more writing—emailing back and forth between friends, chatting with the written word using instant messaging, and chronicling their lives through blogs in a glut of diarists—than we have seen in this country since the nineteenth century. Some things may decay, but in the best-case scenarios, teachers will use these changes to demonstrate to students the power of the written word and the importance of communicating clearly, and teachers will then give students new tools to improve their command of prose.

Chapter 8

Student Presentations

Introduction

Student PowerPoint Presentations

Recording and Editing Audio for Podcasting

Screencasting

Building Simple Web Sites with Google Page Creator

Final Thoughts

INTRODUCTION

Powerful multimedia publishing tools that once could only be found in major studios are now available free with new computers or on the Web. With practice, broadcasting a radio show, making a video tutorial, creating slides for a lecture, or designing a simple Web page can be done in a few short class periods. Using these new tools, we can now let students demonstrate their understanding and learning in a much wider array of media.

Moreover, creative assignments that use technology can help diversify and broaden our assignments and teaching methods. We may also discover that teaching with multimedia tools can help us learn more about our students by providing them with opportunities to excel in areas not consistently addressed in pen-and paper activities.

The Web also allows students to publish their work easily for a wider audience. Student writing can be posted to blogs or wikis, students can upload their videos to YouTube or Google Video, and student podcasts can be presented as online radio shows. Increasingly, students have the ability not just to find things on the Web but also to make meaningful contributions to it.

STUDENT POWERPOINT PRESENTATIONS

We discussed PowerPoint for teachers in Chapter 1, "Lectures," and the principles of good slide design that we laid out for teachers also apply for student presentations. When students will be orating alongside their slides, they need to keep things simple, focus on visual media, and use text as prompts without trying to put an entire lecture on the slides.

PowerPoint, however, can be used to create more than just lecture slides. Students can also create a variety of self-contained presentations, like slide shows with voice-over narration, that can be viewed independently.

In this section we focus on PowerPoint because it is the most commonly used presentation software in schools. But simply being the most common doesn't necessarily make it the best. Apple's Keynote software is an excellent alternative. And while PowerPoint may be the most common presentation software in schools, many students don't have access to PowerPoint at home. If you hope to have students work on presentations for homework, your classroom, college, or school district should seriously consider adopting OpenOffice's Impress, which has many of the same features as PowerPoint, but it is entirely free, as opposed to PowerPoint's $229 retail price tag. For reviews of all three of these presentation products, see Chapter 1, "Lectures."

Tech Specs: Student PowerPoint Presentations

Set-Up Time: You'll need to make sure that you are familiar with all of the features of PowerPoint that you expect your students to use. If you are already using PowerPoint for your own lectures, then you are probably all set

Keep-Up Time: None.

In-Class Time: Plan on a full class to introduce your project and have students learn how to use PowerPoint (see our suggested method below), and then most projects take 3–5 class periods to produce. Be sure to budget plenty of time if you want to show all of these projects in class.

Tech Savvy: Low to medium. Text and images are easy; inserting audio, video, and other features is more complicated.

Teaching PowerPoint

If you aren't a PowerPoint wizard, don't worry about teaching PowerPoint. You very likely have several students in your class who know the software much better than you do. Let them teach your class how to use the software.

One fast, fun way to get everyone in your class up to speed on the basics of PowerPoint is to have a 20-minute Pop Culture PowerPoint Presentation Contest.

Tech Specs: Pop Culture PowerPoint Activity

Set-Up Time: 5 minutes to think of a list of pop culture icons.

Keep-Up Time: None.

In-Class Time: 5 minutes to introduce the activity, 20 minutes for students to work, and then the rest of the period to introduce the real PowerPoint project.

Tech Savvy: Low to medium, depending on which features of PowerPoint you ask students to use.

Tell students that they will be teaching themselves PowerPoint for the first part of class, and then you'll be helping them figure out how to use these skills in an upcoming class project.

1. Break students up into groups of three or four. Try to include one student in each group who knows how to use PowerPoint.
2. List ten elements of pop culture on the board, like Boy Bands, Divas, Reality TV, Talent Contest TV, Animated TV, Blockbuster Films, and so on.
3. In 20 minutes each group needs to create a three-slide presentation where each slide has at minimum:
   a. A title
   b. A text box
   c. An image
   d. Recorded narration (if your computers have microphones)
   e. Some form of animation— a slide transition or moving text
4. Be sure that students have access to the Internet so that they can find images for their presentations.
5. Twenty minutes later, you'll very likely have a barebones PowerPoint presentation from each group. You'll also have students begging you to do pop culture research in every class period. Tell them that everything was more entertaining and morally wholesome when you were a kid, and move on.

Have a few students show their masterpieces off to the class, and then spend the rest of the period introducing the real assignment that they will need these PowerPoint skills to complete.

PowerPoint Design Hints for Students

1. **PowerPoint is a visual medium, so focus on images and graphics**. Often an image and a title are all you need for a great slide to support your own words. Choose powerful images and label them thoughtfully.
2. **Use text as prompts**. The text on your slide should consist mostly of words that will help the audience follow your presentation, like topic headings or concise statements of key points or essential questions. Keep the number of words on each slide to a minimum.
3. **Use simple designs**. When choosing a design template, avoid designs that take up too much space. Stick with basic designs that will keep your audience focused on you and the content, not the window decorations.
4. **Avoid flashy animations and transitions**. Much of what you can do with PowerPoint is a waste of time. Focus on creating great content with effective illustrations, and don't spend your time making words shoot in on rocket ships.

Strict limits on the number of slides in each student presentation can help focus the energy of your students. For instance, for a group of three students, consider limiting the group to nine slides total, or three slides each, for a 50-minute class. The dominant element in each slide should be an image or multimedia feature, not text. Discourage students from reading prepared speeches, and instead encourage them to use slides as prompts for group discussion and analysis. Have them prepare questions to ask the class about the slides. You can have students create a lesson plan (based on a template you provide) that encourages them to think in terms of a two-way, interactive exploration rather than a one-way "stand up and lecture" presentation.

The best way to reinforce effective principles is to create rubrics that grade student presentations heavily on the content and quality of the student presentation and group engagement, minimally on simple, elegant layout, and not at all on flashy extras.

WEBSITE: Here are a few online examples of rubrics for PowerPoint presentations:

- University of Wisconsin–Stout PowerPoint Rubric
  http://www.uwstout.edu/soe/profdev/pptrubric.html
- Evaluation Rubrics for PowerPoint Presentation
  http://www.ithaca.edu/jwiggles/computers/ppt1_rubrics.htm
- Jamie McKenzie's "Scoring PowerPoints"
  http://fno.org/sept00/powerpoints.html

PENCIL: If you have a day of PowerPoint creation planned and the network goes down, you can still have students do some planning with pencil and paper. Have your students plan out what each slide should look like on "storyboards," and if they will be recording narration, have them write out and rehearse what they are going to say. They'll be fully prepared and raring to go when they can get back online.

The speaker icon here indicates that there is an audio segment in this slide, which can be played by clicking on the icon.

Source: Microsoft product screen shot reprinted with permission from Microsoft Corporation.

Using Narration to Create Stand-Alone PowerPoint Presentations

While PowerPoint is most commonly used to accompany lectures, you can also create presentations that anyone can watch and listen to on their own. The key to this is recording audio narration to accompany each slide.

For instance, you could have students create their own museum audio tour. Have them choose five related works of art and create a PowerPoint slide about each work. Visually, the slide should contain the image of the art and some basic information about the title and the artist. Students can then record a few minutes of audio with background on the artist, the history of the work, the historical context of the work, and some criticism. Anyone who views the presentation can then open the PowerPoint, view the slides, and listen to the commentary.

One of the main advantages of this method is that you don't need to spend a week of class watching students deliver these presentations (although public speaking is a vital skill that should be taught!). Students can produce these presentations and then teachers can review and grade them on their own time.

Recording Narration in PowerPoint

With recorded narration on a slide, PowerPoint presentations become stand-alone works that can be viewed by anyone, anywhere, and still carry the distinct voices of their authors. A simple recording tool is built right into PowerPoint, so the creation of these files is fairly easy to do.

With older computers, PowerPoint might start to get a little feisty and prone to melt down if you try to record very long sound files. If you have this problem, break up the narration into several smaller files.

(A new, free online tool called VoiceThread enables you to upload pictures and easily record audio to accompany them. More on this tool later in the chapter.)

Here are three steps for recording narration in PowerPoint:

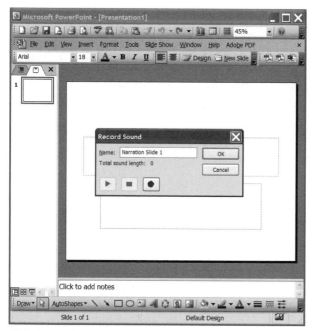

Click the red circle to begin recording your narration and the green triangle to play the audio back.

Source: Microsoft product screen shot reprinted with permission from Microsoft Corporation.

Step 1: Click *Insert→Movies and Sounds →Record Sounds*

Step 2: Record the narration. Click the red circle to begin recording, and click the green triangle to play back your recording. If you want to keep the recording, give it a name and click *OK*. If you want to try again, click *Cancel* and repeat steps 1 and 2.

Step 3: Locate the large half megaphone. This symbol is the button for your new sound file. Click it, either in the design view or when viewing the slide show, to play your recording.

You may want to put a text box near the symbol encouraging viewers to click it. The symbol can be dragged anywhere on the slide, like any other object.

Importing Audio and Video into PowerPoint

In addition to recording audio directly into PowerPoint, students can also record sounds in another program, like Sound Recorder, Audacity, or GarageBand, and then import them into their slide shows. (We discuss these sounds-recording programs later in this chapter, under "Podcasting.") To import these other audio files, click *Insert →Movies and Sounds* →*Sounds from File.* Search for your file, select it, and it will appear as a half-megaphone symbol identical to a recorded narration.

Students can also include short video clips in a PowerPoint slide or create a hyperlink to link to video on the Web. For a fuller discussion of importing audio and video into PowerPoint, refer to Chapter 1, "Lectures."

> **WEBSITE**: Apple's Keynote program is an excellent alternative to PowerPoint for Mac users, and it offers seamless media integration with iPhoto, iMovie, and iTunes. Visit http://www.edtechteacher.org/chapter8.html for our series of video tutorials that demonstrate how to create slideshows in Keynote.

RECORDING AND EDITING AUDIO FOR PODCASTING

In this section we explain how to record and edit audio for podcasting, an increasingly popular means of broadcasting digital audio over the Web.

Podcasting Defined

A *podcast* is typically an audio file, or series of files, that is broadcast on the Internet and can be automatically downloaded by subscribing to the podcast's *feed.* Podcasts often resemble radio programs in that many *podcasters* (podcast creators) add music and sound effects to their oral presentations. Podcasts are typically distributed over the Internet in .mp3 format through a syndicated feed (see "Tech Terms" below for more info). Podcasts can be played on a computer or portable media player. For our purposes here, we define podcasts rather loosely and include downloadable audio files that you don't need to subscribe to.

Podcasting refers to the means through which the podcast is distributed. Podcast combines the words "iPod" and "Broadcast," so many people associate podcasts with iPods. (Apple is very happy that people make this connection!) However, you don't need an iPod or an Apple product to produce, or to listen to, a podcast. Hundreds of educational podcasts are available via Apple's iTunes Music Store and through the Education Podcast Network at http://www.epnweb.org/. Through iTunes and other services, you can subscribe to a podcast series and get future episodes from a particular podcaster. (iTunes is a free download for PC and Mac from http://www.apple.com/itunes/download/.)

Tech Terms

.mp3 is an audio-specific format. The main advantage of .mp3 files is that they are compressed while still maintaining high audio quality, so they sound fine and are small enough to be easily distributed.

A **feed** is a means of distributing frequently updated content from Web pages, such as news sources, blogs, and podcasts. RSS, commonly known as "Really Simple Syndication," is a popular type of feed that lets an **aggregator** (a collector of feeds) know that content from a certain source has been updated. For instance, Apple's iTunes software serves both as an aggregator of podcast feeds and as a place where you can subscribe to and play podcasts. For more on RSS, please see Chapter 2, "Discussion and Communication."

Podcasting in Education

Tech Specs: Podcasting

Set-Up Time: You can learn the basics of simple recording in minutes; it's audio *editing* that can take a lot of time. Recording into a computer or into an iPod is quick and easy. If you really need to edit the audio, plan on an hour to learn how to work with either GarageBand or Audacity.

Keep-Up Time: If you decide to regularly publish your own podcast or a class podcast, you'll need to budget a few hours every week, bi-weekly, or monthly to create a new podcast.

In-Class Time: Students can learn the basics of recording and editing in one to two class periods. Projects based on these skills can range from a class period to several weeks.

Tech Savvy: Medium to high.

Podcasting can be used to record a teacher's lesson or students' conversations. It can be used to create a homework assignment or be part of a test. (Noble and Greenough School French students receive iPods during their final exam as part of an aural evaluation.) Students can use podcasts to interview each other about what they learned during the week. They can create a newscast, hold a debate, or run a radio show. Schools can use podcasts to make announcements via their Web sites. Students can read their own poetry or stories. Podcasts can also be used to record guest speakers and make their presentations available online.

Here are some specific podcasting ideas for Social Studies and English/Language Arts classrooms:

- Students can write a radio drama based on a historical event and record their show. In Tom's U.S. History class, students researched teenage hobos' lives during the Depression and then created a radio show featuring in-character interviews.
- Students can interview relatives about their life histories. Tom's students interviewed their parents about their experiences during the 1970s and '80s. Students recorded the interviews directly into portable recorders.
- Students can combine audio with family photos in a PowerPoint or iMovie project. Middle school students at the Noble and Greenough School create a "Who Am I?" video project that combines personal narrative with family pictures.
- Students can create a "Round the World" podcast that features interviews with individuals from different continents.
- Students can write and record short stories and add music and sound effects. One idea is to create a digital poetry project in which students recite their own poetry and add music and images that evoke the ambience of the poem.
- Teachers can record instructions or a lesson that students listen to on their own. A teacher of English as a Second Language (ESL) can record podcasts for homework assignments to help students' listening skills.
- Students can record music that evokes the spirit or sentiment of a poem or a scene in a play and explain why they chose that particular piece of music.

- Journalism students can interview people for the school newspaper and put the interviews online.
- Children's Literature students can write and record their own children's book and make the recordings available for young people to listen to.
- Students can use portable recorders to take notes during a field trip and record their impressions.

 WEBSITE: Apple has created lesson plans and rubrics for a variety of activities at: http://www.apple.com/au/education/ipod/lessons/.

Podcasting Project Example: "A Day in the Life of a Hobo" Radio Project

Tech Specs: "A Day in the Life of a Hobo" Radio Project
Set-Up Time: Familiarizing yourself with GarageBand or Audacity will take an hour.
Keep-Up Time: None.
In-Class Time: Three to five class periods.
Tech Savvy: Medium. You'll need to become familiar with a recording program like GarageBand or Audacity.

This interdisciplinary creative writing/historical simulation activity calls on students to research the plight of homeless teenagers during the Great Depression and then create their own written fictionalized account of a day in the life of a hobo. Students post their stories on their blogs and read each other's work. Students comment on what they liked about the story they read and what made it seem authentic. (The blogs provide a public forum to present and share student work.) Students are then interviewed in character and recorded as part of a "1930s Radio Show" podcast.

Instructions to students:

In this assignment you are to write from the perspective of a hobo who is "riding the rails." Use your knowledge of the period and your creativity to create a story (500–1,000 words) about a day in your life as a hobo.
Here are some questions to help guide your story:

- How old are you?
- Where are you from and why have you left home?
- Are you traveling alone or with someone? Who? Why did he or she leave home?
- What possessions do you have?
- What are your plans?
- What are your concerns?
- How are you feeling, physically and emotionally?
- What happened to you today?

- What dangers have you experienced?
- What have you been eating?
- What are you wearing?
- What have you seen? How does what you see make you feel?

Once you have written your story, you should post it on your blog. You will be required to comment on the stories of at least two other students. Then we'll spend a class recording interviews with each of you "in character." I will interview you for a 1930s radio show about the plight of teenage hobos. You will need to answer our questions as if you were a teenager riding the rails during the Great Depression.

A Note about Recording the Show

Students were interviewed three at a time as they sat around a Mac computer equipped with an internal microphone. Tom played the role of a sympathetic radio talk show host, and students were required to answer his questions in character as teenage hobos. The interviews were recorded directly into Apple's GarageBand software and were later edited. Music, clapping, and special effects were added to create a live studio audience feel to the program. When finished, the radio show was distributed as an .mp3 file via the classroom blog so that students, parents, and other people in the school community could enjoy the show.

> **WEBSITE:** Listen to a podcast including excerpts of our 1930s radio show and Tom's comments about this activity at http://www.edtechteacher.org/chapter8. html.

Planning a Podcasting Activity

Most podcasting activities consist of three steps:

Step 1: Record the Audio. The first step in podcasting is to record the audio. There are many digital tools available to record audio. For instance, it is possible to record your voice directly onto a computer (the PC has a simple program called Sound Recorder, and Mac users will find GarageBand ideal for this purpose). You can also record sounds on the Internet using Web sites like VoiceThread.com or Odeo.com (more on these tools later in this chapter) or into a portable recording device. Some email programs, like First Class, allow you to record directly into an email message.

Step 2: Edit the Audio. If you plan to edit the audio, then it makes sense to record directly into an audio editor. If so, consider Audacity or GarageBand. Both Audacity and GarageBand offer high-quality audio recordings and a bevy of audio-editing tools, and GarageBand even comes equipped with a variety of special effects. We discuss both of these tools later in this chapter.

Editing is the most difficult step of podcasting, and you might consider trying to avoid it. If you have your students rehearse their readings before they start speaking, then you might be able to just distribute what they record.

Step 3: Distribute the Audio. After you've recorded (and perhaps edited) the audio, the likely next step is to distribute it in .mp3 format for direct distribution over either a Web site or blog. You can also use a service like Odeo, discussed below, to create your own online podcast complete with an RSS feed that people can subscribe to.

If you are eager to avoid learning audio-editing software like GarageBand or Audacity, and don't want to fuss over distributing your audio, then let us introduce you to a great online program called VoiceThread.

Recording Audio into a VoiceThread

FEATURED PRODUCT

VoiceThread

Web site: http://www.voicethread.com
Developer: Steve Muth, co-founder of VoiceThread
Cost: K–12 teachers can apply for a free educator's account.

VoiceThread is a program that enables one or more people to record audio commentary on a single Web page. Users upload pictures, record accompanying audio commentary, and invite others to record commentary as well. VoiceThreads can be hosted free of charge at VoiceThread.com and can be embedded in blogs, wikis, and other types of Web sites.

Tech Specs: VoiceThreads

Set-Up Time: Designing your own VoiceThread might take between 10 and 30 minutes. You will upload pictures, add audio commentary, and invite others to comment.

Keep-Up Time: You will want to come back to listen to the comments students leave and perhaps add more pictures and commentary of your own.

In-Class Time: 15–30 minutes to let students listen to the VoiceThread and record their own commentary. They could also do this at home as part of an assignment.

Tech Savvy: Low.

A VoiceThread consists of an image, or an entire album of images, that is accompanied by audio commentary. This simple combination of visual and recorded media is perfect for creating multimedia presentations using simple tools in a relatively short time frame.

To get started, go to http://www.voicethread.com/. Once you've filled out the brief registration form and signed in, click on the *Create* link in the upper right corner of the page. There are three steps to creating a VoiceThread: *Title, Upload, and Comment.*

Step 1: Add a Title and Description. The first step is to add a title and description for your VoiceThread in the fields provided.

Step 2: Upload an Image. Next, upload a single image, or multiple images, to include in the VoiceThread. Click *Upload* →*Browse* to find an image on your computer.

Step 3: Add an Audio Comment. After you've uploaded your image to VoiceThread, the next step is to comment. Recording into VoiceThread is easy. Simply click on the *Record* button just below your picture and then click *Allow* to enable your microphone, internal or external, to work. Then start talking. To stop the recording, click on the red *OK, start talking . . .* button. Once you do, it will play for you what you just recorded.

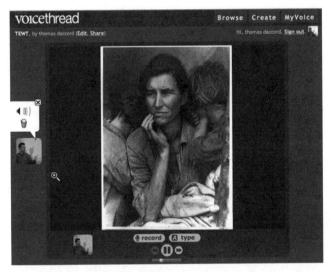

VoiceThread is a great new online program that allows you to upload pictures and add audio commentary. It is easy to use, and you can invite others to add audio commentary as well.
Source: Courtesy of VoiceThread.

If you don't like what you just said, you could click *Cancel the recording* and start over. Otherwise, *Save*, and your comment will be added to the image. Record audio for all the images you include in your VoiceThread. Use the big arrows in the bottom left and right corners to move back and forth between your pictures. (Lost your voice? You can type into a VoiceThread by clicking on the type button just below the uploaded photo.)

If you include a picture of yourself as part of your VoiceThread profile, it will appear beside any image you comment on. But this need not be a solitary experience! You can invite others to view and comment on your photographs. To do so, click the *Share* link located just above the photograph in your VoiceThread. Click *Add a friend* and use the form provided to send your students an email invitation. Once your students receive the invitation, they can view your VoiceThread and leave comments for any, or all, of your images. To hear comments from other people, simply click on their faces or icons beside the image and their comments will start playing. A VoiceThread can hold the comments of hundreds of people and can store hundreds of pictures, so you've got plenty of space to work with!

There are a myriad of educational possibilities with VoiceThread. For example, students can recite and comment upon their favorite poems. They can analyze and comment upon historically significant photographs. A class can create a virtual tour of a place or event they are studying. VoiceThread can even be used as a means to debate a topic. For instance, students could analyze and comment on photographs of the crisis in Darfur and debate the appropriateness of the United Nations' intervention in the area.

Recording Audio onto an iPod

FEATURED PRODUCT

Apple iPod
Web site: http://www.apple.com/ipod/ipod.html
Developer: Apple
Cost: The "fifth generation" video-enabled iPods range from $249 to $349. The iPod Shuffle and iPod Nano are audio only and cost less.

An iPod is a great tool for simple, mobile audio recording and playback.

An iPod is primarily a playback device, but you can record audio with it. A big advantage to recording with an iPod is that it is extremely portable, unlike a desktop computer or even a laptop. Mind you, it doesn't have an internal microphone, so you do have to buy a specially equipped external microphone. We have used Griffin Technology's iTalk Pro and Belkin's Voice Recorder for the iPod, and both products work well. You simply attach the external microphone to the bottom of the iPod and record your voice. You can even pause and restart your recording. The key thing to remember is that you cannot edit the audio with an iPod. You can only record it and play it.

The iPod will store your recordings in a special folder for audio recordings. You can then download its contents directly into iTunes. If you decide that you do wish to edit the audio you recorded, you can always move the files into an audio editor like GarageBand.

Editing Audio on Apple's GarageBand2

FEATURED PRODUCT

GarageBand2
Web site: http://www.apple.com/ilife/garageband/
Developer: Apple
Cost: Included with Apple's iLife suite of software programs at a cost of $80.

GarageBand is a powerful and flexible audio editor great for recording and editing podcasts and music.

If you have access to a Mac computer, GarageBand is a terrific piece of software for recording and editing audio. Below are basic instructions for using GarageBand version 2 to record spoken audio, to put some background music behind it, and to edit your recording.

Step 1: **Open GarageBand.** To find the GarageBand application, open up *Finder,* choose *Applications* from the side bar, and then scroll down to find the program.

- Click *Create a New Project.*
- Click *Save Project* and assign a title to it.
- Delete the piano track (select the track and click *Track →Delete Track*).

Here is the basic interface for Apple's GarageBand. The purple segment is recorded audio. Below it are the basic **Record, Play, Rewind,** and **Fast Forward** buttons, and below them you can see the options for music and special effects that Apple includes with the program.

Step 2: **Insert a New Track.** Click *Track* →*New Track.*

- Select the *Real Instrument* tab and then choose *Basic Track* and then *No Effects.*
- To check the input settings, click *GarageBand* →*Preferences* →*Audio/Midi;* if an internal microphone is to be used, the Audio Input should read, "Built in Audio." If an external microphone is to be used, Audio Input should read something like: "microphone model no. x."

Step 3: **Insert Music**: Hit the loop browser *eye* icon (left of scissors) to sample music tracks.

- Select an appropriate music style. To listen to music, simply double-click on the samples until you find a selection you like.
- Drag the desired track to beginning of your new track.
- Select *Track* →*Master Track* to set the master volume level.
- Select *Control* and uncheck *Metronome.*

Step 4: Record Your Voice. Move the *playhead* (red vertical line) just after your music track. Now record your voice.

- Hit the red record button and speak. Click the play button arrow to stop recording.

Step 5: Edit the Audio. Edit the audio you've added to your new track.

- Select and double-click the segment you just recorded (recorded audio has a purple background).
  - You can split a region in the timeline. (Splitting a region lets you start playing from anywhere in the region and allows you to use different parts of a region in different places in the timeline.) Select the region you want to split and then move the playhead to the point where you want to split it.
- Click *Edit* →*Split*. (Only the region in the selected track will be split, even if a region in another track is under the playhead as well. If multiple tracks are selected and are under the playhead, they will all be split.)
- To delete a section of audio, simply click on the section and hit the *Delete* button or select *Edit* →*Delete* from the menu bar.

Step 6: Export Podcast to iTunes. To export your podcast to iTunes, select *File* →*Export to iTunes* (this might also be under *Share* →*Send Song to iTunes* in other versions).

- When you open iTunes, select the song and then click *Advanced* →*Convert to MP3*. If *Convert to MP3* is not an option, you need to edit your iTunes preferences. To do so, go to *iTunes* →*Preferences* →*Advanced* →*Importing*. Under the *Import Using* tab, toggle select *MP3 Encoder.*
- Now that your file is in .mp3 format, it can be uploaded to a Web page or blog, or perhaps even emailed to students (if the file is not too large).

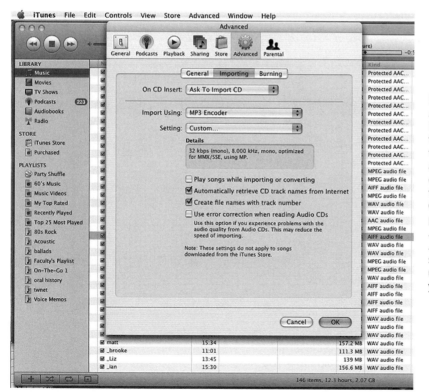

iTunes is an Apple program, but it is available for download on the PC as well as the Mac. You can use iTunes to convert your GarageBand podcast into an .mp3 file. The .mp3 file will be smaller and take up less space on your computer.

PENCIL: If your computers are down when you plan to do some podcasting, you may not be entirely out of luck. You can still have students write and rehearse, and then they can record their audio when things are up and running again.

Editing Sounds on PC Computers with Audacity

FEATURED PRODUCT

Audacity
Web site: http://audacity.sourceforge.net/
Developer: As open-source software, Audacity is created by a team of volunteer developers
Cost: Free

Many serious podcasters regularly produce great shows using this free, open source recording studio. It has many of the features of professional software, and it's *free*.

Audacity is a free sound-editing software for PCs that rivals even professional studio software. (Audacity also runs on Macs, but Mac users are better off with GarageBand.) Many of the best amateur podcasters use Audacity to create their programs. Though the software is loaded with features, the basics are simple. Audacity can be downloaded directly from the Audacity Web site. The download and installation instructions are mostly straightforward, except you will almost certainly want to download one optional file, the LAME .mp3 encoder. You will need to save this file somewhere memorable, like in My Documents, for later.

Three Steps to Producing a Sound File with Audacity

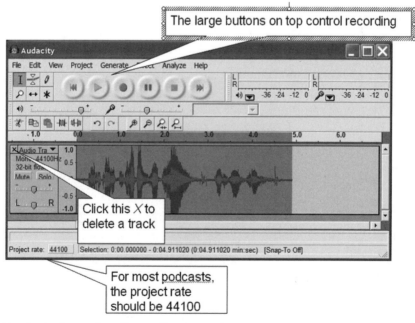

Here is a basic overview of key Audacity controls.

Step 1: Start a New Project. Once you start Audacity, you'll have a new project up and running. The interface is pretty intuitive. The big red button records, the blue parallel lines pause, the yellow square stops. To jump to the beginning, use the *Reverse* button and click the *Play* button to hear your material.

To scrap your work and start over, click the *X* in the top left corner of the audio track.

Step 2: Record a Track. Prepare your remarks in advance and rehearse them a few times. Sometimes it's best to know your script cold; sometimes it's best to speak more off the cuff. It depends on your topic and your audience.

Click the red *Record* button to get started, click *Pause* to take a break, and click *Stop* when you are finished.

If you make a mistake, it's easiest to just pause for a few seconds, catch your breath, and say things again: "In Boston, the capital of the United Sta— . . . In Boston, the capital of Massachusetts." (See the next page for a fix.) If you leave a silent pause after making a mistake, you'll easily recognize the long, flat pauses while editing.

Step 3: Save and Export your Audio. Click *File → Save* to save your work.

Audacity records in very large file formats, so you'll probably want to compress your files, most likely in the .mp3 format. To do so, choose *File → Export as MP3*. Be sure to delete any unwanted tracks before doing this. (The first time you do this, Audacity will prompt you to tell it where you saved the LAME .mp3 encoder.) For long sound files, this can take a very long time, so be prepared to work on another element of your project while waiting.

The Big Hint: If you click *Pause* while recording, you will start up again on the same track. If you click *Stop,* you'll start a new track the next time you click *Play.* The new track appears below the old one. If you are taking a break, it's best just to pause rather than stop.

Four Tricks to Spice Up Your Podcast with Audacity

Trick 1: Design a Sound Studio and Adjust the Input Level. To get higher quality sound, try to find a quiet place to record. If the area has too much echo, try hanging blankets on the walls to muffle the sounds. Another strategy is to adjust the input level of the microphone by adjusting the slider to the right of the microphone symbol. Record a few test sounds and play them back to get it right.

Trick 2: Cut Out and Re-record Mistakes. If you flubbed a line and then paused and re-spoke as suggested above, editing your mistakes is easy. In the top left toolbar there are six tools; choose the selection tool. Search the track to find your error; it should be before your long pause, which will look like a long flat line. Select and highlight the section where you have misspoken, and then hit *Delete* to remove it. Replay the section to see if it sounds right. If not, click *Edit → Undo* and try again.

If you need to re-record mistakes, this will be a little trickier. Press the record button and record your new material. This will appear on a second track. Use the selection tool to select the new material and copy it to the clipboard (*Control-C* or *Edit → Copy*). Find where you want the new material on the original track and paste (*Control-V* or *Edit → Paste*). Select and delete the error in the original track. Delete the extra track by clicking the *X* in the top left corner of the track.

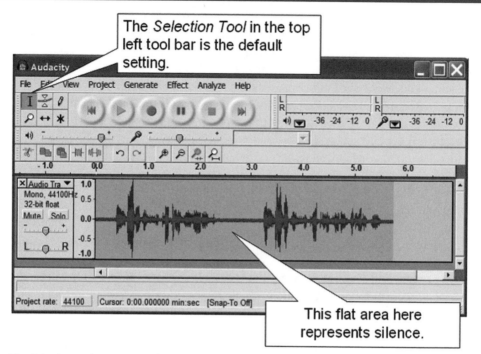

The Selection tool is important for editing recorded audio.

Trick 3: Import Some Music. To give your podcast a professional sound, get some intro and exit music. If students at your school have a band, see if they'll record 30 seconds of music for you and send it to you as an .mp3 or .wav file.

Another alternative is to find royalty-free music, sometimes called "podsafe" music, as in safe and legal to put in your podcast. You can try searching for "podsafe" or "royalty free" in Google or you can try this Web site: http://www.royaltyfreemusic.com/free-music-clips.html.

Once you have found something good, click *Project* → *Import Audio* and choose the file, and it will upload as another track. You can put some of the sound at the beginning or at the end of your track.

Select the section of music you want, copy the selection, and then paste it to the beginning and the end of your original track.

You can also use this technique to compile a single podcast from multiple contributors working from different computers.

Trick 4: Add Effects. Audacity has dozens of effects that you can play with, but *Fade In* and *Fade Out* are probably the most useful. For instance, you can have the theme music fade in or out at the beginning and end of your podcast.

Use the selection tool to select the first or the last few seconds of music. Then click *Effect* → *Fade In* (or *Fade Out.*) The track will automatically be adjusted with the desired effect. (Play with the *Reverse* effect for fun.)

Zooming and Navigating Your Sound Tracks in Audacity

As you produce longer tracks, you'll need to zoom in and out to see the entire piece or choose specific selections. On the bottom tool bar are four *Zoom* buttons. The magni-

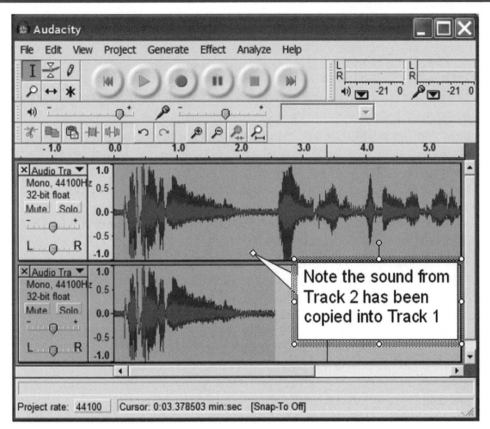

Copying a sound from one track to another is a handy editing feature.

fying glasses with a plus will zoom in; the one with a minus will zoom out. The third button will zoom in on a selection that you highlight. The fourth will zoom out so you can see your entire project.

Sharing Your Sound Files

Whether you use GarageBand or Audacity, once you are finished, you'll have a sound file that you can use in a variety of ways.

- You can play the sound file in class with any regular media player like QuickTime, Real Player, or Windows Media Player.
- You can share the file by exporting the file as an .mp3 file as described above, and then attaching the file to an email to your students. If the file is larger than 10 megabytes, you may need to break it up into several small files in order to email it.
- You can also share the file by posting it to your blog (we discuss blogs in Chapter 2, "Discussion and Communication"). Some blogging platforms, like Typepad and Edublogs, allow you to upload .mp3 files directly. Blogger and several other blogging platforms don't support uploading files, other than images, but in the next section, we'll show you how to get around that.
- You can use an online, Web-based podcasting service to host your podcast.

Publishing Your Podcast with Odeo

Tech Specs: Publishing a Podcast with Odeo

Set-Up Time: It will take at least an afternoon of orientation and fiddling to understand the features of Odeo.

Keep-Up Time: If you decide to publish your own podcast or a class podcast, you'll need to budget a few hours every week, bi-weekly, or monthly to maintain the podcast.

In-Class Time: Once students have produced a recording, you could expect it to take a class period for them to upload it into Odeo and arrange all of the settings. It might be easier not to do this in class, and just have you and a few volunteer students do this outside of class.

Tech Savvy: Medium to high. Producing a podcast, adjusting the settings in Odeo, and then embedding your podcast in a blog could be the final exam for your self-taught class in Web 2.0.

FEATURED PRODUCT

Odeo

Web site: http://www.studio.odeo.com
Developer: Odeo, Inc.
Cost: Free

The Odeo studio includes a simple Web-based recording program, but it also has tools to publish your podcasts on the Web and to embed them in blogs, Web pages, and wikis.

Once you have created your first audio file with GarageBand or Audacity, you may want to create more sound files, save them, and then tell people every time a new one comes out. Podcasting is a little bit like syndicating your own radio show on the Web.

There are lots of free tools on the Web to help you publish your podcast, and one of the best is Odeo. To get started, go to http://www.studio.odeo.com/ and sign up for a free account. Once you sign in you will have a chance to either record new audio or upload audio that you have already recorded with Audacity or GarageBand.

A note about Odeo: right now there is not a podcast publishing tool dedicated exclusively to education. So Odeo hosts all kinds of podcasts, some quite interesting and others unsavory. If you are going to have your students publishing podcasts with Odeo, it is best to review your acceptable use policy, and remind them to stay away from things not appropriate for class.

Step 1: Start a New Podcast. Click the button to *Set Up a New Podcast* and fill in the simple form. Where it says "website," you can put a link to your class Web site or blog, or just leave that field blank. In either case Odeo will create a new Web page for you or blog dedicated to your podcast. Right now, there are no limits to the number of podcasts you can have.

You can create your own podcast by recording it through Odeo.

Source: Courtesy of Odeo.

Step 2: Record Audio in Odeo. Odeo offers a very simple tool for recording audio, though it has no editing tools, so you need to get it right the first time. Follow the *Record Audio* link. Click *Record,* jabber away, and then click *Save Recording,* and you'll have an audio file ready. When you save the file, you need to fill in a simple form to give the recording a title and link it to your podcast.

Step 3: Upload Audio in Odeo. You can also upload files that you recorded in Audacity or GarageBand into Odeo. Follow the *Upload Audio* link and click *Browse* to find your file. When you upload audio, Odeo will attach an innocuous three-second introduction to anyone who downloads the file. It's a brief ad for Odeo. As when recording, you will need to fill out a simple form to title the file and link it to your podcast.

Step 4: Publish with Odeo. Once you have audio files that are associated with a podcast, Odeo will publish a Web page with all of your sound files on it. To find the link to your page, click on the name of your podcast under *My Podcasts* on the right of the Odeo Studio.

Once you create your podcast, Odeo will give you an RSS URL that students can use to subscribe to your podcast, and a second URL that you and your students can go to in order to listen to your podcast directly from the Web. *Source:* Courtesy of Odeo.

You can also embed your podcast into another Web page by copying and pasting the source code.
Source: Courtesy of Odeo.

You will then be taken to a page with all the information that you need about your podcast. If you would like students to subscribe to your podcast through iTunes or another podcast aggregator, you can give them the RSS URL at the top of the page. If you'd like them to listen to your podcasts directly from the Web, share the Odeo Directory URL with them.

Step 5: Embed with Odeo. Embedding refers to taking a file from one Web site and displaying it in another. So you can embed Odeo podcasts in a blog or other Web page. Embedding can get a little tricky, but it's an important technique for connecting different media.

In the Odeo Studio, go to *Audio in this Podcast* and then choose a sound file. At the bottom of the page for each sound file there is a box with the title *Put this Audio on your Website*. In this box will be HTML code, which looks like gobbledygook. Select and copy all of this code.

Try posting this code into your next blog post. Load up your blog editor and choose the *HTML* interface instead of the regular interface. (For example, in a new post in Blogger, you would select the *Edit HTML* tab rather than the *Compose* tab.) Paste the code into the blog post editor and save the post. If all goes well, your blog post will have a little Odeo media player loaded with your sound file.

Now you can have your students visit your blog, read your notes, and listen to your thoughts. Or you can have students record files and post them to your blogs so that they can talk to each other.

We won't lie to you; it's something of an investment to figure out how to record audio, publish it with Odeo, and then post it to your blog, but if you can do all those things, then you will have mastered the basic tools of the new Web 2.0. Once you learn how to do these tasks once, they become much easier in the future.

Here is the embedded podcast in Justin's blog.

Mobile Podcasting

FEATURED PRODUCT

Cast
Web site: http://gcast.com
Developer: iLike, Inc.
Cost: Free

Gcast is a free podcasting service. A key feature is the ability to record and upload a podcast via a cell phone.

Mobile podcasting is essentially podcasting by cell phone. You dial a special number and record your voice, and your voice then gets published online. Mobile podcasting opens up a new realm of possibilities for teachers. For instance, you could take your students on a field trip, and they could record and publish their observations via cell phone. You could tour a museum or historical site, and everyone could record and publish commentaries online, almost instantaneously.

There are several online services that enable you to record and publish a podcast via a cell phone or a landline. One of the best is Gcast, located at http://gcast.com. Gcast enables you to record a podcast and host it at the Gcast site for free. Once registered for the service, you call a special number, enter your ID and PIN code, and start recording. Your podcast will then be automatically added to the site!

SCREENCASTING

A screencast is essentially a recording of what's on your computer screen, often including audio, for later viewing by others. You can use a Web-based program or downloaded software to do the recording. In a screencast you can perform three basic operations: record what you see on your screen, record any sounds on your computer, and record your voice. And you can do all this at the same time!

Both teachers and students might create screencasts. As teacher, you might capture video of a historical event off your computer screen and add audio commentary. Or you might capture a poet reading one of your favorite poems and inject your impressions. In essence, you can capture what you see on your computer screen and, if you wish, explain or describe it as you capture it. You can include questions for students to answer or outline tasks for them to complete.

You can even use screencasts to create video tutorials to teach content or skills that perhaps you don't have enough time for in the classroom. For instance, if you want students to explore a large Web site, you can create a video tutorial of you navigating the site, directing them to the most important pages to visit and explaining the content as you move through the site. You could also create a screencast in which you edit a document in a word processor, pointing out structural and grammatical errors in the essays, and then actively demonstrate ways of correcting them.

Students could create a screencast as part of an individual or group presentation or assignment. For instance, students could add audio commentary to video of a silent movie from the 1920s or describe footage they watch of American factory life in the early twentieth century. English and Language Arts students might view an online video of a scene played out from a Shakespeare play and record their own commentary. They can point out specific instances where the actors faithfully represented Shakespeare's work. They might add even add music clips they feel add to the atmosphere of the scene. Students can create video tutorials for other students, demonstrating how to identify a comma splice, perform a Google image search, or insert a video clip into PowerPoint. Kids can get pretty creative with these tools once they understand how to use them.

You have probably surmised by now that one way of using screencasts is to capture scenes from a DVD or online video; however, here we potentially venture into murky copyright waters, so we strongly recommend that as you experiment with this, you hire an army of lawyers to scrutinize your every move. Or maybe you could just talk to your library media specialist.

For many teachers, there just isn't enough class time to show a whole DVD movie or even a whole scene, and it can take time to ready scenes to show in class. With screencasting you could capture the exact film clips you wish to show and save them in a single file. You can take clips from multiple movies and even add your own commentary.

Now, if you do this with videos that you have created or that have no copyright restrictions attached to them, then there's no problem. However, doing this with most commercial video would likely involve copyright infringement, much like creating a mix tape or CD of songs involves copyright infringement. So while it's true that it may seem very convenient to pre-record just the clips you want to show in class, and while it's true that if you only show these clips inside your classroom it is unlikely that the big studios will come after you, we do not recommend that you use screencasting to copy selections of copyright-protected commercial DVDs.

WEBSITE: Visit http://www.edtechteacher.org for plenty of examples of screencasts, including video tutorials.

Capturing a Video Recording of Your Screen with Screencast-o-Matic

FEATURED PRODUCT

Screencast-o-Matic
Web site: http://www.screencast-o-matic.com/
Developer: Big Nerd Software
Cost: Free

Screencast-o-Matic is a program that allows you to capture video and audio on your computer screen into a media file and upload it for free.

Tech Specs: Screencasting with Screencast-o-Matic

Set-up Time: Little, except for planning what you want to capture on the screen. Screencast-o-Matic is quick and easy to use.

Keep-Up Time: None, really. Mind you, video files are big, so if you want to keep many screencasts on your computer, you will need space on your hard drive.

In-Class Time: If you plan to screencast in class, then allow 10–30 minutes for preparation and recording.

Tech Savvy: Low for just recording. Medium if you want to export your video to your own Web site.

Screencast-o-Matic is available at http://www.screencast-o-matic.com/ and works with both Windows XP and Mac OS X. Screencast-o-Matic is free, and any video recording you make with the product can be uploaded, also for free, to a Screencast-o-Matic server. Screencast-o-Matic is in beta (test phase), so if you encounter any problems along the way, please make sure to notify the creators.

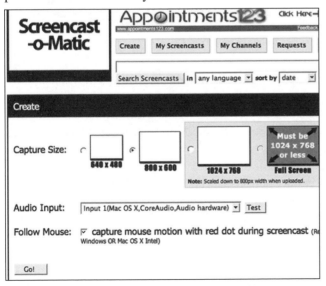

You can choose how much of the screen you would like to capture for your screencast.

It's a pretty straightforward process to create a screencast with Screencast-o-Matic:

Step 1: Select a Capture Size and Audio Input Type. To begin, simply click on the *Create* button. You can choose among four capture sizes: 640 x 480, 800 x 600, 1024 x 768, and full screen. Keep in mind that capturing more of the screen creates a larger file. Notice that the two largest capture sizes are scaled down when the screencast is eventually uploaded.

You also need to determine the audio input type if you plan to add audio to your screencast. *Input 1* is your basic choice for the internal microphone.

If you check the *Follow Mouse* box, you can capture the movement of your mouse during your screencast.

When ready, click the *Go* button.

Step 2: Record Your Screencast. Click the red record button to start recording the part of your screen inside the black frame, and click the *X* button when you're finished. If needed, there is also a pause button. It's that simple. Note: Unfortunately, you cannot resize the black frame for a more accurate area selection.

Screencast-o-Matic does a good job of explaining to you how to use its program.

Step 3: Export or Upload Your Screencast. It will take from a few seconds to several minutes to process your recording depending on its length and a few other factors. You can preview your screencast by clicking on the green triangle play button at the bottom left of the screen. If you are unsatisfied, click *Discard Screencast* and try again. When you are happy with your screencast, you have the option of uploading your screencast to the Screencast-o-Matic server or exporting a screencast to your computer. Note the upload and export buttons in the lower right corner of the page. Before you do either, you might want to fill out a title and description of the screencast in the form provided in the right column. If you upload your screencast directly to the Screencast-o-Matic server, you will be given a URL that you can then give to those you wish to view the screencast. If you choose to export your screencast, it will be in QuickTime format, which you can then upload to a Web site like YouTube.com or TeacherTube.com (a clean alternative to YouTube). Instructions for uploading videos can be found at both of those sites.

BUILDING SIMPLE WEB SITES WITH GOOGLE PAGE CREATOR

Google, source of all manner of amazing free things, has added a free, simple Web page builder to its suite of products: Google Page Creator. You will need a Gmail account to get started, but once you have one, you and your students can easily create simple Web pages without needing to learn any programming languages, like HTML.

Ten Ideas for Student Web Site Projects

1. When reviewing for an AP exam, have students create review pages for different topics and post them to a Web site.
2. Have students write character studies for a novel, and hyperlink their pages together. As students learn about relationships in the novel, they can jump from one character to another.
3. Have students research a piece of local history that is not well documented on the Web (maybe a local civil rights action or colonial settlement) and create a Web site.
4. Have students analyze a poem or short story, and then have their page link to other criticisms of the work.
5. Have students create an annotated search directory for a particular topic, using the Best of History Web Sites (http://www.besthistorysites.net/) as a model. Find the best Web resources for researching a particular topic, then rank them and annotate them.
6. If students create visual projects for a class—maps, posters, newspapers—have them take digital photos of the works and then publish the works on a Web site.
7. Have students maintain a page about a global climate change, with analysis and links to important reporting on the issue.
8. You might use a Web page to collectively maintain important lists for students—like commonly misspelled words, clichés, or weak verbs. That way, as students are writing, they can pull up the Web site and reference those lists.
9. If you have set up an international "ePal" project where you are emailing with students from another part of the world (see Chapter 2, "Discussion and Communication"), have each student in your class set up a Web page so that your ePals can learn more about your students.
10. Publish an online version of your school, grade, or classroom newsletter to keep parents and your community in the loop with all the great things happening at your school.

Getting Started with Google Page Creator

Step 1: Register for Gmail and Create Your Google Pages Site. The first thing you will need to do is set up a Gmail account. You can do this from a link at http://pages.google.com/. Once you have done that, you can create your own Web site sub-domain, which will be some version of yourname.googlepages.com. You can also choose a starting layout for your first page.

Step 2: Create your First Page. Once you select your site name, you can create the home page for your site. The WYSWYG (What You See Is What You Get) editor for Google Page Creator allows you to do some basic text formatting—changing font size, adding bullets, changing text color and text size, and using boldface and italics.

Google Page Creator makes it fairly easy for you to manage your Web page, and you won't have to worry about any of that html code.   *Source*: Courtesy of Google.

Step 3: Add Links. Every good Web page has hyperlinks to help readers navigate to other related pages. With Google Page Creator, you can link to other Web sites, other Google Pages, files that you upload, or an email address. Simply click on the *Link* button on the editor, and you will get a menu of link options. Type the text you would like displayed, and then tell the Google editor what you would like that text to link to.

With the file upload option, you can attach documents, presentations, or any other file that students might need for your class, which is a handy way to distribute important documents.

You can add links to other Google Pages, to outside Web pages, or to files on your computer
Source: Courtesy of Google.

Step 4: Liven Things Up with Images or Gadgets. Putting an image on your page is equally easy. Click the *Image* button and then upload an image or find one on the Web. When you find an image on the Web that you like, you will need to give the Google editor the picture's URL. The easiest way to do this is to *right-click* (*Control-click* for Apple) on the image and select *Copy Image Location.* Then paste that image location into the box that says *Image URL.*

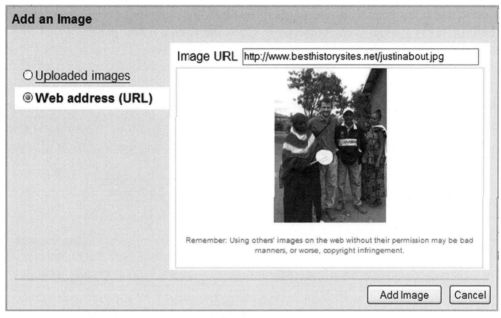

You can add an image either from your computer or from another Web site.
Source: Courtesy of Google.

Once the image is in the Google editor, you can click on it and drag it around the page to change its location, and you can also choose to reset the size to small, medium, or large. You can also click *Remove Image* to throw the image away.

The Google editor also has a series of gadgets that you can put on your Web site, which are mini-programs. Useful ones include calendars, mini–Web browsers, and maps. Not so useful and downright counterproductive ones include PacMan and Super Mario Brothers.

To add a gadget, click the *Add gadget* link in the bottom right of the page, and then you'll be taken to a menu of gadgets to choose from. If your project is of a strictly academic nature, it is best to steer students clear of this one.

Step 5: Change the Look or Layout. Two links in the top right of the page let you change the "look," or color scheme, of the page and the layout of the boxes on the page. If you want to experiment with different options, follow those links.

Editing the HTML: If you want to dig around in the code of any box on the page, then click the *Edit Html* link in the bottom right of the page. Of course, if you know how to edit HTML, you probably could have figured that one out on your own.

Step 6: Publish or Perish! Once you have things looking good, click the *Publish* button and your Web site will be available to the world. Click *Preview* to see what it will look like, or just open a new Web browser window and put in your brand, spanking new URL. If you want to pull your page off the Internet, there is an *Unpublish* button at the bottom.

Step 7: Create New Pages. Once you finish your first page, click on *Back to Site Manager* at the top left of the editor. The Site Manager lets you see what pages you have created and it lets you create new pages. When looking at the list of pages, the one with the little home symbol is the home page. Click the *Create a new page . . .* link to get started on your next page.

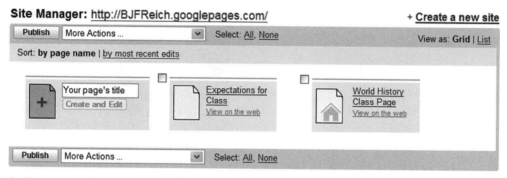

The Site Manager allows you to look at all your different pages in one window.   *Source*: Courtesy of Google.

When you click the *Create a new page . . .* button, a window will appear where you can give the page a title. Choose something short and relevant. Then click the *Create and Edit* button below the window and you can get started on your new page! Don't forget to create links on your home page to your new pages or people will have a hard time finding them!

The Google Page Creator editor is easy to use, but you can use it to create sophisticated Web sites with all the formatting, images, bells, and whistles that you would normally need knowledge of HTML to create. There are some space limits to Google Page Creator, but they are quite generous. You can create up to five sites with unlimited pages, and your sites can hold up to 100 megabytes of data, files, and images. And if you run out, just register for another Gmail address and start over!

FINAL THOUGHTS

Whereas writing was the basic medium of communication of our culture for centuries, writing now needs to make room for video, audio, and the emerging forms of interactive media of the Internet.

Students' lives are immersed in these new media, and teachers can harness their enthusiasm for these forms by designing assignments that challenge students to think through problems in writing and with audio, video, and images. Students love having the opportunity to express themselves creatively, and they find it empowering to contribute their creations to the world via the Web. For teachers, these projects offer an opportunity to assess skills that don't normally get graded in the sequence of the regular class rou-

BLOGS VERSUS WIKIS VERSUS WEB PAGES: WHAT'S THE DIFFERENCE?

The short answer to that question is "not much." All three are vehicles for publishing information on the Internet, with differences in formatting and authorship. Most projects could be published in all three formats, but here are some guidelines:

Web pages are a blank slate with single authorship. Most Web sites come with little pre-formatting. Google Page Creator, for instance, will set you up with a few columns, but that is it. They are usually authored by a single person or small team, and they are designed to stably reside on the Web without needing much changing or tinkering. If you want to have a simple publication of information, Web pages are a great choice.

Wikis are collectively written and edited. The distinctive feature of a wiki is that anyone can contribute to and change any page. When you have a project that you would like an entire class or a large group to contribute to, the wiki might be the easiest way to handle multiple authorship.

Blogs are chronologically ordered and singly authored, and allow readers to talk back. Blogs have two distinctive features. First, they are chronologically ordered, so they function well as journals or portfolios where you want to trace the development of ideas over time. Second, they have built-in features to accept comments from readers, which means that they are a natural medium for dialogue and communication. Blogs are probably the simplest of these tools to set up and maintain.

Most projects can be conducted, with modification, in any of these three platforms. Start your online ventures by experimenting with one, and once you get familiar with it, try assigning a project in another medium. Whichever you choose, your students will appreciate the chance to be creative and publish their works to the world!

tine. Most importantly, the fun and wow factor involved with these projects will generate enthusiasm and energy in your classroom that you can direct toward covering important content in your curriculum.

It's also worth a word at this point to consider technology and gender. For decades, computers and boys went together like peanut butter and jelly, and in higher education, fields like Computer Science continue to be dominated by men. The creative applications discussed in the chapter, however, focus on communication and collaboration, which appeal just as much to girls as to boys. If you find that the computer lab in your school is a boys' club and if your Computer Science classes have a decidedly male bent, incorporating these kinds of projects into your curriculum can help invite female students to consider the future possibilities of technology.

Chapter 9

Assessment and Grading

Introduction
Online Tests and Quizzes
Giving Tests in an Online Environment
Electronic Commenting and Grading
Online Rubrics: Finding Them, Designing Them, and
  Grading with Them
Electronic Gradebooks
The New Frontiers of Online Plagiarism
Final Thoughts

INTRODUCTION

Though this chapter is dedicated to assessments, just about anything that you have read up to this point could be used to create an assessment. You can evaluate students by having them post to blogs, record podcasts, contribute to wikis, design presentations, build WebQuests, or use any of the other tools that we have discussed.

This chapter will add to the arsenal of assessments that you have already accumulated. First we explore more ideas for designing electronic assessments, and then we'll consider how to design rubrics to evaluate new assessments; the rubrics, of course, will be composed using online tools. We also spend some time looking at the art of grading and commenting on electronic copies of papers, and we examine a few different online gradebooks to help teachers track their grades.

Then we do some undercover investigation to look at the dark, steaming underworld of online writing: the market for plagiarized papers. We explore the sites where students can get plagiarized materials and arm ourselves with tools to educate and catch potential plagiarists.

ONLINE TESTS AND QUIZZES

Creating a secure, stable testing environment with computers is tricky, and most schools probably are not yet ready for it. You need to have enough computers for all your students, security measures to make sure that each student is doing his or her own work, an IT staff member around to make sure things will work, and backup computers in case machines fail. The good old pencil and blue book are looking pretty good for now.

Even if your students won't take their final on a laptop, there are still plenty of great uses for online tests. Online testing provides opportunities for students to practice in test-taking environments or test their knowledge before diving into the real assessment. As SAT and other high-stakes tests move onto computers, giving students practice taking tests in an electronic environment is more important than ever.

Computers cannot decode anything beyond the simplest of answers; they cannot effectively read an essay or even a single-sentence response. Online tests, therefore, tend to ask simple kinds of questions—multiple choice, fill in the blank, true-false—where there is exactly one right answer. These may not be the best tools to plumb the depths of student understanding, but they are useful tools to help students get their facts straight. Some online testing tools enable you ask more difficult questions but also require you as the teacher to complete the grading.

Finding Online Tests and Quizzes

Many teachers have come before you, so why reinvent what they have already done?

In History and Social Studies, many teachers have posted multiple-choice, true-false, and other types of simple tests on their class Web sites. AP History teachers in particular have made plenty of their work available. In addition, many textbooks with companion Web sites have quizzes available for students online.

Carla Beard's Web English Teacher at http://webenglishteacher.com is a great resource for lesson plans, activities, and assessments in English and Language Arts. Study guide companies also provide assessments. Both SparkNotes (http://www.sparknotes.com/) and CliffsNotes (http://www.cliffsnotes.com/) have short online quizzes for all of the books that they annotate.

Another option is to create your own quizzes through Quia, a tool for designing online tests and quizzes.

> **WEBSITE:** Not only does each page on the Best of History Web Sites portal (http://besthistorysites.net/) include links to great history resources on topics like World War II and the U.S. Constitution, but each page also has links at the bottom to activities, lesson plans, and more. In these sections, you can often find online quizzes and tests.

Creating Your Own Online Tests and Quizzes with Quia

FEATURED PRODUCT

Quia
Web site: http://www.quia.com
Developer: Quia Corporation
Cost: $49 for one teacher for one year. Discounts are available for groups.

Quia allows teachers to create quizzes, with ten different types of quizzes ranging from multiple choice to matching and sixteen types of games from flash cards to hangman. If you register your classes and students, Quia can also be set up to automatically grade and track students' results. Teachers have already created over 2 million activities that you can borrow or adapt for your students.

Quia is a tool for generating and automatically grading online quizzes and games. The tool costs $49 a year, but it offers an incredible variety of activities and test questions for teachers to design and use. Everyone, even non-subscribers, can also access the 2 million activities that teachers have already created, in categories from Accounting to Zoology. Visit http://www.quia.com/shared/ to search through a wide variety of teacher-created activities, including a list of the top 100 games.

> **Tech Specs: Designing a Quia Quiz or Game**
>
> **Set-Up Time**: Plan on a few hours to learn your way around the interface and make your first quiz or game. With practice, future quizzes will take 15–30 minutes to design.
>
> **Keep-Up Time:** Editing quizzes can be done regularly, so if you change your syllabus a bit you can adapt your questions in just a few minutes.
>
> **In-Class Time**: Depends on the length of the quiz, though the great advantage of these online quizzes is that students can take them on their own time.
>
> **Tech Savvy**: Medium. It's not particularly difficult, though the interface will be unfamiliar.

Five Steps to Designing a Quia Quiz

Step 1: Register with the Site for a Subscription. You can start with a free 30-day trial before paying. Go to http://www.quia.com/web and click on *Get a FREE 30-day trial.* You'll need to provide some basic information to get your free account.

Step 2: Create a New Quiz. Enter the Instructor Zone at http://www.quia.com/instructorZone. Click on the *Quizzes* tab and then *Create a New Quiz.* Note: the Z in the URL may have to be capitalized for the site to load properly.

Step 3: Fill Out the Form to Create Your Quiz. Give the quiz a title and description, and then you can begin adding questions.

In *Section 2: Questions,* there is a yellow bar where you determine the number and type of questions to include in the quiz. Set these variables, and then click *Add.* If you would like your quiz to have multiple types of questions, just reset the information in the yellow bar and click *Add* again. If you get stuck, there are handy help icons next to each section with good tips about designing the quizzes.

Step 4: Design Your Questions. For each question you will need to fill out the question, provide possible answers, and indicate the correct answer.

If you look under other options, you can also give feedback to students for correct or incorrect answers. It can be useful when students supply incorrect answers to give them hints on where to study to be able to better answer the question.

Step 5: Give the Quiz URL to Your Students. When you finish designing your quiz, click *Done,* and you'll be given a URL for your quiz that you can give to your students.

If you want Quia to be able to grade your quizzes for your students, you will need to go into the *Classes* tab, select *Roster,* and begin the process of setting up your classes, either by typing in a roster of your students or giving them a randomly generated password that will allow them to sign up.

Creating classes will give you access to a host of new grading features, but the steps are unnecessary if you just want to give students quizzes for review or for fun.

The Quia interface includes a series of forms and check boxes so that you can easily design all kinds of quizzes and activities.   *Source:* Courtesy of Quia.

For each question you write, you can also write a series of answers and you can even write feedback for correct and incorrect answers.

Source: Courtesy of Quia.

Four Steps to Adding Images and Audio to Your Quizzes

Your quiz questions can include more than just text; Quia allows you to add audio and images as well. You could have students choose the right caption for an editorial cartoon, identify a work of music, or answer questions based on a map.

Step 1: Upload Image and Audio files to Your Folder. You will need to upload to the Quia Web site any images or audio files that you want to use in Quia quizzes. From your main instructor page, click on the *Files* tab and then click on *Upload.* Click on *Browse* to select the file from your hard drive. You can change the name of the file before you finally upload it.

Step 2: Start a New Quiz or Edit an Old One. Go back to the *Quizzes* tab and choose to start a new quiz or edit an old one.

Questions can include not just writing, but images and audio as well.
Source: Courtesy of Quia.

Step 3: Choose Other Options for the Questions Where You Would Like to Add Images or Audio. When you are designing your questions, click on *Other options* to open another menu. Here you can upload images or audio files to add to your questions.

Step 4: Select the File You Would Like to Include. When you click *Get Image* or *Get Audio* you will see the list of files that you have uploaded to your Quia folder. Choose one of these and upload it to the question. The file can only be associated with the question, not the answer.

When students take the quiz, they will see this file when they get to the question. Images will be automatically displayed, and audio files will have a mini player that they can click on. You can preview any quiz by clicking on the *Preview* button at the bottom.

Four Steps to Creating Games and Activities with Quia

In addition to quizzes, you can create over sixteen types of games with Quia to help students learn specific content like vocabulary, dates, and important people. Before a big vocabulary test, you might create a few of these games and tell students that you've made them. They may be fun enough that kids don't even realize that they are studying.

Step 1: Click on the Activities Tab. Activities are kept in a separate section from quizzes. Although these activities can be more complicated and sophisticated than quizzes, they are often much easier to set up.

Quia makes it easy to create a wide variety of games and activities using your questions and content. *Source:* Courtesy of Quia.

Step 2: Select a Type of Game or Activity. There are sixteen types of games or activities, from Battleship to Rags to Riches, a *Who Wants to Be a Millionaire?* clone. If you want to preview a type of activity, click on the *Sample activities* on the right side of the window. (Don't you wish they would make the helpful links bigger?)

Step 3: Complete the Form. Once you select a type of activity, you will be taken to a form to fill out with questions and answers. Each activity has its own particular form to fill out.

Step 4: Share the Activity URL. When you finish designing your activity, click *Done* and you'll be given a URL for your activity that you can give to your students, just like with the quizzes.

WEBSITE: Visit http://www.edtechteacher.org/chapter9.html for more Web tools to design games and quizzes. You can also visit http://www.besthistorysites .net/Multimedia.shtml for sites with history games and animations.

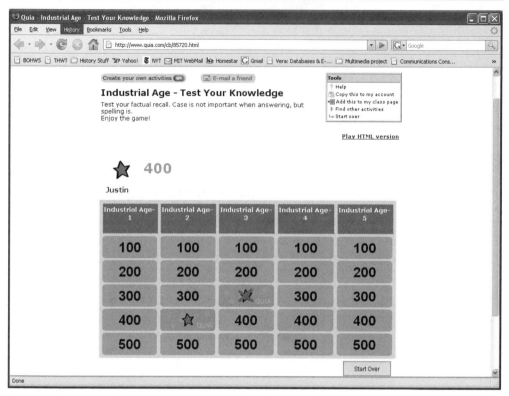

Tom uses Quia regularly to create review games, like this Jeopardy quiz clone, for his students.
Source: Courtesy of Quia.

Sample Online Tests and Quizzes

Here are the URLs for a few Quia quizzes and activities that Tom created for his students and a few other good ones that we found online. Give them a try, and good luck!

1. Tom used Quia to create this Jeopardy-style game to test his students' knowledge of Gilded Age America: http://www.quia.com/cb/85720.html.
2. This is a World Religions quiz: http://www.quia.com/cb/24385.html.
3. *Life of Pi* Quia vocabulary quiz: http://www.quia.com/cb/24385.html.
4. This is a Quia game to help learn the past tense of irregular English verbs: http://www.quia.com/cb/8111.html.
5. Use this as a game to test knowledge of the Greek and Latin roots of English words: http://www.quia.com/jg/66094.html.

GIVING TESTS IN AN ONLINE ENVIRONMENT

Proctoring tests with computers presents special challenges. Students have always found devious ways to cheat, but the potential for mischief significantly increases when computers are connected to the Internet. Computers also can fail catastrophically and delete a student's work, whereas the worst failure of a pencil merely requires sharpening.

For all of these risks, though, testing with computers can bring some important benefits. When students write on computers, they have the chance to do far more editing and polishing than when writing with pen and paper. Many computer-literate students can also write much faster with computers, though some poor typists are slowed. For students with documented learning disabilities, the use of a computer for tests and quizzes can be a helpful, and even mandated, solution.

Here are some tips for safely and fairly proctoring tests in an online environment.

1. **Make each screen visible**. Set up the room in a horseshoe with you at the center so you can watch the students work. If you must have students seated in rows, sit in the back of the classroom where you can see their screens.

2. **Require students to make their word processor full screen**. Make sure that students are not working in windows that allow them to look at anything other than their work.

3. **Disable the Internet until the end**. If the test does not involve the Internet, ask your IT administrator to disable the Internet in the lab or classroom until the end of the period when students are finished with their test or writing.

4. **Save, save, save.** Remind students to save their work every five to ten minutes.

5. **Bring a thumb drive**. Even if you plan on having students email their work to you at the end of class, bring a thumb drive (see Chapter 1, "Lectures") in case the connection fails.

6. **Write cheat-proof questions**. When you ask students common or standard questions about literature or time periods, they can use the Internet to find common answers. If you ask creative questions, students will have a harder time finding ready-made answers.

7. **Get your IT staff on call**. Tell your school's IT staff when you are giving the test, and see if they can spare someone to help you.

8. **Practice with smaller, low-stakes assignment**s. Before you offer your final exam in the lab, give an online quiz to a few classes so that you and your students can practice in the computing environment.

9. **Be aware of stressed students**. If students have always taken tests on paper, taking their first few tests on computers can be very stressful. Remind them that they are smart and have a great teacher who prepared them well.

There are some excellent rewards from letting students take tests on computers: no more messy handwriting, more carefully revised student writing, and the option to grade and comment either on paper or online. You can also allow students who initially do poorly to revise their answers from their original document file. If you have a computer lab in your school available and a supportive IT team, try giving your next test or quiz there.

PENCIL: Whenever you give a quiz or test in an online environment, be sure that you have a paper backup of the test ready to go in case something goes wrong with the computers or the network.

Designing Online Assessments with Templates

Templates allow students to create documents from foundations instead of from scratch. Thus, templates allow students to focus on solving a particular type of problem instead of figuring out how to solve a type of problem.

Here are some documents and projects you could ask students to take on with templates:

1. **Cover Letter and Resumes**. Help students get ready for the summer job market.
2. **Business Plan**. Have students invent a business and then think through the steps to bring their ideas to life.
3. **Book Reviews**. For students just starting to learn how to write book reviews, give them a structure to get started.
4. **Newsletters**. Keep parents involved with the news from your classroom.
5. **Flyers**. Have students invent an event and think through the planning.
6. **Brochures**. Imagine a product and then have students decide how best to sell it.
7. **Poetry Templates**. Help reluctant poets get started with structure.
8. **Essay Templates**. Most of these are based on the five-paragraph essay model, which is perhaps a good way to get students to start writing.
9. **Lesson Plan Templates**. One of the best ways for students to try to understand material is to think about how they would teach it. Even if you don't have time for students or groups to teach a class, it can still be worthwhile to ask students to plan out a lesson or a whole unit.

Templates for many different types of documents can be easily found online, and some even come included with Microsoft Word and other word processors. You can find free Word templates at http://office.microsoft.com/en-us/templates/. Education World, an online resource for educators, has an excellent set of templates at its Web site, http://www. education-world.com/tools_templates/index.shtml. To find other templates, try performing a Google search for a type of document plus "template." When you find one you like, copy the document, paste it into a word processor, and then make changes to adapt the document to your class's needs. Be sure to give credit to the original author of the template!

---

iPods and Assessments. iPods are starting to find their way into exam rooms. For instance, Tom brought iPods into his U.S. History final exam last spring and had students watch and analyze historical clips as part of an essay. Mark Sheeran, a French teacher at the Noble and Greenough School in Dedham, Massachusetts, has been using video iPods in his final exam for years. The first part of Mr. Sheeran's assessment focuses on the auditory component: he records mp3 sound files that are downloaded onto the iPods, and students write down answers to questions. The next two components involve video. First, students watch flashcards of vocabulary terms that they are then required to identify. Next, students watch a short movie clip on the iPod from which the sound has been deleted. The students are then asked to write a script of what they imagine the dialogue to be.

ELECTRONIC COMMENTING AND GRADING

If you can get your students writing electronically, then you as a teacher have the chance to grade and comment electronically. Like many technological tricks, it will take an initial investment of time to figure out how best to grade papers online, but after climbing up the learning curve, you can offer significant feedback in much less time.

Receiving Assignments

Depending upon your system, students will be able to submit their assignments to you in a variety of ways. If your school system uses a course-management system like BlackBoard or Moodle, your students may be able to submit assignments through that. You could also have students post their online work to a blog or a wiki so that you can interact with the writing together (See Chapter 2, "Communication and Discussion," for info on blogs, and Chapter 7, "Writing," for more on wikis). Each student can also sign up for an online portfolio like Xdrive and upload their work to their portfolio (See Chapter 1, "Lectures," for more on Xdrive). You might also have them submit their work to a plagiarism detection tool, like Turnitin.com, that will forward you the checked work (more on that below).

If you have students email you their work, be sure to set up a separate "Turn In" account separate from your regular email account. Having a separate email account exclusively for receiving, filing, and returning schoolwork will help manage the communication between you and your students.

If students email their work to you or post their work to a school server or Web tool, be sure that they save their work as a file that you can read. Most word processors can save in a generic format called rich text format (.rtf), and this format can be read by Word, OpenOffice, AppleWorks, and most other word processors. You can save a document this way by using *File→Save As* and then selecting rich text format as the *File Type*.

The Basics: Bold, Color, Parentheses, and Highlighting

The easiest way to comment in a student's paper is by inserting bold text. The ability to make text bold is universal in word-processing software, so you don't have to fear that your comments will be erased if you edit in Word and your student writes in Appleworks. Your comments will stand out from the rest of the paper, and you can switch to boldface just by pressing *Control-B*. If you want to be certain that students can tell their text from your comments, you can also put your boldface comments in parentheses, **(like this)**. Bold text works well for statements that need to stand out, as when you want to offer encouragement, contest a point, ask a question, or make a statement.

Another simple tool for marking up papers online, common to most word processors, is the highlighter, which colors the background of text much like a real highlighter. In Microsoft Word, the highlighter button can be found in the formatting toolbar, and it looks like a little highlighter. Other programs have a similar button. To highlight text, simply click the *Highlight* button and select an area of text. The newly highlighted text will be surrounded by a background color—yellow by default—that makes the section stand out. The highlighter works well for marking grammar and style errors in essay drafts. If the error is simple enough for students to figure out the problem, the highlighter gives them a chance to solve it. If the error requires some explanation, go back to using the bold text.

Another option for making distinctive comments is the font-color button, which in Word looks like a capitalized *A* with a bar of color below it. Clicking this will change your type to another color, and clicking the downward-facing triangle next to the button will open a menu so that you can choose different colors. You could use different colored text for different types of comments, though all the clicking and selecting is time-consuming. We tend to not use this tool in favor of the boldface, mostly because it is so much easier and faster to just hit *Control-B* (*Command-B* on a Mac) than doing all the clicking, and boldface stands out as well as red or blue type.

With these three tools, you can make basic comments on an essay, but these are mostly things you could have done with a pencil, red pen, and highlighter on a paper copy. If you are a fast typist and enjoy working in a paperless environment, these alone may be attractive reasons to grade online. But let's look at a few features from Microsoft Word that are much harder to replicate with a pencil.

Useful Editing Features in Microsoft Word for Grading: AutoCorrect and Track Changes

Tech Specs: Using AutoCorrect and Track Changes for Grading
Set-Up Time: It may take an hour or more to familiarize yourself with all of these features.
Keep-Up Time: None. Hopefully it will cut down on your grading time!
In-Class Time: None.
Tech Savvy: Medium. There is some "programming lite" involved

AutoCorrect

In teaching the craft of writing, you end up writing many of the same things over and over. How many times a week do you write the word "paragraph"? It's a long word, and the keys are all over the board, so it's time-consuming to type. One way to make typing "paragraph" easier is with the AutoCorrect function.

You may have seen the AutoCorrect tool in action if you have ever typed "teh," "ovre," or "adn," and had Microsoft Word automatically change those errors to "the," "over," and "and." If you have words that you commonly misspell that are not in the AutoCorrect tool, you can add those easily. For instance, if you have the habit of spelling "precedent" as "precident," then you can program Word's AutoCorrect to fix that for you. Go to *Tools→AutoCorrect Options* and look for the windows that say *Replace* and *With*. Put the offending spelling in the *Replace* box and the correct spelling in the *With* box, and click *OK*. From then on, Word will make the change for you.

While AutoCorrect was designed to fix spelling errors, there is no reason you can't use it to make typing easier. For instance, you can tell Word to change "pgh" into "paragraph" and "pghs" into "paragraphs" as the first step toward letting you use something like a secretarial shorthand when typing. To do this, simply put "pgh" in the *Replace* window, put "paragraph" in the *With* window, and then click *Add*. You could create a

The AutoCorrect tool was designed to automatically fix common spelling errors, but we can configure it to do much more work for us.

Source: Microsoft product screen shot reprinted with permission from Microsoft Corporation.

whole library of these little codes: "ts" is "thesis," "tss" is "thesis statement," "sn" is "sentence" and so on. It can also be useful to sometimes add temporary ones when you are working on a particular unit, like "qsh" for "Qing-shi Huang-di," the great Chinese emperor or "tgg" for "*The Great Gatsby.*"

To take this a step further, you can also program your ten or twenty most common comments into the AutoCorrect tool. Don't you wish you had a dollar for every time you typed, "This sentence is too vague," or "You need more details here!"

In the illustration that follows, we've put the text "v1" in the *Replace* window and we've put a comment in the *With* window: "Your sentence is too vague, and your point is unclear. You need to use precise vocabulary and incorporate an example or illustration that will clarify your statement." That sentence is so long you can't even see the whole thing in the *With* window, but Word will happily take all of those words. By clicking *Add* on the bottom right,

AutoCorrect: English (US)

AutoCorrect | AutoFormat As You Type | AutoText | AutoFormat

☑ Correct TWo INitial CApitals
☑ Capitalize first letter of sentences
☑ Capitalize names of days

Exceptions...

☑ Replace text as you type

Replace: With: ● Plain text ○ Formatted text

v1| Your sentence is too vague, and your point is unclear.

youare	you are
your a	you're a
your an	you're an
your her	you're her
your here	you're here
your his	you're his
your my	you're my
your the	you're the

Add   Delete

☑ Automatically use suggestions from the spelling checker

Cancel   OK

In this example from Tom's Mac computer, we're creating a list of automatic comments for essays.
Source: Microsoft product screen shot reprinted with permission from Microsoft Corporation.

every time we type "v1" and then hit *Spacebar* or add some sort of punctuation, Word will automatically replace that with the two sentences that we've programmed into it.

You might create not only ten to twenty generic comments, but also five to ten comments specific to a particular assignment. These assignment-specific comments could be deleted after the assignment. Say you have assigned a documents-based essay to fifty students and you have a good sense of which documents will give students difficulty and why. In advance of correcting the essays, you might set up some AutoCorrect comments that explain to the students why they might have misinterpreted a specific document.

You could use the *Insert → Comment* tool in the Reviewing toolbar (PC) to insert your feedback at any point in the document. (See more about inserting comments below.) Or you might simply place your comments at the end of each essay. You could even correct the essay with pen and paper and just create a Word page for AutoCorrect comments.

Initially it can be difficult to remember your codes, so put a sticky note on your monitor (or an electronic sticky note on your screen if you have that software). After a few stacks of papers, you'll have your codes down cold and be ready to add new ones.

Here is a sample from Tom's AutoCorrect sheet:

	BODY PARAGRAPHS
b01	Your body paragraphs have clear and strong topic sentences that relate directly to the topic of the essay and support the thesis statement effectively.
b02	You provide much relevant supporting evidence that illustrates and substantiates your arguments. Bravo.
b03	You provide well-chosen evidence to support your thesis, but your thesis is narrow in scope. Thus, your answer to the question is incomplete.
b04	Your essay is not particularly well written, nor partcularly descriptive.
b05	You should make a more concerted effort to distinguish between relevant and tangential points.
b06	Constantly ask yourself whether the information you wish to include is central to illustrating and supporting your thesis. If not, discard it.
	SUPPORTING EVIDENCE
se 1	You do wonderful work in incorporating relevant and detailed information.
se 2	The essay lacks balance because you rely predominantly on the documents and incorporate little specific outside information.
se 3	The paragaph lacks balance because you rely predominantly on outside information and incorporate few specifics from the documents.
se 4	You have not provided adequate supporting evidence to bolster your arguments in this paragraph, nor in the remainder of the document.
se 5	Your supporting evidence is well chosen and accurately conveys the arguments outlined in the documents.
se 6	Your analysis of the document is not particularly clear, nor thorough.
se 7	You have provided adequate supporting evidence from the documents to substantiate your arguments, but you don't seem to understand the full message being conveyed in the documents.
se 8	Your essay is constructed in a logical and reasonable manner, but lacks balance. Much space is allocated to direct quotations and correspondingly little to analysis.
se 9	You have some excellent ideas, but they are not carefully developed and supported. You make abrupt transitions in this paragraph, which makes it seem disjointed.
se 10	You demonstrate a solid recall and understanding of the main themes and details of the unit.

Track Changes

Track Changes is a powerful editing tool, which makes it somewhat problematic as a grading tool: it lets you do too much of the work of editing the paper. It also requires you and your students to have Microsoft Word; if one of your students uses AppleWorks, Writer, or another word processor, the comments may not translate. The instructions for using Track Changes can be found in Chapter 7, "Writing," in the discussion of peer-editing tools.

When you are working closely with a student on a particular piece of writing or a particular writing problem, Track Changes can be very helpful since you can make changes to a document in a way that allows students to see exactly what you added and what you deleted. Many teachers will find they don't have time to devote this kind of attention to every paper, but for students who need or ask for extra attention, this can be a great way to offer detailed feedback.

If you do know that all of your students have access to Microsoft Word, then you could use a few of Word's functions for grading student papers. With Track Changes on, every comment you leave will be colored and underlined for your students. Students will need to choose to *Reject/Delete Changes* to get rid of your comments as they work on revising their drafts. If you fix problems for students, they can also *Accept Changes* to agree with your corrections, but why should you be the one fixing their papers?

The Comment function can be also very useful. These comments appear on the margins of the page in newer versions of Word (2003 and later), and they appear on a bottom split-screen in older versions. In newer versions, the comments have a little dotted line from the insertion point to the margin, so the comment doesn't interfere with reading the text. The AutoCorrect tool works automatically in the comment box, so you can insert comments and then use AutoCorrect to fill the comment boxes with your automatic comments. Comments can be easily added by leaving your cursor in the text or selecting a section to comment on, and then clicking the *Comment* button on the Reviewing toolbar, or choosing *Insert→Comment.*

These tools are perhaps a slight improvement over just typing something in boldface at the end of a sentence or the bottom of a paragraph. If students don't have Microsoft Word, they won't be able to see them, and it can be more confusing for students to *Accept* or *Reject/Delete Changes* than it is to simply delete teacher comments on drafts and make the changes themselves.

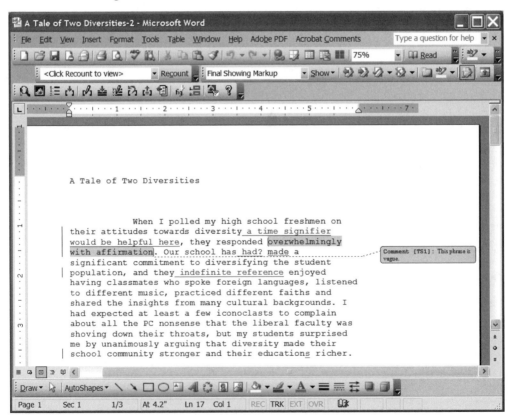

An example of Track Changes, with comments on the side and in the text.
Source: Microsoft product screen shot reprinted with permission from Microsoft Corporation.

We use Track Changes frequently with advanced students who are working with us on independent projects and with friends and colleagues who help edit our own writing, as Track Changes is an excellent tool for collaboration. Many teachers also choose to use Track Changes as their main tool for online marking and grading, though the other, simpler techniques that we discussed earlier may be easier and faster.

ONLINE RUBRICS: FINDING THEM, DESIGNING THEM, AND GRADING WITH THEM

Rubrics are grading matrices that allow teachers to give students more specific feedback than a simple letter grade without doing much more work than assigning a letter grade. Rubrics typically evaluate student performance on a scale of 1 to 4 in a series of categories, and the rubrics often spell out performance benchmarks for each rating in each category. If you have 4 benchmarks in each of 5 categories, that's 20 benchmarks. Creating rubrics can be time-consuming. Fortunately, finding them on the Internet and borrowing or adapting them can be quite easy. There are also some great free pieces of software to help you create rubrics. Once you settle on a format you like, adapting and updating your favorite rubrics can also be fairly simple.

We showed a few of our favorite rubrics in Chapter 7, "Writing," during our discussion of peer editing, but we have more to say here about finding and editing rubrics. Many rubrics of varying quality can be found throughout the Internet. A simple Google search using "rubric" and your assignment, like "Book Report," as search terms will lead you to many examples. Rubrics can also be found by visiting the Web sites of the rubric generators that we discuss below. An excellent collection of rubrics for English teachers is located at http://webenglishteacher.com/rubrics. html, which is part of the Web English Teacher Web site maintained by veteran English teacher Carla Beard.

When you find a rubric that you like, it usually can be easily edited in a word processor. A few hints:

- Go to the Web page with the rubric and select the entire page either by typing *Control-A* or by choosing *Edit→Select All*.
- Copy the page to your clipboard with *Control-C*.
- Open a new word-processing document.
- You will almost always be happier if you change the page orientation to landscape, where the 11" side is on top. Go to *File→Page Setup* and click on *Landscape*, then *OK*.
- Paste your rubric into the new document with *Control-V* or by choosing *Edit→Paste*.
- If the formatting looks good, then you can make changes to the text, change the size of the boxes, add new rows for new categories, and delete unnecessary ones.
- If the formatting gets messed up in the process of copying it, it may not be worth the time to fix if you can easily find another rubric that you like. Search a bit for an alternative before you try to fix a garbled copy.

- Be sure that you credit the source you borrowed from for your rubric. What is good for the goose is good for the gander!
- Be sure to give your rubric to students *before* they set off writing the assignment. When students are armed with expectations, they can begin their assignments with the end in mind.

One change to almost always make to a rubric is to add a space to write or type comments. You can use this space to copy and paste a particularly strong or particularly weak phrase or sentence, to further clarify a point in the performance benchmarks, or to add a general comment (perhaps a ready-made one using AutoCorrect).

When using rubrics with performance benchmarks, you might mark different benchmarks from different grades on the rubric. A student's introduction might provide excellent context but present no clear thesis; thus, it "Exceeds Standard" in one way but is just "Getting Started" in another. Referring to different benchmarks lets teachers offer more refined feedback. When grading with rubrics on a computer, it is quite easy to highlight specific benchmarks using boldface type. Two examples are below.

One section of a rubric:

	Getting Started	Approaching Standard	Meets Standard	Exceeds Standard
Evidence	Minimal evidence presented.	General evidence supports thesis. Significance of evidence unclear. Evidence seems to be from one source.	Specific evidence supports the thesis. Significance of evidence is clear. Evidence is gathered from multiple sources.	Significant, specific evidence persuasively supports the thesis. Clear indications of original interpretation of sources.

Comments:

The same section completed:

	Getting Started	Approaching Standard	Meets Standard	Exceeds Standard
Evidence	Minimal evidence presented.	General evidence supports thesis. Significance of evidence unclear. Evidence seems to be from one source.	**Specific evidence supports the thesis. Significance of evidence is clear. Evidence is gathered from multiple sources.**	Significant, specific evidence persuasively supports the thesis. **Clear indications of original interpretation of sources.**

Comments: Very good work with evidence . . . some research into the new border crossing with Palestine might have helped.

WEBSITE: A few of our sample rubrics can be found at http://www.edtechteacher.org/chapter9.html.

PENCIL: Keep printed copies of any rubric handy just in case. If you have trouble with your computer, you can have students print out their papers and hand them to you, and then you can grade them on copies of the printed rubric.

Creating Rubrics with Rubistar

FEATURED PRODUCT

Rubistar
Web site: http://rubistar.4teachers.org/
Developer: 4teachers.org
Cost: Free

Rubistar allows you to search through over 100,000 teacher-created rubrics, edit those rubrics, and design your own rubrics from templates.

Tech Specs: Designing a Rubistar Rubric
Set-Up Time: With help from the tutorial, you can get your first rubric designed from the available templates within about an hour.
Keep-Up Time: Editing rubrics, or modifying older rubrics for new assignments, is simple and can take just a few minutes.
Tech Savvy: Low. The design tools offer an easy-to-use Web interface.

Rubistar is a program designed by 4teachers.org, which got off the ground with a Department of Education grant. Rubistar lets you find and create rubrics using very clever templates. You can easily create rubrics for grading class debates, oral presentations, persuasive essays, timelines, Web sites, and many other projects. Rubistar can be found at http://rubistar.4teachers.org.

Rubistar has an excellent tutorial on its homepage (click on *Tutorial*), so we won't re-create one for you here, but we will show you some of the handy features.

To get started with Rubistar you will need to register.

To find rubrics, use the search engine on the right-hand side of the home page. Put a few keywords in the window, like "English essay," and then click *Search*. You will then be able to search through a bank that includes over 100,000 rubrics.

To get started creating your own, click on one of the template buttons at the bottom of the page. This will take you to a page with a variety of customizable rubrics. Choose one of these templates to easily get started.

Once inside, you will be able to name your rubric and decide whether to make it temporary, lasting online a week, or permanent. You then will get into the meat of creating your rubric.

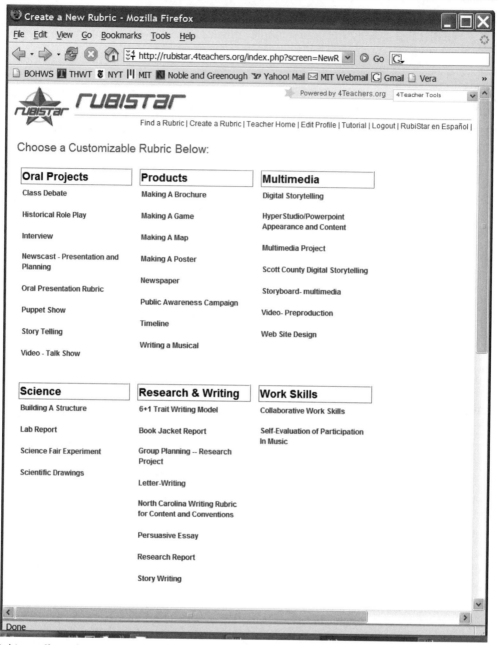

Rubistar offers a diverse array of customizable templates for rubrics.
Source: Courtesy of 4teachers.org.

Each Rubistar rubric starts as a series of blank categories. If you like, you can completely custom design a category, by giving it a name and describing performance benchmarks in four different grades. But why start from scratch?

In any category, toggle a drop-down menu, and you will see options for several different categories. When you choose a category, performance benchmarks will automatically appear in each grade level. You can edit these performance benchmarks and customize them to any degree you see fit.

You can create a rubric in Rubistar by adding pre-crafted components. You can also modify any component or benchmark, or even create elements on your own from scratch.   *Source:* Courtesy of 4teachers.org.

Then you can submit your rubric and choose whether to print it, download it into an Excel spreadsheet file, or save it to the Rubistar online database.

This program takes very little time to learn and will enable you to very quickly customize rubrics for your assignments.

ELECTRONIC GRADEBOOKS

Tech Specs: Setting up an Electronic Gradebook

Set-Up Time: Many electronic gradebooks can be found on the Web in just a few minutes of searching. Setting up an electronic gradebook might take between 30 and 60 minutes to enter course information and set preferences.

Keep-Up Time: You will need to take a few minutes after every assessment to enter scores. If you use your gradebook for attendance records, plan on spending a couple of minutes every schoolday to enter the information.

In-Class Time: The expectation is that you will enter data outside class time.

Tech Savvy: Low to enter scores; medium to create reports and charts.

There are many excellent electronic gradebooks available to help you calculate grades, keep attendance records, create student reports, and perform a variety of other tasks. Electronic gradebooks can also be put on a network for students (and perhaps parents) to see teacher grades. An obvious advantage of the electronic gradebook over pen and paper is the automatic mathematical calculation of grades. But electronic gradebooks can do so much more than just calculate grades.

There are several electronic gradebooks we could recommend to you, but we are going to focus on our favorite: Easy Grade Pro.

An Easy Grade Pro Tutorial in Ten Steps

FEATURED PRODUCT

Easy Grade Pro
Web Site: http://www.orbissoft.com/
Developer: Orbis
Cost: A single license for a Mac OS X or Windows computer is $49.

Easy Grade Pro is a powerful, flexible, and popular electronic gradebook to manage student grades, attendance, and other information. An Easy Grade Pro gradebook can be placed on a network, allowing access from any computer to teachers, students, and parents.

Step 1: Create a New Gradebook. To start an Easy Grade Pro gradebook, click the *Create a New Gradebook* button, give your gradebook a name (e.g., "US History Daccord 08-09), and choose a location for it on your computer.

Step 2: Add Classes. The next step is to add classes. Once you create your new gradebook, a window will automatically appear directing you to add classes. For each single subject in a single term add a list of student names and related information. (We find it works best to add a class to the gradebook for each class you teach in your *current term* only and add classes for future terms later.) At any point you can select *Add Class* from the *Tool* option in the menu bar to add an additional class.

Type the name of the class—use a unique name for each class—in the *Class/Subject Name* field and press *Key Tab*. Feel free to edit the term labels so that they match the term labels used by your school. For instance, you could insert "First Semester, First 6 Weeks, Quarter 1, Semester 2," or whatever you like. Select the current term for the class by clicking in the box to the right of your current term's label. A checkmark should appear.

Don't worry about Class Weight. Unless you have a class that is worth half of a normal class, the class weight should be left at 1.0.

To add more classes, click the *Next Class* button and repeat the steps above. Click the *Done* button when finished.

Step 3: Add Student Names. Now you're ready to enter student names. You'll be prompted to enter first and last names and gender. ID is important only if you plan to let students access the grades online and want to assign them a unique identification number. You may want to use the *Custom Data* fields on the right to enter relevant information about the student. (Perhaps you wish to note accommodations for a student with a learning disability.) Click *Next Student* to proceed through your list, and click *Done* when you finish your list. To switch to different classes, use the Class menu or the *Prior Class* and *Next Class* tools.

In Easy Grade Pro's class options you can set the grading scale, decide how you wish to round up scores, and set other features. *Source:* Courtesy of Orbis Software.

Step 4: Set Class Options. Class options are important because your selections will impact how Easy Grade Pro calculates and perhaps weighs the scores you enter and how it organizes information. It is a good idea to set the class options to match the way you work before creating any additional classes. Keep in mind that you can set different class options for different classes or copy class options from one class to the next.

In the class options menu you can adjust the following options:

- **Scale:** You can use the default grade scale and corresponding percentages, or you can edit them by clicking in the appropriate field. Grades can be letters (A, B, C), words (Excellent, Satisfactory), or numbers (4.00, 3.50).
- **Rounding:** Determine if you would like to round up scores by whole numbers, tenths, or hundreds.
- **Category:** Again, you can use the default categories, but it is likely that you will want to customize them to reflect how you organize and weigh assessments. Perhaps you want to include a final exam as a category, or class participation. In any event, if you use weight categories, they must add up to 100 percent.
- **Footnotes:** You can define up to seven footnotes to add to student scores. You can edit the footnotes by simply clicking and typing in the appropriate field.
- **Score:** This tab is for marking and tracking such things as missing or incomplete work.
- **Attendance:** This tab is for marking and tracking such things as absences and lateness to class.

- **Calendar:** The calendar is important to set up if you wish to keep accurate records of student absences and lateness. Select all the days you teach that class and click on the corresponding dates for the beginning and end of the term and any holidays.
- **Term, Seat, Color:** Term is useful if you wish to copy student data from one term to a current class. The other two categories can help you organize your classroom seating arrangement but do not impact the calculations of grades.

Click the *Done* button when finished.

Step 5: Add Assignments. By default you should now be in the Score view. To add an assignment, simply double-click the vertical *Add Assignment* button. Give the assignment a name and determine its maximum points and score. For many teachers maximum points and score will always be the same. However, some may wish to score a particular assignment out of, say, 100 points but only want the assignment to count for 50 points toward the student's overall grade.

If you are weighting categories, it is important to designate a category for each assignment. Simply toggle the category selections and make your choice. There are additional options you may consider. For instance, Special Scores can be used to provide special meaning to a score, such as "extra credit" or "not for grade." You can also display scores as percentages or grades and add a customized note.

Click *Next* to add more assignments and *Done* when finished.

Step 6: Add Scores. By default Easy Grade Pro will open up a cell to record the first grade of the first assignment. Enter a score. If you wish to enter a Footnote or Note to accompany a grade, simply double-click on the cell. The box that opens is for adding your custom note. You may also wish to select a footnote from the menu. Just select the appropriate number and hit *Done*. If you add a footnote, a little squiggly symbol will appear in the bottom left corner of the cell in question in the scores. If you add a note, a little square will appear in the top right corner of the cell.

Note: you must enter a 0 for an assignment that is not done or enter an attendance code such as "AE," absent excused. (Refer to Class Options.)

As you add scores to assignments, Easy Grade Pro will calculate them as grades as per the settings from Class Options. The overall student grade will appear to the right of each student's name.

Step 7: View the Mini Summary. A Mini Summary palette appears in the upper-left corner in Score view. (If the palette is not visible, choose *Edit* → *Tool Options* → *Show Mini-Sum*.) Toggle the arrow in the top left corner of the palette to display an assignment graph or a graph of other information, such as student grades and student attendance.

Note: You must enter at least six assignment scores for any particular student to see a graph of individual student scores.

Step 8: Print Notes for a Student or Class. To view and copy the text of any note you've added to any score, double-click on the cell that contains the score you put in. The note can be copied and pasted into another type of document and application. To see, copy, or print all of the notes you've added to any assignment, for

| | Score | Attend. | Seating | Student | Assign. |

Term 1: U.S. History (8)

Mini-Summary

davis, john
OVERALL GRADE   88.4/100 =   88
• Essays & Tests (6379.5/425 =   89
• quizzes & homework 104/125 =   83
• effort/portcipation 92/100 =   92
• Completed.........88.4/100 =   88

#	13 of 13 Students	Mi..	Overall	pop quiz 1 (10)	pop quiz 2 (5)	Ragged Disk paragraphs (40)	class participation (50)	corrected paragraphs (NG)	Essay 1 Industrial Age (100)	Industrial Age test (100)	extra credit q1 (EC)	20s Magazine editorial (50)	20s Magazine design (25)	30s hobo story (50)	Quiz units2-3 (70)	effort & participation (50)	assessment (100)
1	brown, jane		84 B	3	4	33	46.5		84	78		43	23.5	43.5	55.5	44.5	83
2	davis, john		88 B+	5.5	4	33	46		88	85	2	46	23.5	46	61.5	46	89
3	miller, tucker		81 B-	3.5	0	32.5	45.5		83	83		43	23	43.5	39	44	84
4	smith, henry		92 A-	7.5	4	35.5	47.5		89	91		47	23.5	46.5	67	47.5	94
5	jones, mary		88 B+	7	4	34	46		87	86		44	23	45	61	46.5	87
6	johnson, sara		84 B	5	2	34.5	46.5		83	83.5	2	43	23.5	43.5	47.5	46	87
7	miller, diane		89 B+	9.5	3	34.5	46.5		86	90.5	2	42	23.5	45	61	47	87
8	lewis, laura		93 A-	6.5	4.5	34	48		93	89.5		47.5	23.5	47	64.5	48	94
9	williams, caroline		86 B	7.5	2.5	35	47.5		86	85.5		41.5	21	42.5		44	85
10	rodriguez, jerome		84 B	7.5	5	34	38		87	86		43	23.5	44	52.5	43	86
11	walker, stephen		86 B	6	1.5	33.5	46		87	87.5	2.5	44	23	43.5	53.5	45	88
12	hernandez, elizabeth		83 B-	2	1	35	47		84	81.5	3	43.5	21	45.5	43	46	84
13	young, greg		91 A-	ex	5	36	48.5		92	89		47	23	43.5	61.5	47	89
14	ADD STUDENT +																

The Mini Summary makes a wide variety of information available to you at a glance.
Source: Courtesy of Orbis Software.

any student, you can generate a Student Notes Report with the *Student Notes* option turned on.

Select *Print* from the menu bar and click on the *Other* tab. Scroll down and select *Student Notes*, the bottom item in the list. Click on *Next*. In the *Student Notes Report Options* window, be sure to check the *Include Student Score Notes* option. Click on *Preview* to be sure this is the information you want and then click on the *Print* button.

Note: You can choose to print the report for all of your classes, for the currently selected class, or for selected students only.

Step 9: Print a Score Chart Report with Footnotes. Select *Print* from the menu bar and click on the *Chart* tab. Select *Score Chart* from the top of the list. Click on *Next* and make sure you check the *Include footnote key* box. Click on *Preview* to be sure this is the information you want and then click on the *Print* button.

Step 10: Post Your Easy Grade Pro Gradebook Online. In order to put a gradebook online, each student must have a password between six and eight characters long, containing letters and numbers. To move your grades online, choose *File* from the menu bar and select *Internet*. The rest depends on your school's online setup. Your school might use Edline, an Internet platform that serves as a Web site, and Easy Grade Pro has an *Edline* tab that you can select to choose student data and single-class and multi-class reports.

If your school doesn't use Edline, another option is to use Basmati to post grades online. Basmati is a free open-source application that students, parents, and staff can access using a specific login and password. Go to the Easy Grade Pro Web site for more information about Basmati.

Make sure to talk with your school IT director to ensure that your school allows grades posted online, and also review your school's acceptable use policy for technology. Your IT director will likely have specific technical information for you for posting grades online that are not included here.

THE NEW FRONTIERS OF ONLINE PLAGIARISM

While the Internet has made millions of incredible primary sources and scholarly articles available to students, it has also spawned a massive industry for cheating and all-too-easy opportunities to plagiarize. Intellectual property, citation, and plagiarism are complicated subjects, and the Web has made them even more complicated. Helping students write honest, fair, well-documented papers requires teaching good research and writing habits and understanding how students can fall into the new bad habits of the Internet age. Let's start by walking through some of the seedier places on the Internet.

Paper Mills

In March of 1999, the librarians at Kimbell Library at Coastal Carolina University began keeping a list of "virtual paper mills," which can be found at http://www.coastal.edu/library/presentations/mills2.html. These are Web sites where students can download papers on a variety of subjects. Sometimes the papers are free and the sites make money through advertising; sometimes students need to pay for their papers with a credit card. Many of the sites also provide an opportunity for students to sell original papers to the Web sites. Almost all of these sites harvest papers from one another, so many of the papers found at free sites can also be found for sale. As of November 2006, the list had grown to over 250 sites.

Some of these sites also offer custom papers, where students can order essays on any topic and specify a minimum number of sources, required sources, minimum length, and other factors. Many sites claim that they have PhDs and retired professors writing these essays which doesn't sound like a very good retirement to us. Custom papers don't come cheap, with sites charging around $20 per page.

Fortunately, some of these sites are kind enough to explain to students that these papers are only meant to be used as examples and, if used, should be properly cited. A1 termpaper.com comes with this stern warning:

> I understand that plagiarism may be **ILLEGAL**, that it is **always** UNETHICAL, and that I **MAY NOT** publish or represent this report as my own work. I understand that legal and/or academic censure may result if I do so. I agree that I will use this paper for research purposes only. **By clicking the button below, I am indicating that I accept these terms.**

There must be some kind of reverse psychology at work here. For students with a little time to search or a little money to spend, a paper on almost any imaginable topic is easy enough to find.

In addition to paper mills, it is also easy enough to copy and paste material from legitimate Web sites. Many of the topics studied in school have extensive commentary on a variety of Web sites, including Web sites created by students.

While copying other material wholesale is a problem, many sophisticated students have also developed more subtle means to take ideas from other sources. Some students will browse through online term papers looking for thesis statements, arguments, and pieces of evidence, and then take those ideas and write papers in their own words. If students are clever, this form of plagiarism can be much harder to detect.

Copying and Stealing from Friends and Classmates

Copying things by hand is very time-consuming, but sending a schoolmate an email with an assignment is awfully simple. Change a few words here and there, and the same response to an online homework assignment can be handed in by a few people.

Even worse, students can also attempt to get into each other's email or server space. Many students are careless about sharing passwords and logging out of programs when they finish, and other students can take advantage of such carelessness to steal academic work.

Recently Justin received a pair of identical assignments. He summoned one student to his office and showed her the two papers, and she agreed that they were identical. She said she had copied the work, and she would talk to the other student. When Justin summoned the second student to his office, she explained to him that she and her friend had been editing her MySpace page. While doing so, she had given her friend her MySpace password and had casually mentioned to her that it was also her school email password. It became clear that her friend had taken that password, hacked into her email account, copied the assignment, and tried to pass it off as her own. Needless to say, the honest student felt heartbroken and angry that her friend had taken advantage of her trust, and she felt pretty foolish as well.

Sloppy Research Habits

Careless research habits have always greased the slope to plagiarism, but again computers can amplify the problems of sloppy research.

Imagine that a student begins research and starts a word-processing document to keep notes. The document is not organized as a research journal (see Chapter 4, "Guided Inquiry"), and so ideas, quotations, and passages pile atop one another. Some of the material is original ideas, some of the material is copied and cited, and some of the material is just copied. The student gets confused about what material is his and what is not; eventually, it all makes it into the paper.

When students get busy enough, even the best can make mistakes. Justin, on one occasion, detected plagiarism of this nature by an honor-roll student who served on the student disciplinary committee. Plenty of hard working, honest students can make these kinds of mistakes in the absence of strong guidance about how to organize their research materials.

With so much material to be borrowed, bought, and stolen from the Web, how can teachers prevent and detect plagiarism?

Preventing Plagiarism

A one-time lecture on plagiarism is no longer enough to prevent students from intentionally or inadvertently committing acts of plagiarism. You'll need to emphasize good research, writing, and citing habits throughout the year to help kids stay on the right path. Here are ten ideas for doing so:

1. **Educate students about plagiarism.**
   The first thing any student will tell you when caught plagiarizing is that they did not understand that what they were doing was wrong. At the beginning of every term, teachers need to refresh their students on the meaning of original work and intellectual property and the skills of proper citation. Be sure to explain to students that plagiarism is one of the only serious academic crimes that can be committed without bad intention. To show up to class drunk, you need to put some work into it. But unlike other trespasses, carelessness and sloppiness can lead to plagiarism.

2. **Explain how the best scholars read and cite widely.**
   Many students think of citation as something that you do to stay out of trouble. This negative interpretation needs to be reversed. Students need to learn that the best scholars cite widely to support their ideas and demonstrate their intellectual breadth. Students should come to see citation as a means to demonstrate their good research skills.

3. **Know your students as writers.**
   Many of the tools of plagiarism detection work best if you have an inkling that something is amiss. Get to know your students as writers so that when you read language that sounds borrowed, you can run some of the tests described below.

4. **Design plagiarism-proof assignments.**
   Many of the essays that can be found online are based on generic topics like "Arguments Against Stem Cell Research" or "The Tragic Flaws in MacBeth." To prevent students from using these topics, design more creative assignments. Ask questions that relate to class discussions, compare unlikely passages or events or consider topics in unusual ways. If you ask unique questions, it will be much harder for students to find generic answers.

5. **Limit the allowed sources.**
   If you control the data set students can use, then you can much more easily predict the kinds of conclusions students will draw and the kinds of essays they will write. Also, if you force students to write using less common sources and to make more unusual comparisons, they will be much less likely to find helpful essays online.

6. **Break up the writing process into pieces, and give deadlines and collect drafts throughout.**
   Students cut corners more when they are under pressure. Help students relieve that pressure by breaking long assignments up into smaller pieces, and collecting their work at the completion of each step. If students need to hand in brainstorming maps, outlines, drafts, corrections, and other products, it will be much harder for them to simply turn in an essay from the Internet.

7. **Devote some in-class time to writing.**

   Make students do some of their writing in class so you can float around the room and watch their ideas develop. If students try to discard the work they do in class, it may be a clue that there is sneaky business afoot.

8. **Demonstrate to students that you know how to detect plagiarism.**

   At the beginning of the semester, give your students a tour of paper mill sites, CliffsNotes and SparkNotes, and the plagiarism-detection tools that we discuss below. Show some examples of students who turned in plagiarized papers and explain how you caught them. Make it clear to students that you are familiar with the new ways students can make bad decisions and that you are committed to helping them not make those decisions.

9. **Let students submit their drafts to a plagiarism-detection tool.**

   The most popular plagiarism-detection software is a Web tool called Turnitin .com, and we discuss this tool later in this chapter. Turnitin.com can be set up so that teachers submit assignments, but you can also allow students to submit papers on their own.

10. **Promise students that you will vigorously preserve a fair classroom.**

    One of the most common reasons students give for cheating is that they feel pressure to compete with other students who are cheating. (The University of British Columbia has a good synopsis of why students cheat here: http://www.arts.ubc. ca/Why_Students_Cheat.116.0.html.) So if a handful of students cheat in your class and get away with it, then others will feel pressure to cheat in order to keep up. Then you have a room full of students who feel like they need to cheat to succeed. Crack down early, and your best students will appreciate the opportunity to work in a fair environment.

Detecting Plagiarism

Computers and the Internet have given students a wide variety of tools to commit plagiarism, but fortunately teachers have their own suite of resources to keep up with cheating students.

Searching for Plagiarism with Google

The simplest place to start detecting plagiarism is with the Google search engine. When you detect a paragraph, sentence, or phrase in an essay that doesn't sound like something your student would write, turn that phrase into a search term in Google. Google will accept up to 32 words. You might start by taking the most unlikely short phrase and searching for that in quotation marks, so Google looks only for that exact phrase. You can also put a longer section into the search engine without quotation marks and see what comes up. Try a few phrases, both with and without quotation marks, and you will be able to find most cases of copying from Web sites.

Each search result that Google displays provides the title of the Web site as well as an excerpt from the page that contains your search terms. This excerpt can help you easily detect where students have borrowed or adapted whole phrases.

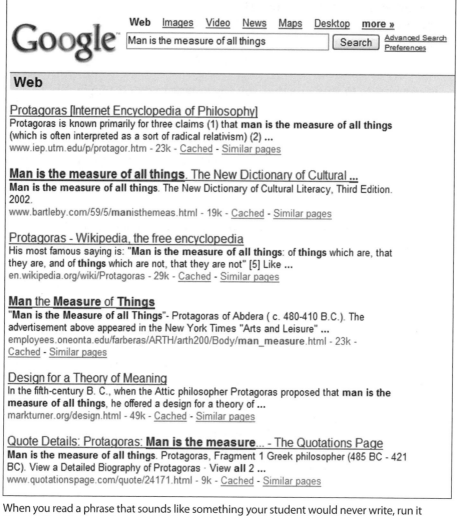

When you read a phrase that sounds like something your student would never write, run it through Google to see if you can find it somewhere else.   *Source:* Courtesy of Google.

If you have a good eye for when a student is not using his or her own words, Google can be very effective in establishing plagiarized materials.

Turnitin.com

FEATURED PRODUCT

Turnitin.com
Web site: http://www.turnitin.com/
Developer: iParadigms
Cost: Depends on the size and nature of the institution, but our school of 500 students was charged $700 for a license in July 2007.

Turnitin.com allows you to submit student papers to be checked for plagiarism against an enormous database of Web sites, online databases, and Turnitin.com's database of every paper ever submitted to it.

If students are copying from downloaded papers or from each other, you may need to use a more sophisticated tool than Google. Currently the most popular tool is called Turnitin.com, though there are several others. A list of plagiarism-detection services can be found at this Web site by the Shapiro Undergraduate Library at the University of Michigan: http://www.lib.umich.edu/acadintegrity/instructors/violations/detection.htm.

Turnitin.com compares submitted papers to three databases. First, it will check the paper against papers and other sites from the Web. Second, it will check the paper against commercial databases of online journals and news articles. Finally, it will check the paper against every other paper that has ever been submitted to Turnitin.com. Turnitin.com will then produce an "Originality Report," which will indicate the percentage of the paper borrowed from other sources and will provide links so that you can see where each borrowed section came from. It includes features like *Omit Quoted Materials* and *Omit Bibliography* so you can focus even more quickly on likely sources of plagiarism.

Keep in mind, though, that while Turnitin.com checks an enormous number of public Web pages, there are many more "hidden" Web pages—such as those in private online databases—that Turnitin.com is not able to access. Thus, while Turnitin.com accesses a great amount of Web content, it is hardly able to access the "whole" Web.

Turnitin.com users have two main options for employing the tool in their classrooms. One option is to have students email the teacher their papers, and have the teacher upload those essays into Turnitin.com. Teachers can routinely search all essays, spot check a few at random, or upload only essays that may have problems. Teachers can then use the tool to catch students in the act of plagiarism.

If you choose to use this method, you will probably want to notify your students that you are doing so. Consider a statement in your syllabus like this: "In this course I am committed to maintaining a fair working and grading environment for all students. To preserve this fair environment, I am committed to trying to prevent students from copying or plagiarizing the writings of others, and I will use both conventional and new online methods to identify plagiarism."

Another method for using Turnitin.com is to set up accounts for each of your students and have them submit their own papers, often at the rough draft stage. That way, if students make errors related to citation and plagiarism, they can fix them before submitting their papers. This option is almost always less time-consuming, and it lets students correct errors (and bad judgment) before submitting final drafts of papers. It can also be used, of course, to figure out how to dupe the program and plagiarize anyway. There are pros and cons to both methods of using Turnitin.com.

If many of your students have Internet connections at home, then some of them are almost certainly plagiarizing in their papers—either intentionally or through ignorance. If you aren't detecting cases of plagiarism, don't be fooled into thinking that it isn't happening in your classroom (but *my* students respect me and would never do that in one of *my* classes). At our school, we find a strong correlation between teachers who detected plagiarism regularly and their level of technological savvy. This suggests to us that plagiarism is a problem throughout the school, and tech-savvy teachers seem best equipped to detect these issues.

Getting Started with Turnitin.com

Tech Specs: Getting Started with Turnitin.com

Set-Up Time: It will take you an hour or two to set up your classes and practice submitting a few old papers to see how things work. (It's best to learn the system with a paper that you know was plagiarized from an online source.)

Keep-Up Time: Spot-checking a few papers now and then will take perhaps 30 minutes each time you do so. Submitting an entire course's worth of papers can take an hour or more.

In-Class Time: If you want your students to register with your Turnitin.com account so that they can submit their own rough drafts, plan on a class period for this.

Tech Savvy: Medium. Turnitin.com has numerous ways to submit papers and a variety of tools for evaluating them, so it can take some time to learn your way around.

As mentioned earlier, you can submit student papers yourself or you can set up accounts for each of your students and have them submit their own papers.

Once you have registered for the service, the first step is to log in with your username and password at http://turnitin.com.

Step 1: Set up *My Classes*. Click on the My Classes tab in the upper right corner and select *Add classes*. Use this feature to organize documents by classes. First, add a class name. Add a password if others are to be given access to this class and its documents. Set an end date for the class. From here you can also allow students to view their "originality reports," Turnitin.com's determination of how original, or unoriginal, a particular document is.

Click *Submit* when you're done.

Your class is now active. You should see your class name in the form of a link on the page. Click it.

Step 2: Create a New Assignment. Before you or your students can submit a paper, you first need to create an assignment. To create your first assignment, click the *Create a new assignment* link. You can label the assignment a "paper" or "revision" assignment. Give it a title, such as "Essay 1," and choose a start and end date to submit papers for the assignment. Make sure that *Generate originality reports* is set to yes and click *Submit*.

Step 3: Submit a Document. You are now ready to begin the originality report process. First, you should see your assignment as a link and various options to the right. Look for the submit icon and click it.

Next, determine how you want to submit the file. For instance, you can upload a single file or a batch of files from your computer or copy and paste from a document. Toggle the options beside *Submit a report by*.

If you are uploading student papers yourself, then have the students email you their documents and save them on your computer. Hit the *Browse* button, find a student paper on your computer, and choose it. (Turnitin.com accepts many different file formats.) Once a file is selected, the *Browse* button will become a *Submit* button. Click it. In a few seconds Turnitin.com will show you text from the first page of the document and ask if that is indeed the document you wish to submit. Click *Yes submit*.

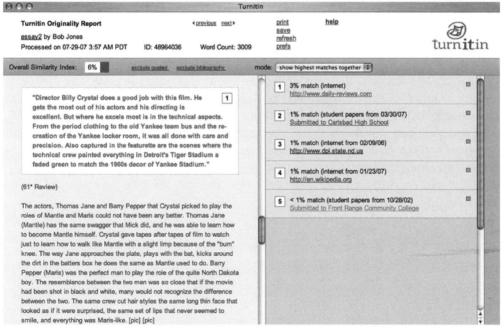

To submit a paper, locate the paper you want to submit on your computer by clicking the "browse" button and enter a title for the paper. Select an enrolled student using the student pulldown to associate the submission with a student and click the submit button to upload the paper.

Turnitin.com accepts many different file formats, and Turnitin.com will generate an "originality report" for each document you submit.   *Source:* Courtesy of iParadigms, LLC.

Step 4: Check your Inbox and Originality Reports. Click the inbox icon that appears above the document. In the inbox you will see the author and title of any documents you have uploaded for that particular assignment. To the right you will see a category called Report. If Turnitin.com has finished its originality report on a particular document, you will see a percentage and color associated with the document. The higher the number, the higher the degree of unoriginal material in the document. If the report color is orange or red, then Turnitin.com has detected a high degree of unoriginal material in the document.

To look at the full originality report, click the report icon with the percentage and color. If Turnitin.com finds an exact match between text in the essay and text in its databases, or

You have the option of excluding quoted text from the originality report via a link near the top of the page, and it is a good idea to do so. Direct quotes from books, articles, Web sites, and such are likely to be marked red and can skew the originality report.   *Source:* Courtesy of iParadigms, LLC.

the Web pages it searches, then the student's text will be marked red in the originality report. Turnitin.com will also flag other, less exact, similarities between text in the document you submit and text in its databases, or in other Web pages. In the left column is the document you submitted. In the right column are links to the sources that contain similar text to the student paper. The degree of similarity is indicated by the color code. If you click on the links on the right, you will be taken to the source and can compare the similarities between them and the document you submitted.

Turnitin.com is a plagiarism-detection service, but only you can make the final determination that a particular paper is plagiarized or not. Consider using Turnitin.com regularly as a plagiarism-*prevention* tool by asking students to upload a draft of their essay to Turnitin.com before they turn it in to you. They can assess the originality of their own writing, make changes if necessary, and hopefully become more mindful of the need to cite their sources.

FINAL THOUGHTS

There is much to be said for curling up on a sofa with paper in your hands when it is grading time. For years we did just that, even after we were teaching with laptops. However, the long hours every other weekend spent grading essays by hand took its toll on us. Like many others we tried rubrics and other devices to shorten our grading time, but nothing has more dramatically reduced our grading time than the use of the AutoCorrect tool in Microsoft Word. No more writing out the same comment over and over again every time we grade. No more wondering whether students can even read our handwriting. AutoCorrect made the process of adding comments to student papers so quick and easy that the problem is now restricting the number of comments we leave. Now if we can just figure out how to program Word to do all of this *automatically,* all our grading dreams will be fulfilled!

Of course, more efficient grading of papers with technology is only one part of the message of this chapter. Online quizzes, tests, and games provide us with an opportunity to diversify our assignments and assessments within a framework that can really motivate and engage students. (Our students often clamor for online review games before a unit test.) Quia.com and other services provide us with interesting and flexible tools to help students master content and have fun in the process. They also prompt us as teachers to think more creatively about our assignments. With more creative assignments and assessments come varied opportunities for students to display their abilities. We have a terrific opportunity to learn a lot more about our students as a result.

Chapter 10

Class Management

INTRODUCTION

Change is scary. When your students are lined up in rows, and you are lecturing from the front of the room, that can feel much safer and more comfortable than when students are spread out in a classroom or computer lab, working on different tasks at different speeds. Hopefully, though, we have convinced you through the various chapters in this book that computers can enhance great teaching and put students in the driver's seat of their own learning. We also hope you have come to share our belief that the opportunities provided by new technology are worth the risks and challenges. In this chapter we step back from the different facets of teaching to consider the best techniques for managing the educational technology environment as a whole.

We start by looking at best practices for teaching in computing environments and then we look at tools that can help you manage your classes and curriculum, such as email, course-management systems, and class Web sites. We also consider some of the big pieces of technology administration at the school level, like acceptable use policies, so that you can be familiar with schoolwide issues of technology management and be prepared to contribute to conversations at your own school. Finally, we gaze into our crystal balls and give our predictions for where all this is heading.

TEACHING STRATEGIES FOR COMPUTING ENVIRONMENTS

While a notebook and pencil, or a classroom window, offer significant opportunities for distraction in class, computers open a Pandora's box of ways for students to ignore you and goof off during class. Here are some tips for keeping students focused when computers are in use.

- **Design your classroom or lab so you can watch screens**: If possible, set up the computers in a horseshoe so that you can view all student screens at once. Rows of computers can work too, although it can be difficult for students to see past each other's monitors, and you will need to teach from the back of the room, behind students, if you want to watch everything.

  If you need to set up your classroom into clusters of machines, or with a big cluster in the middle of room, then you may want to consider a piece of software called Vision. Vision allows the teacher to watch all of the screens in a classroom at once, which allows for easy tracking of wayward students and coaching of individual students who need help. Check it out at: http://www.genevalogic.com/index.php?id=us.

- **Move around and hover**: Teaching in a computer classroom means teaching on your feet, moving around, checking in on every student and keeping them all on task. Assume that whenever you are not watching, they are surfing the Internet or playing Minesweeper.

- **Design activities that are challenging and engaging**: The best way to keep students on task is to design activities that students are excited about and challenged to complete in the allotted time. Give them high-quality assignments and hold them accountable, and you stand the best chance of keeping them focused.

- **Build in time for getting started and logging off**: When you are crafting lesson plans for computer labs, be sure to budget in the time it will take for students to get logged on and to save their work and log off. You will lose a few minutes at either end of the period, since it takes students a little longer to save their work than it does to shove their notebooks in their bags.

- **Have extra computers available**: If at all possible, have a few extra computers ready for students to use if a machine gets stuck or shuts down. It can often be easier to start over on a new computer than to try to resurrect a quirky machine.

- **Provide different benchmarks for different students**: For most tech activities, it can be helpful to have a main goal and then a secondary goal for fast-working students. For instance, if you want students to write on a topic, it might be worth also giving them a second topic to write on in case they finish early. If students find themselves with enough free time to start playing with the computer, it can be very hard to get them back on track.

- **Hold students accountable for staying on task**: Students need to know that there are consequences for goofing off with their computers during class. Write up a contract in the beginning of the year and be prepared to revoke computing privileges if a student cannot responsibly use the machines.

- **Balance routine with variety**: Since using computers as learning tools will take practice for you and your students, settling into a routine in the computer lab can help everyone get oriented. That said, if you overuse the same routine, students will lose some of their focus. Just as good teachers balance lecture, discussion, and projects in a normal classroom, teachers who use technology need to provide a variety of activities for students as well.

- **Have a backup plan:** Take a few planning minutes before class to figure out what you will do if the computers or the Internet is not working. Hopefully some of the suggestions for backup plans in this book will inspire your thinking.
- **If students share computers, make sure that everyone has a task**: If you have your students work on computers in groups, be sure that the shy girl with poor social skills isn't stuck doing all the work. Give each person in the group a specific task that requires him or her to split time between the keyboard, taking notes, and processing information offline.

EMAIL: GETTING ON THE SAME ELECTRONIC PAGE

One key to successful classroom management is for teacher and student to use the same, flexible email system. At the very least your email client should allow you to organize and store email messages as well as allow you to attach documents to email messages. If you and your students adopt the same email system, it will be easier for you to share and organize materials as a group and exploit whatever advanced features the system may have. If your school already integrates a popular email client such as Outlook—or a more specialized system such as First Class—that's great. Or perhaps you use a course-management system like Moodle or Blackboard. If so, use it. If not, an easy way to organize for email exchanges is to sign up for Gmail.

WEBSITE: Our school uses First Class, a powerful email client that is popular with many educational institutions. To see how we use First Class in our classes, you are invited to watch some instructional videos on our EdTechTeacher Web site: http://www.edtechteacher.org/chapter10.html.

Gmail is Google's free Internet-based email system, and anyone can get a Gmail account. (You no longer have to be "invited" by a current Gmail subscriber to get an account.) You can also have more than one account, so you might even set up a "turn-in" Gmail account solely for collecting essays and assignments from your students.

Note: Once you have a Google account, it's also easy to sign up for other Google services such as its online blogging tool (Blogger), online photo editor (Picassa), and online video sharing (YouTube).

Getting Started with Gmail

FEATURED PRODUCT

Gmail Email Account
Web site: http://www.gmail.com
Developer: Google
Cost: Free

Gmail offers free email accounts with spam protection, antivirus scanning for attachments, and about 6 gigabytes of free storage. It has a clean, easy-to-use interface and plenty of customizable features for advanced users.

Tech Specs: Setting up Gmail Accounts

Set-Up Time: 10 minutes.

Keep-Up Time: It takes no time to maintain the account, but you can sure waste plenty of time checking email.

In-Class Time: The first time you have students set up their email accounts, plan on spending 20 minutes getting everything set up and teaching students about the features

Tech Savvy: Low. Gmail is a very easy email system to use.

To get started with Gmail, go to http://www.gmail.com and click on the *Sign Up for Gmail* link in the bottom right corner. After filling in the required fields, you should receive email confirmation. Armed with your login name and password, go back to gmail. com and sign in.

Gmail has some unique features that you should find especially helpful. For starters, Gmail users don't have to delete messages. Gmail users are given plenty of space in their Gmail accounts, and Gmail's storage capacity is continuously growing. Practically speaking, this means students can store the messages that you send them, indefinitely.

Gmail also has a nifty search feature (it is Google, after all!). You can search the content of email messages, the "From," "To," or "Subject" headings, or you can just search chronologically. Gmail thus makes it very convenient for you and your students to locate emails you have sent each other at any time during the academic year. Moreover, Gmail groups messages by "conversation," or replies to a particular email. As a result you can easily view conversations with your students. Very convenient!

Our Gmail account makes it easy to manage suggestions for our Best of History Web Sites and sign-up requests for our newsletter.   *Source*: Courtesy of Google.

Once you and your students are on email, there are some simple, but effective, ways of using email to help you administer the class. First, get in the habit of emailing students homework assignments, class notes, and related course materials. With Gmail they will have those emails for as long as they like and can search for them with ease. If you teach in a computer lab or laptop classroom, begin by emailing the day's homework to students before class. Once they arrive, ask your students to sign in to their Gmail accounts (they'll want to check email anyway) and read the homework. If the assignment entails visiting a Web site, the students can click on the URL you put in the email message and go straight to the site. If you have a handout to share, you can attach it to the message. It can save you a lot of time at the photocopy machine! Keep in mind that you are not limited to attaching only text files; you can attach audio, video, and other sorts of multi-media files as well.

Gmail includes some clever tools to keep your emails organized. As mentioned earlier, emails sent back and forth are saved as "conversations," so when you click on the most recent email from your uncle Bob, you can easily see all of the emails that you and Uncle Bob have been sending to each other each time either of you replied to a message. You can also apply "labels" to emails or conversations, which put those emails in a category. You could encourage students to use Gmail labels to organize specific messages per unit, theme, author, or book. In this way, you are encouraging students to create their own online filing system of notes and assignments for the year. And will they ever be pleased come exam time to have all this information in one place!

To create a new label, like Homework Assignments, click on *Edit Labels,* and then look for the *Create New Labels* window. Type in the label name, and click *Create.* To apply a label to an email or conversation, click the box to the left of the email and then click on the *More actions* drop-down menu. Choose the label you want to apply at the bottom of the menu. To view only the emails associated with a certain label, click the name of the label from the list on the left-hand side of the inbox. In essence you've created a well-organized folder classification system to manage electronic materials for your course.

COURSE-MANAGEMENT SYSTEMS

An increasing number of public and private schools are investing in some kind of course-management system to coordinate the technology needs of their schools. Some of the most popular programs include Moodle, Blackboard, Angel, and a host of other smaller providers. Different products offer different services, but the most sophisticated allow faculty and students to set up blogs, chat rooms, digital portfolios, and class Web pages, and share syllabi, readings, assignments, and grades all through a single interface.

These systems are designed to meet the needs of many different shareholders in a school community—teachers, students, parents, administration, and IT staff. As a result, rarely is everyone completely happy with the product. (See our discussion of "You and Your IT department" below.) Unfortunately, of all those shareholders, sometimes course management tools can seem to respond to the needs of teachers the least. Course-management software can be great for the IT people and administrators who need to use the tool everyday, while not being as easy to use for the teachers who need to integrate it with many other teaching strategies.

Nevertheless, many schools are moving in this direction, and teachers need to be ready to keep up. Throughout this book we have discussed specific tools—often free or open-source tools—that can enhance teaching and learning. A blog can be set up for free on the Internet with a Web tool like Blogger or Edublogs.org, but many course-management tools will also have features that let students or teachers start blogging. If your school uses Moodle or Blackboard, then you can adapt the activities that we describe in this book to work with these systems. Hopefully this book can spark conversation between teachers and IT staff about how best to implement new teaching strategies with the tools that your school has.

SETTING UP YOUR OWN CLASS WEB SITE

Teachers are constantly communicating information to their students. You can write notes on the board, make announcements in class, or pass out handouts to keep students current on your expectations. But students space out in class, lose their class folders, and find other ingenious ways to not get your message. All of these communication media have their strengths, and adding a class Web site to your communication strategy can offer a persistent, accessible location for information that your students need. Forget a homework assignment? Lose a handout? Look it up on the Web. While it can certainly be an investment of time to set up a class Web site to help manage your communication with students, once it is up and running, it can certainly save you plenty of time.

How Web Sites Work

Despite the prevalence of Web pages in our lives, most folks don't really understand how a Web page works. You don't need to understand Web pages to teach with them, but sometimes knowing how they work can help you make the most of them or help you when they are not working.

The lingua franca of the Internet is hypertext markup language, or HTML, which is the programming language used on most Web pages. At the heart of this language are "tags." Tags tell Web browsers, like Firefox, Safari or Internet Explorer, how to display information. For instance, the <b> tag tells Firefox to put the subsequent text in bold-face. The </b> tag tells Firefox to stop using boldface.

So if I programmed the following line in HTML:

"Hello World . . . <b>Hello World</b> . . ."

then it would look like this on your Web browser:

"Hello World . . . **Hello World** . . ."

When you put a Web address, a URL, into your Web browser, you are telling your browser, "Hey, go to this page, read the HTML code there, and present the information the way the page tells you to." The HTML code at a URL is stored on another computer. Your Web browser takes the information from another computer, and displays it on your computer. Web pages are just text and tags that tell Web browsers how to present the text.

But what about images, videos, and sounds? Again, these are all done with tags. The images you see on a Web page are not actually stored in the Web page. They are stored somewhere else on the computer hosting the Web site, or sometimes even somewhere else on the Web. The Web page uses an image tag, <img>, which can be made to say "Make a box on the left-hand side of the page 100 pixels high and 20 pixels wide; then go to the images folder and put the picture called tomandjustin.jpg in that box." If you translated the above sentence into HTML, it would read <img src="images/tomandjustin.jpg" width="20" height="100" align="left">.

The same trick works with videos, sounds, and other elements on a page—they are just separate files that your Web browser tracks down and displays when the page tells the browser to do so.

All of these Web page and media files are stored in folders. When you see a Web address that says www.thwt.org/workshops/registration2007.htm, that means you are looking at a page called registration2007 in a folder called workshops at a site called www.thwt.org. If you get lost in your surfing, it can be helpful to delete everything after the .com, .edu, or .org in order to get back to the home page of the site you are browsing. Sometimes if a site has lots of interesting images, you can see if it has a searchable image folder by going to www.nameofthesite.com/images. Sometimes folders are protected, but sometimes they are freely searchable.

Blogs as Class Web Sites

Few tools are easier for getting a class Web page online than the free blogs provided by blogger.com or Edublogs.org. Edublogs use a blogging system, called WordPress, that makes it very simple to write both posts and pages. Posts are the chronologically ordered bits of writing that make up the bulk of any blog, whether they are the daily homework assignments or the student-prepared notes of the day. Pages are static pages that are linked to the sidebar of the blog. Unlike posts, pages are designed to remain up for a while, so they are perfect for sharing syllabi or course expectations and policies. They are easy enough to change, so that you could easily have a weekly homework assignment sheet on a page that you updated every weekend.

With this blog as a course Web site, you can create a simple communication medium for your students where they can get the information they need to succeed in your course. Blogs also allow interested parents to keep up with the goings on in your classroom, and they can also allow you to share your work with your colleagues. For much more on blogging, refer to Chapter 2, "Discussion and Communication."

Free Teacher Web Sites

Over the years, a variety of Web sites have offered free hosting services for teachers to create their own Web sites without needing to know HTML, the programming language of the Web. Currently SchoolRack.com is making that offer, and they have a Web tool that allows you to create basic teaching Web sites with different pages for your different sections and central pages for information common to all of your classes.

SchoolRack.com has a very good video tutorial that walks you through the steps of setting up your Web site. The pages are built through a series of forms where you can supply basic information about each class, create additional pages for common information, host a page where students can download files, and even have students or parents sign up to a mailing list so you can easily email your whole class. For a free service, the quality is quite impressive, though there are Yahoo ads embedded in the top of your pages. Another free and simple option for teachers would be designing a Web site using Google Pages, which is described more thoroughly in Chapter 8, "Student Presentations."

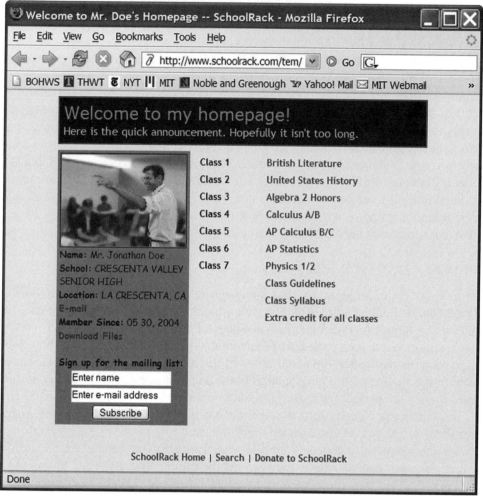

SchoolRack.com is a great resource for teachers looking to create their own Web sites.

Source: Courtesy of SchoolRack.

Starting Up Your Own Web Site

When you are really ready to dive in, it can be worth creating your own Web site where you can share your assignments, lesson plans, syllabi, and so on. A Web site is a great place for teachers to express themselves creatively, share their work, and communicate with students, parents, and other faculty. A few of the most popular teacher Web sites that share lesson plans and curriculum ideas get millions of hits every year, and they can actually earn money through the sale of advertisements.

Building a Web site is a project beyond the scope of this book, but here are some hints to get started.

- To have your own space on the Web, you will need to register a domain name and find a server to host your Web site. You can do this through a variety of services, like Yahoo Web Hosting, HostMySite.com, or the well-advertised GoDaddy.com, though their SuperBowl commercials are terrible.

- Next you will need to learn a little bit about HTML, the programming language of the Web. A very good free online class is available at w3schools.com.
- Once you understand a little HTML, you can start designing Web pages. Microsoft FrontPage and Macromedia DreamWeaver are two popular pieces of software for designing Web sites, but all you need is a simple text editor—like NotePad from Windows or TextEdit on Apple's OS X.
- One of the easiest ways to design a site is to borrow elements from other sites. All Web browsers have a feature that lets you look at the source code for a given Web page. In Firefox it's *View→ Page Source* from the menu bar. One of the best ways to learn HTML is to copy this source code and then start manipulating and changing it.
- Finally, you will need a means to move your files from your computer to the server hosting your Web site. Often this is accomplished via an FTP (file transfer protocol) program. FrontPage and Dreamweaver have built-in tools for FTPing your files, but other programs can be used to send your files to your Web host. FileZilla is a popular free, open-source FTP tool.

Designing and maintaining your own homepage can be a great way to develop your skills as a teaching professional. Get good enough at it, and maybe it can turn into a second job for those summer months as well!

YOU AND YOUR IT DEPARTMENT

We'd love it if after reading this book you have come to feel fairly enthusiastic and knowledgeable about many of the technology tools we have shown you. When we run workshops for teachers, they often get very excited about a particular tool and are determined to use it in their classrooms. We're excited when that happens, but we also know that the teacher may not get permission to use it. When classroom teachers start popping into their school's IT office to ask permission to use certain online services or software, sometimes IT departments say no. These requests can lead to frustration, for both the classroom teacher and the IT staff member. (Tom is both a classroom teacher and an IT staff member, so he is constantly frustrated with himself!)

Classroom teachers and IT departments look at technology problems from two very different vantage points, and it can be quite helpful for both to try to see issues from the other side's point of view. IT departments have limited resources to support the growing technology needs of teachers, and as such they have an interest in getting teachers to all use a smaller number of tools that the department is confident that they can afford and support. For instance, fixing misbehaving or broken computers is a much simpler task if every computer has the exact same software loaded onto it. When teachers request to put a particular program in one computer lab, the IT department often envisions either putting that program on every computer in the school or facing the problems of having to deal with dozens of different "builds" on computers in different labs, libraries, and classrooms.

Of course, the teacher making that request often isn't concerned with all of those details; he or she just wants to use the best possible tool or service for the students. There are already so many bureaucratic obstacles that impede teachers' work, teachers who approach IT teams are hoping that those teams can solve problems rather than create new ones.

So IT teams and classroom teachers need to be constantly working to find their way to middle ground, where teachers have access to tools that meet their needs and IT staff keep the number of different programs and services to a manageable number. Solving these kinds of school wide and district wide issues can be made easier by teachers and IT staff taking time to view problems through their colleagues' point of view. Many teachers also find that IT departments are prompted to act and make changes when a teacher comes forward to act as an advocate for a particular tool. As such if you present yourself as an enthusiast, you may be in a great position to sway your school's adoption of a tech tool or service, such as an online blogging service or maybe the use of iPods in the classroom.

If you'd like to effect change in the manner in which your school or district adopts and incorporates technology, consider sitting on your school's technology committee (or asking your IT staff to start one). Too often schoolwide technology decisions are made without the input of classroom teachers. With the knowledge gleaned from this book and your experiences in the trenches, we hope you feel in a position to influence technology usage at your school in a positive way.

ACCEPTABLE USE POLICIES

Acceptable use policies (AUPs) are designed to establish principles and set guidelines for computer and Internet use in a school community. An AUP typically covers issues of legality, netiquette (or online behavior), and online safety and should serve to remind students, teachers, and staff of proper behavior regarding computer usage.

If your school has an AUP, make sure to review it before the school year begins, and check that your educational technology initiatives fall within its guidelines. Go over the AUP with your students at the beginning of the year if they are not already aware of its provisions. If the AUP language is technical or complex, explain it in language that your students will understand. Keep in mind that it is especially helpful to provide examples of both acceptable use practices and *unacceptable* use practices. Think about any provisions you would like to emphasize as they pertain to your classroom.

It's a good idea to outline specific guidelines and policies for computer usage in your classroom. If you teach younger students, make them aware of basic Internet safety rules before you allow them to surf independently. With all students, discuss issues of online plagiarism and inappropriate Web sites. Remind students that they shouldn't write anything in an email that they wouldn't want seen by a parent, teacher, or guardian.

Some states have specific directives that schools need to follow in creating their AUP, so don't arbitrarily eliminate your school's AUP provisions. Of course, there is also the danger of including too much information in an AUP, to the point where teachers and students cannot realistically read the document. While there is no single right or wrong way to create an AUP, the best are often relatively short. Also, consider the tone of your AUP. Some AUPs are cold, technical, and legalistic, while others are gentle, informal, and instructional. The consequences of violating an AUP can be serious, but try not to adopt a threatening tone in the document.

WEBSITE: The Virginia Department of Education offers an excellent online handbook on acceptable use policies at: http://www.pen.k12.va.us/VDOE/Technology/AUP/home.shtml.

Try to reinforce a few key principles in your AUP:

- There should be no accessing or transmitting offensive or inappropriate materials.
- Accessing or disrupting another user's computer account without permission is prohibited.
- Unauthorized copying or distribution of software or multi-media is illegal and prohibited.
- Use of any software to compromise or monitor the school's network system is prohibited.

We stress the following in our classroom AUP:

- Use of school technology, such as laptop computers, is for educational purposes only.
- Visiting unauthorized Web sites or checking email during class is disruptive and can result in punishment.
- Your email communication on our school communication system is not confidential and may be monitored if we suspect inappropriate use.
- Downloading unauthorized software or tampering with school computers is prohibited.

WEBSITE: Here are a few online examples of acceptable use policies:
http://title3.sde.state.ok.us/technology/aup.htm
http://www.westmont.dupage.k12.il.us/jrhigh/FYI/techpermission.html

ONLINE SAFETY AND HEALTH

Conversations about online safety start with discussions about dealing with stumbling across some of the more unsavory elements of the Internet. Research black history and you might run into hate speech; research women's studies and your students might pull up post-feminist pornography. Filters can solve some of these problems, but they can also prevent students from accessing legitimate sites.

The best way to prevent these occurrences is by limiting activities that let students roam the Internet freely. When working on projects, give students a restricted number of sources that they can look at, or have students start their research from a search directory like the Best of History Web Sites (http://www.besthistorysites.net) or WebEnglishTeacher.com (http://www.webenglishteacher.com), where the Web sites will have been vetted in advance.

When you are ready to let students get involved in more open research, it is important to set expectations for what should happen if a student stumbles on to something untoward; generally that the student should close such a thing quickly and move onto the next task tactfully.

Teachers should also reinforce with students that they should not give away personal information over the Internet—like phone numbers, addresses, social security numbers, or even their last names. School projects should be designed so that students can digitally sign their work with just a first name and last initial. Students should be instructed to tell their teacher if they find information that appears inappropriate. Likewise, they should also be instructed not to respond to messages that appear inappropriate or make them feel ill at ease. They should also never share their passwords, even with friends.

Teachers should also be aware of the possibility that bullying and student conflict can easily move from the schoolhouse into online realms. Teachers should be aware that cyberbullying through email, cell phone text messages, or even a blog posting can be just as cruel and harmful as face-to-face bullying.

While online safety probably deserves top billing in these conversations, teachers should also keep student health in mind when considering online work. If a student spends 45 minutes in class on a computer, has a half hour of homework online, and then spends a few hours at a screen recreationally at home, what percentage of the day is that student at a computer? What are the social and health effects of students working, playing, and socializing online and through technology for hours every day? Are student social lives healthier because they can manage more friendships? What are the effects of young people staring at screens throughout their lives? What is the relationship between computer use and physical fitness?

There is more punditry than research on the answers to these questions, but teachers should pay attention to conversations about these topics and think seriously about how they can influence the online lives of students. As we begin to teach the first generation of students who have lived their whole lives in the digital age, we will all have to come to terms with how the new technology changes us as individuals and as a society.

As teachers we have a role in preparing students for a workforce where understanding and manipulating technology will be essential skills for advancement in many industries. We need to coach them to be good computer users—staying away from harmful content, behaving appropriately in online communities, and learning how to be focused and productive in an environment full of distractions and diversions. At the same time, though, we also need to make sure students spend enough time away from their computer screens to learn the social skills they will need to be successful, happy people. We also need to make sure they get outside and stay active enough to be healthy people. Schools need to discuss these complex issues and help students navigate the uncharted waters ahead.

Which Sites Should Schools Ban?

Just how to keep children safe elicits considerable debate among teachers, parents, students, school administrators, the media, technological experts, and others. There is some general agreement that sexually explicit sites, hate sites, and sites that contain offensive content should be blocked on school computers, but banning Web sites can be just as controversial as banning books from libraries. How exactly should schools determine what is offensive, and what should be done if filters for offensive materials block out legitimate resources?

Some schools also place restrictions on what research tools students can use. For instance, some schools ban, or at least demand students not use, the Google search engine, arguing that students should do online research only with vetted academic sources. Along the same thinking, some schools ban the use of Wikipedia, the popular Internet encyclopedia. (See our discussion of the Wikipedia controversy in Chapter 5, "Open Research.") Literature "study guide" and "paper mill" Web sites are also a problem. Students can read in-depth summaries and analyses of commonly taught books and write and speak intelligently about them without having read the books. Or they can find Web sites that offer a slew of essays for download on the book. What's a school to do?

A third problematic issue is online social communities, sites where students socialize by leaving (sometimes inappropriate) messages and photographs for each other. The online social community Facebook (http://www.facebook.com) is extremely popular with high school students, and many schools prohibit students from accessing Facebook and other online social community Web sites while at school. (Some ed-tech specialists and teachers have attempted to co-opt the Facebook and MySpace concept and bring it to their schools to enhance community.) Also related to e-socializing is instant messaging and chat rooms. Both of these are banned at many schools, but other schools allow them and even encourage their use by students and teachers as a means to communicate.

In all of these cases, we are of the opinion that banning sites is often counterproductive, as it takes away opportunities to teach students appropriate evaluation and use of online materials. Filtering sites inhibits the ability of students to use critical-thinking skills to evaluate Internet content, and these are skills that kids will need as adults. It seems that the best way to ensure Internet safety for children in the long run is to teach students how to use the computer responsibly. That's one reason why teachers should establish an acceptable use policy that instructs students on how to navigate the Internet. Unfortunately filtering software intended to stop student access to pornography and offensive materials often blocks legitimate content and sometimes fails to block the content it was purchased to filter. Filtering software can also cost a school district a good deal of money and sometimes is used as a crutch in place of a well-thought-and regularly enforced AUP. There are seedy and dangerous parts of the Web, but schools are a great place to teach students how to navigate past such places safely.

RECOMMENDED PROFESSIONAL DEVELOPMENT RESOURCES

One of the things we get asked at our workshops is how we keep up to date on educational technology. While there is quite a lot we don't know, we do make a concerted effort to use an assortment of email lists, newsletters, blogs, RSS, and Web sites to keep abreast of ed-tech developments.

Here are a few of our favorite sources:

- **The Scout Report**
  The excellent Internet Scout Report for the Social Sciences offers bi-weekly reviews of select Internet sites in the humanities as well as reviews of new tech tools. http://scout.wisc.edu/
- **TechLearning: From the Classroom**
  TechLearning is full of articles by teachers who have successfully integrated technology into their courses. http:// www.techlearning.com
- **PBS Teacher Source**
  PBS Teacher Source offers lessons and activities arranged by topic and grade level. Sign up for its weekly newsletter to get previews of upcoming shows and associated teaching resources. http://www.pbs.org/teachersource/soc_stud.htm

- **November Learning**
  Alan November is an ed-tech visionary, technology consultant, keynote speaker, and university lecturer. He has international experience guiding schools, government organizations, and industry leaders in improving quality with technology. For his articles, recommended sites, and more, click on *Resources* on his website. http://novemberlearning.com

- **Will Richardson's blog**
  One of the nation's leading edubloggers, Will Richardson is an ed-tech author and keynote speaker whose blog is dedicated to discussions and reflections on the use of Weblogs, wikis, RSS, and other Internet-related technologies in the K–12 classroom. http://weblogg-ed.com/

- **David Warlick's blog**
  David Warlick is a programmer and educational technology consultant. He has created Landmark for Schools, the Son of Citation Machine, and Rubric Machine, among other tech tools, and written a book on blogging. He is widely respected in the ed-tech community. http://davidwarlick.com/wordpress/

- **Web English Teacher newsletter**
  Carla Beard, webmaster of the impressive Web English Teacher, offers an informative bi-weekly newsletter that includes resources and tips for teaching English and Language Arts with technology. Her Web site is chock full of resources for English and Language Arts teachers. http://webenglishteacher.com

- **The Schools of California Online Resources for Educators (SCORE)**
  At SCORE you'll find plenty of rated lesson plans and resources arranged by grade level and content. For periodic bulletins about "What's New on SCORE H/SS," subscribe to Listserv on the SCORE H/SS homepage. http://score.rims.k12.ca.us/

- **History and Social Studies Online: H-Net Discussion Networks**
  H-Net has over 100 email lists to choose from that are populated primarily by professors, teachers, and students. The ED-TECH educational technology discussion network is our favorite. http://www.h-net.org/lists/

- **Learning Page: The Source**
  The Library of Congress Learning Page provides activities, tools, ideas, and features for educators and students. The *Source* is a monthly online newsletter with practical ideas for teachers for Library of Congress American Memory users. http://lcweb2.10c.gov/ammem/ndlpedu/community/am_newsletter/index.php

- **Teaching History with Technology Newsletter**
  We publish our own newsletter with more great new Web sites, tips, resources, and workshop updates. It's generally published four times and year, and you can sign up for it at http://www.thwt.org/membershipform.htm.

- **National Science Digital Library**
  Funded by the National Science Foundation, the digital library provides useful links to quality resources supporting science, technology, and mathematics across grade levels. Searchable and indexed, it is a great resource in support of a science curriculum. http://nsdl.org/

- **Interactivate**
  Interactivate features free, online courseware for science and mathematics that includes engaging activities, lessons, and discussions. It is aligned with a number of common math texts. http://www.shodor.org/interactivate/

VISIONS OF THE FUTURE

It is difficult enough to predict the future (especially the fast-changing world of technology!), but we are going to take this opportunity to look into our crystal ball and discuss some technological changes we see having a considerable impact on schools and classrooms. The following are ten trends that we see developing in educational technology in the years ahead:

1. **Google nudges Microsoft out of the classroom**

   There is a significant turf war going on these days between companies that offer free Internet-based programs and companies that sell software programs. The titans at the center of this struggle are Google and Microsoft. Google offers an increasing number of free, Web-based programs that rival Microsoft's expensive software products. For instance, Google offers a free word-processing program and a free online spreadsheet program that compete with Microsoft Word and Microsoft Excel, respectively. Google "Docs & Spreadsheets" applications also offer the ability to share files and collaborate in real time (you can investigate them at http://docs.google.com). Google offers many other free programs, such as a free presentation program, a free Web page creation service, a free calendar system, a free videoconferencing system, and more, and so it appears to be developing a well-rounded arsenal to do battle with Microsoft on several fronts.

   Schools are paying close attention to the availability of free, Internet-based programs because they represent a huge potential cut in school expenditures and manpower. Microsoft software is prohibitively expensive for many school districts and it is costly and time-consuming to install major updates to Microsoft programs. (Microsoft is not the only one selling expensive software; Adobe's Photoshop is an expensive image-editing program found at many schools. It has been replaced in some schools by the free GIMP program.) Additionally, teachers typically use only a fraction of the features available in these programs, so schools end up spending a lot of money on software that teachers are not fully exploiting. Moreover, as Web access becomes more widely available and connectivity speeds improve, the lure of 24/7 access and lack of Mac/PC compatibility issues makes Internet-based programs even more appealing.

   That being said, familiarity and comfort are important considerations. Teachers and students are most familiar with Microsoft products, and it may be hard to convince them to switch programs. These are also really good products, with powerful and convenient features, so letting go will be difficult. Our bet is that schools will look at the bevy of free Internet programs available to them and the cost benefits associated with leaving Microsoft and eventually take the plunge.

2. **More open-source applications in schools**

   Related to the growth of free, online applications is the growth of open-source applications. Open-source programs are usually free to the public, but they go one step further than some free applications, like those offered by Google. Open-source programs also make the coding that runs their programs available to the public. In a collaborative spirit, software engineers and others are invited to improve the coding of the program for the benefit of all and can modify it for their own purposes.

Interestingly enough, major corporations and software communities are putting in much time and money to develop free, open-source software. A well-known example is Firefox, the popular Internet browser developed by a foundation that includes ex-Netscape engineers.

One open-source software that is making significant inroads in schools is Moodle, a course-management system discussed earlier in the chapter. Moodle is a great alternative to costly subscription-based course-management systems. It is powerful and flexible enough to accommodate most teachers' technology needs.

Another open-source program that is making inroads is OpenOffice, discussed in Chapter 3, "Note Taking and Organization." OpenOffice includes a word processor, spreadsheet, presentation manager, and drawing program, and is compatible with other office suites, including Microsoft Office. The Open Office suite of programs is not as feature rich as the Microsoft Office suite, but when you calculate, say, $99 for Microsoft Office, and multiply that by the total number of computers in a district (tens of thousands in some), that's a considerable amount of savings. Imagine if that money went into your technology funding!

3. Portable software everywhere

As the storage capacity of thumb drives (see Chapter 1, "Lectures") continues to grow rapidly, and as their costs continue to stay relatively low, we expect thumb drives (or similar devices) to become a staple in schools. In the near future, students and teachers will be moving not only files on their portable drives, but entire software programs. We hope that teachers will not have to worry about whether a student has a particular software program on a computer at home. Instead, the software program the student needs will be on a thumb drive the teacher provides him and will play off the drive. So, the student will not even need to download the program to a home computer! We're not sure how proprietary, legal issues will be worked out, but we sure love the freedom and productivity that portable software would bring.

4. Broadband as a national utility

Eventually, nearly every American home will have some form of access to broadband Internet. Assigning students to watch a video clip on the Web will be no more arduous than asking them to watch the nightly news. In fact, it will probably be much easier than asking them to watch the news since the news is on for only a few hours a day, and the Web is open for business all the time. Once teachers can reasonably expect that every one of their students has a functioning broadband connection at home, teachers will be able to reliably assign a much wider array of online assignments.

5. Vlogs and video casts rule

Blogs and podcasts have been all the rage on the Internet the last few years. Mind you, the content of these technologies is primarily text, image, and audio based; video is incorporated only sparingly. We expect that to change. Quicker and easier distribution of video over the Internet should lead to a growth of video logs, or vlogs, and vodcasts, or video podcasts. We anticipate seeing video displayed much more frequently on blogs, wikis, and Web sites, and we expect teachers to use video with increasing regularity.

6. **Virtual classrooms galore**

As both synchronous and asynchronous online course-management software improves, we expect to see more and more schools and universities offering online courses. We ran online courses a few years ago with little more than a blog, some pictures, and text. Nowadays teachers have access to free and versatile videoconferencing options such as Skype and iChat. More revolutionary is Second Life, an online virtual world where people can buy land, create objects and buildings, and communicate, and its ability to provide a forum for virtual schools and classrooms is exciting. We see teachers using Second Life, or similar virtual environments, to hold classes, show presentations, invite guest speakers, and lead virtual trips.

7. **More control over computers**

Fifteen years ago, computers could do much less, and so managing classrooms of students using computers was much easier. For instance, when computers could run only one program at a time, teachers never had to worry about students playing games when they were supposed to be keyboarding. And of course before the Internet, teachers didn't have to worry about students wandering around the Web, because there was no Web to wander. Right now, teaching with computers is fraught with ways for students to get off track. Giving the students the freedom to do their best work often means building fences so they more easily avoid bad choices.

One way to build these fences will be to have schools control the hardware in schools. As prices of computers drop, schools will move away from programs where students own their own laptops that they bring into school, and simply have enough computers for every student at school and offer scholarships so that students can have their own computers at home. Market forces and programs like the One Laptop per Child program out of the Massachusetts Institute of Technology, which aims to develop $100 laptops for students in developing countries, are going to eventually bring notebook computers down to the cost of a few textbooks. When schools control the computers, they'll have more control over what students can do with them.

Similarly, one of the most important next frontiers for educational software design will be programs that help teachers view and control student computer screens, like the Vision program discussed earlier. Already some programs are making headway in this regard, and eventually these will be in every computer lab and classroom in the country. Students won't be able to sign on to the network without surrendering some measure of control of their computer to a teacher, who will have a separate screen at the teacher's desk to view the screens of every student in the room. A student playing pinball while everyone else is writing an essay will be much easier to spot. Who knows; maybe they'll go back to doodling on the desk!

8. Either an end to textbooks or a new beginning for custom publishing

Textbook publishers look at the future, and they are very, very afraid. Respected academics are increasingly making their writings freely available online—lectures, essays, and even texts for an entire course. Why buy a U.S. History textbook when Steven Mintz publishes his at http://digitalhistory.uh.edu? Why buy a World History textbook if Richard Hooker makes one available at http://www.wsu.edu/~dee/? And if there are a few other options out there, why not pick and choose exactly the sections that you want from various sources, and supplement it all with an astounding array of primary-source writing, audio, and video on the Web? Why spend $100 on a textbook and $30 on a book of supplemental readings when it's all available for free online?

Textbook publishers are going to have to decrease the costs and increase the availability of their custom-publishing units in order to compete with the Web. Right now, teachers and schools can order custom-designed textbooks and readers, where they can select chapters and sections from a menu of options, but these custom publications are still expensive. Look for these prices to go down as vanguard teachers start disposing of print media all together. In the long run, teachers should hopefully find themselves with the best of both worlds—reasonably priced custom options alongside the infinity of sources on the Web.

9. Cell phones as portable computers

While we are a long way from getting every student access to his or her own laptop, nearly every student already has access to a portable computer in his or her pocket, a cell phone. Cell phones have already developed into powerful multimedia platforms for voice, still, image, video, and text communication, and their potential for educational uses hasn't yet been tapped.

We discussed briefly the possibilities of mobile podcasting, in Chapter 8, "Student Presentations," and other services exist for mobile Web surfing, email, and blogging. As these technologies develop, expect clever teachers to find innovative ways to make them applicable to the classroom.

10. When all the old teachers retire, things will change

Tenure systems in schools have some wonderful advantages in terms of protecting teachers' freedoms, but there is no question that they infuse a certain conservatism into school cultures. In many systems, teachers need to adopt new technologies only if they want to, and while some old-timers have courageously taken on the challenge of learning about new tools, some are content to teach as they have always taught. But eventually this current generation of teachers will retire, and the recruits who come to replace them will be born of a different era.

Soon enough, nearly every pre-service teacher will be a digital native, immersed in the Internet from birth, and expecting to bring technology and connectivity into the classroom. As this generation of teachers replenishes the ranks of our national teaching corps, schools will place greater emphasis on teaching with technology. Right now the education sphere lags far behind business, government, and individuals in adopting new technology, but hopefully we can count on the new generation of teachers to help us catch up.

PARTING THOUGHTS

The most important message we have for our fellow teachers is that all this is not about the technology; it is about great teaching. Nothing that we can offer can replace the power of a heated discussion or the impact of a passionate lecture. With all the tools that we have at our disposal, will our classes ever measure up to the discussions that Socrates held in Athens without a laptop, without a pencil, without even chalk and slate?

Socrates asked his students to wrestle with the most profound questions of his day and the most profound questions of the human experience. His students, and there have been many of them over the past 2,000 years, have wrestled with Socrates because his questions were so engaging that we are compelled to try to answer them, generation after generation. We still want to know how best to be ethical, to be virtuous, to be human.

Technology will never replace Socratic questions and dialogue. As Picasso elegantly explained, "Computers are useless; they can only give you answers." Great teaching is driven by great questions, and great questions for the foreseeable future will remain in the realm of the human and the real. Technology won't help us ask better questions, but it can enhance our conversations.

Today any student connected to the Internet can read the original conversations of Socrates, translated into dozens of languages. Not only can we read the first discussions in Athens, but we can also read centuries of commentary, debate, and discussion. In the tradition of Socrates, face-to-face conversations are an essential part of a complete education, but we can now enhance those conversations with asynchronous dialogue among not just our local classmates, but fellow students around the world. We can talk to each other anytime, from almost anywhere. We can put our opinions and comments in the public view and hold our students to higher standards of accountability as they engage in conversation with the rest of the world.

With this technology we can expand the conversation in all directions. We can expand it geographically, so that our students can talk not only in class, but also at home, in the lab, and in the library. Our students can converse with their classmates, their schoolmates, or their peers around the world. They can communicate with experts in the community or anywhere.

The conversation also expands temporally. Students can base their opinions on a massive compilation of human thought, more accessible and freer than at any other time in human history. They can share their ideas in class, but they can also share their ideas outside of class with more time to reflect on and craft their opinions.

We may never ask better questions than Socrates, but we can certainly expand the conversations that might lead us to the answers.

We've talked for a few hundred pages; now it's your turn. Come visit us at http://www.edtechteacher.org/ and tell us about how you are using technology in the classroom. Ask questions, and join in the conversation.

Index

Tom Daccord and **Justin Reich** run EdTechTeacher.org, which publishes a series of Web Sites for teachers—The Best of History Web Sites (besthistorysites.net), Teaching History with Technology (thwt.org), Teaching English with Technology (tewt.org), and The Ed Tech Teacher (edtechteacher.org). EdTechTeacher also offers customized workshops and consulting services for schools. Both Tom and Justin have extensive experience teaching in 1–1 computing environments and have spoken at conferences and schools across the country. Tom is currently an Academic Technology Advocate at the Noble and Greenough School in Dedham, Massachusetts, and Justin is a doctoral candidate at the Harvard Graduate School of Education.